For
the Time
Being

For the Time Being

A MEMOIR

MICHAEL FISHER S.S.F.

First published in 1993

Gracewing
Fowler Wright Books
Southern Ave, Leominster
Herefordshire HR6 0QF

Gracewing Books are distributed

In New Zealand
Catholic Supplies Ltd
80 Adelaide Rd
Wellington
New Zealand

In Australia
Charles Paine Pty
8 Ferris Street
North Parramatta
NSW 2151 Australia

In Canada by
Meakin & Assoc.
Unit 17, 81, Auriga Drive
Nepean
Ontartio KZE 7YS
Canada

In U.S.A.
Morehouse Publishing
P.O. Box 1321
Harrisburg
PA 17105
U.S.A.

Cover illustration, 'Horizon', by John Miller

Typesetting by Action Typesetting Limited, Gloucester
Printed and bound by The Cromwell Press

ISBN 0 85244 242 4

Contents

"To those who have seen
The Child, however dimly, however incredulously
The Time Being is, in a sense, the most trying time of all.

Remembering the Stable where for once in our lives
Everything became a You and nothing was an It."

For the Time Being
A Christmas Oratorio
W.H. Auden

Dedication

This is not the whole story, either as history or autobiography, but a Memoir — a bundle of memories. Some of the people who have meant most to me are barely mentioned, though they helped to make it possible.

I offer it in love and gratitude to them and to the Brothers and Sisters of the Society of St. Francis

Introduction

A young woman came up to me recently at a Confirmation service, asked me to sign her prayer book, – and added "I didn't know Roman Catholic monks were allowed to do confirmations in the Church of England!"

It is only too true that there are still congregations, even clergy, unaware that we have monks and nuns in the Anglican church, and that a habit is not a disguise for 'infiltrating' Roman Catholics!

There have been Religious in our branch of the Church for a hundred and fifty years. On 6th June, 1841 (Trinity Sunday) a young woman, Marian Rebecca Hughes, promised God, in the presence of Dr. Pusey in his rooms in Christ Church Oxford, that she would live the dedicated life. Later, as a sign of that commitment, she received Holy Communion from John Henry Newman at the University Church. Four years after that, the first Religious Order for women began in London. In the years that followed many more were established to work among the poor in parishes, nurse in hospitals, to teach, or to live the life of prayer and seclusion in a convent.

At the height of the nineteenth century as the reign of Queen Victoria reached its industrial and intellectual zenith, and as the Empire grew at a staggering rate, Religious Orders for men also sprang up to challenge on the spiritual and social level the confidence, even the arrogance, of a world where great wealth and security relied on a working class that often lived in appalling conditions and real poverty.

In 1866 the first Order for men was started in Oxford and between 1890 and the end of the century several more followed. Some of these Orders, both for women and men, immediately established branches overseas, in America, Australia, Africa, India, wherever colonial expansion was taking place. Peter Anson in his survey of the Religious Orders in the Anglican Communion, published in 1955, listed no less than one hundred and thirty one different Orders for women and eighty three orders for men in the Worldwide Anglican

Communion. Some of them had by then died out, a few had become Roman Catholics. Many more have died out since that time, and yet more have diminished in numbers. Nevertheless, at present, in England alone there are forty-six Orders for women and ten for men, and signs that once again vocations are beginning to increase.

Among the new Religious Communities to be founded for men was one which began its life in 1894. This Order was distinguished from the others by being the first deliberately to follow the example of St. Francis of Assisi. They called themselves the Society of the Divine Compassion, lived and worked among the poor, wearing the Franciscan habit. This was the first of many such Orders and in the course of the next thirty years no less than twenty-two different Franciscan Communities for women and men were started in various parts of the world. Some of these no longer exist while others have merged together as their numbers diminished or they recognised a common goal and ideal.

Like so many of the first Anglican Orders, they were led by striking, determined and occasionally brilliant personalities, who combined holiness of life with single-minded determination, and sometimes a certain degree of eccentricity. It was true of Fr. Benson of Cowley, Bishop Gore of Mirfield, – and of Douglas Downes, who combined his Order with that of Algy Robertson to create the Society of St. Francis. Both Orders began in 1922, one in England the other in India. They linked up in 1937, and in the course of the next twenty-five years, absorbed the remaining brothers of five more English Orders and merged, first with an Order of Franciscan Sisters, and then the Order of St. Francis for men in America.

Like many things in the Church of England these beginnings are difficult to follow, and sometimes untidy. But out of them has come a Society of Franciscans which acknowledges the primitive Rules of St. Francis and St. Clare and also has its own chief guide-lines, called *The Principles,* (first drawn up in India for one of the original component parts of the Society), and embraces not only brothers and sisters who are actively engaged in prayer, preaching, and care of the underprivileged, but also sisters who live the contemplative life, and men and women in all walks of the secular world who dedicate themselves to the same Rule and Franciscan ideal.

In 1994 there will have been Franciscans in the Church of England for a hundred years, and I have had the privilege of watching and sharing in the growth of one part of that movement for half of that time.

I began making some notes in 1983 towards the end of my time in Cornwall, and owe a great debt to Eileen Johnson – "Mrs. J." - for her patient interpretation of my writing and unfailing forbearance as my secretary. I continued in Cambridge, with many lapses for illness and travelling, encouraged by the generosity of David and Elizabeth Walser who gave me a "room of my own" in their home in which to work or be still, and by my good friend Fr. Douglas Gale who never tires of word-processing my manuscripts and has been unstintingly generous in time and trouble. I am also indebted to Dr Peta Dunstan who with great skill and charming ruthlessness helped knock the manuscript into shape. Last but not least a good deal of revision was made possible during holidays and times for reflection with John Miller and Michael Truscott at Sancreed in Cornwall, in a house which they have made a place of peace and renewal, that is truly Franciscan and not for me alone but for so many others.

In 1991 Brother Kenneth, the last of the founding Brothers, died in Dorset. His death marked the end of the beginning of the Society of St. Francis. I met him first just fifty years earlier, in 1941 when I went down there to join the Society.

This book is a personal account of my experience in this Community during those fifty years, some of its personalities, and the way it shaped my early life.

A Brief Bibliography

For a comprehensive account of the whole Franciscan movement in the Anglican Church.

The Franciscan Revival in the Anglican Communion. Barrie Williams.

For the Society of St. Francis – S.S.F.

Brother Douglas by Father Francis S.S.F.
Father Algy by Father Denis S.S.F.

For Christa Seva Sangha and Christa Prema Seva Sangha – C.S.S. and C.P.S.S.

The Eyelids of the Dawn Jack Winslow
Christa Seva Sangha Jack Winslow
A Wheat Corn in India

For the Society of the Divine Compassion – S.D.C.

The Life and Letters of Father Andrew Kathleen E. Burn

For the Community of St Francis – C.S.F.

Corn of Wheat Mother Elizabeth C.S.F.

For the Brotherhood of the Holy Cross – B.H.C.

Father Potter of Peckham George Potter B.H.C.

Chapter One

My Mother and father – "In Service"

Lady Juliet Duff – the name haunted our childhood, as did her signed portrait by Cecil Beaton, which stood almost like a shrine on the piano, such was mother's pride at having been her 'lady's maid'. My mother was born in 1885 and grew up in a country cottage in Fife, one of a large family, and retained a singular and determined loyalty to her Scottish origins. She was the only one of her generation to come South, going, as a young girl, "into service" at Rievaulx Abbey in Yorkshire.

Life as a servant in Edwardian households has been well chronicled. My mother never tired of telling endless stories of life below stairs; the maids, nursery maids, scullery maids and "between maids", butlers, gardeners and cooks; the intrigues, romances and feuds, the titillating knowledge of the goings-on at the house- parties, and who among the Lords and Ladies went with whom. The drudgery of it as well. Very early-morning cleaning of grates, rooms, shoes, guns. The strict pecking order and the tyranny of housekeepers. The casual kindness of the wealthy, and the loving devotion that it some-times won.

My father, born in Sussex, had just one brother, and hardly any recollection of his father, who deserted my grandmother when the boys were young. He was rarely spoken of, but I caught some glimpses of him in stilted photographs and relished his name, Jabez. My grandmother married again, a large man with a florid face and huge walrus moustache. As children we hated being kissed by him. He was a mean, miserly and selfish man.

Sussex and Scotland were the places to which, as the poor rela-tions, we went for holidays. Hove and Brighton were however our more frequent destinations. I was baptised at Brighton Parish Church, but first experienced the exotic world of Anglo-Catholic worship in a setting of Byzantine splendour at St Bartholomew's, taken there by my grandfather on Easter Day when the church was so full that, together with several others, we had to stand in the pulpit. When I visited St Bartholomew's a year or two ago, I

1

found none of its glories diminished, nor Wagner's extravaganza less exciting than when I first saw it. The towering baldachino, the huge candles soaring behind it, the silver and the gold, the colour, the sheer glamour, and something of the beauty of holiness as well. The great ark of brick, so vast that the aspirations of man might fail to reach into those dusky heights. There were not quite so many people.

My father also "went into service", and between them my parents notched up quite a considerable little Debrett of their own: a footman with Lord Beauchamp, something else with Lord Crewe, and Lord Bath, and a marvellous life between country and town houses as they travelled round with them. They met during a London "Season" when he looked after Lord Bath, and they were married in St Mark's, North Audley Street, not long before the 1914-18 war broke out. During the war he went to work in the munitions factory at Greenwich, and I was born in 1918. They had a boy before me, but he did not live long. After me, there were two more, girls: "Brownie" (whose real name is Margaret Mary) and Sybil.

I'm always a little surprised that neither of them was called Juliet, so large did she figure in my mother's life. A romantic beauty, very tall, like her mother who brought the Russian Ballet to London, Juliet Duff knew everyone in the artistic and theatrical worlds, and shared a lot of her thoughts and feelings with Jane. My father always called my mother Jeannie, though she had been baptised Martha Lindsay. Jeannie got corrupted into Jane, so that is what we sometimes called her. We seem to have had an odd way of changing our names. I was baptised Reginald Lindsay, following my father and mother, but was always known as Roy, until I became a friar.

During the lean years in the late twenties and thirties, we were sent large hampers from Fortnum's and helped out with money as well, I expect. Jane lived on the stories of the gay days of her youth, the parties and romantic encounters, all the name-dropping of what this Earl said to her, or that Baron; the scandals and wickednesses, marital involvements, beauty and wealth of that era.

Juliet Duff never forgot Jane. When my father died, she invited her to stay at Wilton, near Salisbury, and the two picked up all over again, only now Jane was there as a friend rather than a servant, and my mother tried to help Juliet with a memoir which she was writing. It became an annual holiday of several weeks. Over the years, I have come to stay myself in some of the houses that I once heard described from "below stairs", recognised the names, the family portraits, heard even, from another point of view, the same familiar anecdotes, scandals, successes. Sometimes, from the guest room in a stately home, I sent Jane a letter with a familiar address at the top. She took it in her stride, only commenting with a sniff that they were no longer running the place as they did in "the old Lord's" time! "They didn't do it like that when *I* was there!"

My father was a gentle, insecure, lovable man, living in the shadow of his capable and charming brother, who was something of an "officer and a gentleman", killed in the First World War. The picture of "Uncle Wilfred" also had a place of honour, a handsome smiler in uniform, and I think that my father might have suffered a bit by comparison, though he, too, had infinite charm, reckless generosity, and a hopelessly unbusinesslike life. So Jane really kept the show on the road. After the second war, he worked in pubs all over London, and she would travel up from the suburbs every day to help him until she was nearly seventy.

We left Clapham when I was sixteen, and moved from time to time into a variety of slightly odd homes. First, the basement of a big house in Clapham Park which, for the first time in our lives, gave us the use of a large garden, apple trees and all! It also meant a room of my own for the first time. Then to rooms over a corner pub in Tulse Hill, and from there to rooms over a corner shop by Tooting Bec Common. Reg found the places, but Jane supervised the moves, as she really ran everything. We were living there when the war broke out, and I was called up, and left home, in a sense, for the last time.

Later, she was always "seeing me off", invariably with a stoic determination to show no sign of the pain and anxiety that she felt. Seeing me off in uniform, slipping a little crucifix into my pocket, kissing me Goodbye (no doubt remembering Wilfred whom, I now know, she loved as much as Reg) — a fairly familiar story of integrity and devotion to an only son, probably all the more precious because she had lost the first one. She combined extraordinary strength, fortitude, and determination, with a capacity for love and devotion, a discernment of purpose that was unique, and a never-ending source of fascination and amusement.

Early in the war, a bomb dropped somewhere near and she moved again, lock, stock, and barrel, more-or-less single-handed, to a house in Thornton Heath. At last, a whole house of our own! She went up to London every day from there, sat it out under an Anderson Shelter when more bombs dropped, and when I became seriously ill visited me in my various hospitals.

Still the family moved on — to half a house in Herne Hill after the war. There my father died. He had been ill for some time with internal problems which I thought were cancer, collapsing suddenly in the street and being rushed into Charing Cross Hospital. It was in 1956, not long after I had become a priest. Alas, he had been unable to come for the ordination service. I was with him when he died, after yet another operation. Sitting beside his bed, I thought he was unconscious, but he shortly opened his eyes, finally focused them and found my face. I held his hand and, in the dim light of the ward at three in the morning, we seemed alone and as intimate as I had ever known my relation with him to be. "This is it" he said.

"Yes, I think it is"

There was a lengthy silence and I was about to speak when he said hesitantly, "I've not lived a very good life"

I tried to reply honestly and gently — "You have sometimes been a foolish man and done some bad things as we all have. But you have done some good things as well. There is one thing I can do for you now: tell you that God has forgiven you"

So I said the words of absolution, the only sacrament I ever gave my father. Then I kissed him and he slowly smiled, the old, charming smile, closed his eyes, and died. He was sixty-seven.

I learnt a little more about grief. It was my first funeral, and my friends and brothers seemed surprised that I should take it. It had never occurred to me to do otherwise. The cemetery in Streatham seemed vast, cold, impersonal — acres and acres of empty stones, paths, with little unreal figures going about their solitary business of burial, the removal of dead flowers, the mournful standing at graves, the wordless, determined sorrow, and ritual loss. It was a dull and colourless day. We bought a double grave, and my sister patiently paid for it to be looked after. At the end I was offered a fee for taking the service and stood unbelieving with the packet in my hand, understanding then for the first time what had happened.

People sometimes say, "You talk so much of your mother, what about your father" If there seems an imbalance then perhaps it is understandable. She lived for thirty years after he died, and indeed even while he lived, I think she overshadowed him. He was tall, dark, very good-looking, fastidious about his appearance, and very attractive to women. When he died, he left so little, so very little. He was sometimes foolishly generous, and the first to "push the boat out" in a group of men; but he was feckless with money and, ultimately, as dependent on my mother as we all were. My eldest sister inherited all his charm and endless good will towards others. He was a Tory, and detested my Socialism which could whip him into a sudden rage (I inherited that!), but it was soon over. I suspect that he was a lonely, frustrated man in some ways, but I never really knew him. Brownie knew him, by instinct, better than any of us, and loved and protected him. When he died, my mother went to live with her, though, like him, she was always a bit broke, a victim of her own impetuous generosity. In fact, we have always been a remarkably united family, demonstratively affectionate and loving, living emotionally beyond our means.

Brownie had married a merchant seaman, whom we all loved, and they took Jane to another corner house, this time, in Southend. Underneath was a Marriage Guidance Clinic. Sometimes, their doors would be confused by visitors, with amusing and embarrassing consequences. Brownie was equal to it all, welcoming shocked or shy couples who had come to the wrong door, or taking in parcels of contraceptives! They were not there long before Ron was drowned, and there was another move.

Sybil went to a Central School, and not long after leaving it, met Edgar, a friend of mine from the Young Communist League. They settled in a tallish house in Streatham, and generously invited Jane and Brownie to live with them — the top of another house! They both had two children, but there was room for all, and space for me whenever I could get there. Indeed, not only for me, but brothers who needed a bed for the night, friends, or people that I wanted to interview in London. They were all there until the children grew up, married, or departed for universities. Edgar presided over the extended family, though Jane was queen. I baptised some of the children, married others. We always seemed to be crowding into one room, celebrating something.

They came to hear me preach in London — "Darling, please don't be so political!" — shared my apparent successes, mopped up my tears and suffered my fears, and always there has been a bed and a bottle of wine whenever I passed through. For many years, a great event for Jane was an annual week in Bruges, which she loved, staying at a small, homely hotel, the "Cornet d'Or", which she instinctively took over, discovering the secret lives of the other guests, making new friends, and making impossible remarks in her exaggerated stage whisper that could be heard by everyone. "Those two at the next table — I don't think they're married." Scarlet faces.

Then the house seemed too large, the children gone, and those who remained, too old. For a while, Jane and Brownie moved to a flat in Cheam but finally settled in Upper Norwood, next to Pearson's marvellous church, St John's.

She could lie in bed and hear the Angelus. All her life she remained an intermittent communicant, and read her Bible every night before she slept, taking for some time the children's edition of the Bible Reading Fellowship notes, to keep in step with her granddaughter, Lindsey, who was lonely at a boarding school.

She was only nursed away from home in the last few weeks of her life, with Sisters of St Margaret at their Nursing Home in Chiswick. So she received Communion and was anointed and felt safe and secure with the ministry of the Sisters. Not bad for ninety-eight. Her Requiem and funeral in St John's was a triumphant occasion. The church was full of all the Scottish relatives, a crowd of Brothers and Sisters from the Community, flowers and friendship, tears and triumph. Afterwards, the party was all she would have enjoyed. My sisters had produced marvellous food, and a steady flow of wine.

We buried my mother's ashes at the Sisters' Convent in Somerset, in a patch of sloping lawn high up behind the Old Manor House, next to the grave of old Annie Medway. The Sisters at that time had a Nursing Home for old ladies where my mother had been many times for a rest. Annie had been brought there, to the depths of the country, from the East End of London, to be cared for in her old age. How she hated it! "What is there here? I ask you! No noises. Just cows and owls and bloody cuckoos!" When I took her Communion, she would slip me a pound. "Get yourself a drink on the way home. A man *needs* a drink." She loved to have a really good hug and a kiss, sitting up in bed, with her little bright eyes and round, red, blotchy face, her few remaining wisps of hair tied in a tight knot on top of her head with a blue bow. It was like hugging a badly-filled bolster. She was ninety-five when she died, almost as old as my mother.

The Sisters who had nursed my Mother together with Brownie, my sister, and Brother Malcolm, who carried the ashes, were the only witnesses. We walked in a little procession to the grave, a small, square hole, lined with fresh flowers. It was a restful, quiet January day, with a still, pale sun, and spring flowers breaking through. The air carried the smart, sweet smell of damp earth. The old Sisters had made cakes and scones for the occasion, and gave us flowers and apples to take home.

We returned to London in an almost empty, dirty, rather rattling train. Brownie went to sleep over a book. It was the old, familiar journey which I'd known for so long, taken so many times, on trips to London with Father Algy, who was also in my mind. I had buried his ashes at Hilfield years before, so now the two greatest influences in my life were dead. It was an end, and a beginning. And it was then I thought I might try to write some of it down.

I thought I could take it all in my stride, arranging the funeral, celebrating, preaching, and settling into life without her in the world. She had lived to see me become a Bishop. Another couple of years, and she would have shared my sense of fulfilment as Minister General. Her room was a clutter of pictures of me, sometimes to the good-humoured, mocking dismay of my sisters, and I know that she bored them to tears with her anxieties and concern over my welfare. So it was not perhaps surprising that a sharp reaction set in.

I became threatened, conscious of criticism, obliged to explain, defend myself. Vast letters were sent to bewildered friends by whom I felt irrationally rejected. No doubt it was unresolved bereavement, but I refused to believe that. It was six months before I came to my senses.

Was she so special and unusual? I think so, though I expect that I needed to build up a slightly exaggerated picture of her. Nothing however could detract from, or deny, the sheer charm which drew so many to regard her as their special friend; her amusing, sometimes devastatingly perceptive, remarks; her enthusiasm for life, getting up to dance reels late at night until she was eighty; the conscious warmth of her love; her understanding acceptance of all the odd and lonely people in life. People could bore her, and often did, yet she'd let them come back at her.

I never once heard her complain about the life I lived, though there were long times when she had no idea where I was or what I was doing.

She loved the Community for my sake, and would slip them all a tip for "something on the train". Unconsciously, she taught me something of the generosity of love, the infinite patience that leaves you waiting on platforms and airports, the night watches of late arrivals, of forgotten engagements, mislaid messages and letters never written or appointments that were never kept. Never giving up on love, and, as a consequence, sharing the foolishness as well as the fulfilment of God.

She believed in us, and so we tried to please her and make her happy, but her faith in us never encroached on our independence. So it became something, a part of life, a way of looking at other people, a family trait that I have looked for and, perhaps, hoped and prayed for in the wider family of the Franciscans. It was, in the best sense of the word, a foundation of my faith as much as the stubborn Scottish streak that comes out in us all.

Chapter 2

Growing up in Clapham

Elmhurst Mansions, Edgeley Road, Clapham. Rather a pretentious address for artisan flats, built in Edwardian times. A gloomy corridor of three-storeyed blocks, winding down a road from off the High Street. Each dark entrance smelled of gas, and led to six flats. We lived at the top. Each flat had four rooms; the large "front room", facing the street; a kitchen, complete with big wooden dresser, coal-fired kitchen range with an oven of iron, just like any cottage in the country; a small scullery, much of which was taken up by a stone copper for boiling clothes; a bathroom and lavatory; a large bedroom; and another very small one. At first, we had just one room, my father, mother, sisters and I; and the tenants − another family of four − occupied the rest of it. In 1923 we acquired our own flat, No. 29, which was my home until I was fifteen.

The boundary of my life began with Edgeley Road, the streets on the way to school, the High Street, the seemingly endless Common, and the church which I started attending at the same time as I went to school.

I was born in 1918, so this was all within a few years of the end of the First War. Our corner of Clapham lived, I can now recognise, as a local community struggling against the eroding tide of unemployment, poverty, and the Depression which marked the twenties and thirties. Yet I do not remember it as depressing, though there must have been some very grim times for the grown-ups.

A car hardly ever came down the road, and, when it did, we'd stop and stare; and we all ran out into the street if a plane flew over. One marvellous aerial sight was the silver shadow of an airship − the R101! Lamplighters still came round for the gas lamps; and, in the winter, the muffin men, wearing a green apron, with a flat box on their heads, and ringing a bell. "Muffins", "Sweet violets", "Rags and bones", "Coal---man", "Milk--- man" − all were called out at regular intervals.

Clapham still had a dairy, close to the school, with a herd of poor, captive cows. You could take your can to the yard, or wait for the churn to be brought round. By the late twenties, that had gone, and, of all the other cries in south London, the only one that I have heard in recent years is the rag-and-bone man, still going round with a horse and cart and ringing a handbell, as once the coalman and all the others did. "Rag-bone".

One occasional excitement was the Concert Party. A group of five or six men and women, with a barrel organ for music. The women wore long dresses,with feathers and bright make-up. They danced, kicked their legs, and did the "splits" It was a long time before I discovered that *they* were men as well! — and the whole party a hangover from the war.

There were seasons for everything: tops, hoops, five-stones, grottoes (a collection of cigarette cards, flowers, stones, anything that caught the eye, arranged in a group on the pavement, and good for a halfpenny or a penny from a passer-by, if you were lucky).

One unexpected element in Edgeley Road was the Art School. The end of the road closest to the High Street had small houses and, in the middle of them, a School of Art, which gradually became an intriguing source of interest. As I grew older, I would loiter along towards the High Road, hoping that the students would be standing about outside — the doors wide open and a possibility of a glimpse of the interior. Once or twice, I sidled in and, for a moment, watched while an old man sat stock still surrounded by silent men and women, drawing and painting. Once, it was a naked woman who looked, if anything, older than the man, standing like a statue. Nobody noticed me. In any case, they all had their backs to me, standing at easels or straddled on donkey stools, but *she* knew, as she looked right through them and saw me, standing at the door. We just stared intently at each other, almost secretly, but without embarrassment, and then I turned and walked away. A few years later, I saw the same old man in a life class in Fleet Street, but he did not seem so old.

The degree to which London is a series of inter-connected villages has always seemed to me to be more marked south of the Thames. There is a sense of "place" which the large open spaces, parks and ancient commons have given. When we were a bit older, we would sometimes go for a long Sunday walk. As soon as I was of age, it was more like a rambling pub-crawl, which extended across common land. for miles. Wandsworth Common, Clapham Common, Tooting Bec Common, Streatham Common. Wimbledon Common was like being in the country, and we went to such places by tram for the day, as a family, or for the Sunday School treat. Crowded trams of shouting children, all rolling and rocking along, to run races, play games, get sick from heat or too much sweet cake.

Clapham Common was the playground that we graduated to from Edgeley Road. I first played football there; but mostly I went to wander, my sisters trailing behind me. Clapham has the long history of a large village a few miles from the metropolis. Around the common were the lovely Georgian houses which I liked just to look at, long before I knew anything about architecture. There was one – the only one – which I came to know from the inside as well, The Hostel of God – a house for the dying. It is where Brother Douglas, the founding father of the Society of St Francis, died in 1957.

Later I went to school in London, just by the house in Gough Square where Dr Johnson completed his Dictionary. I became captivated by the 18th century, principally, I think, because I loved the music and literature just as much as the houses. Imagine the old man rumbling down to see Mrs Thrale at Streatham; rolling around in his carriage across Clapham Common. The evocative world of place-names suggested a marvellous mixture of London sophistication and rural retreat. "Acre Lane", "Nightingale Lane", "Larkhall Rise". Later still, I discovered the significance of Clapham as the home of high principle. The roads and streets spell out the story. "Macaulay Road", "Wilberforce Road", and "Henry Thornton School". I walked down "Venn Street" every day for years, little knowing that the Clapham Sect had been a force to reckon with, or that the "high" church, St Peter's, which was almost my home as a lad, had been built to accommodate the spiritual needs of the affluent ladies and gentlemen who lived in Clapham Park, and who found the insistent evangelicalism of the Parish Church, with its big emphasis on the Clapham Sect, more than they could stand.

How changed it all is. Grafton Square, a large plastered Victorian counterpart of Belgravia, had by the twenties become a slum. As children, we were warned against playing with anyone who came from *there*. Now, refashioned, it is once more "gentrified", and has even discovered a new way of talking. Clapham has become "Cla'am". The Parish Church stands by itself on the common, near the parish pond. Close by is all that remains of the old fire station, and, beyond that, "The Pavement", which was, I suppose, the *only* pavement at one time.

It was here that my mother worked. As we went to school, so she went to clean and be something of a slave to a selfish, demanding woman whose husband, a gentle and somewhat kind and distant man, had a large, rambling second-hand bookshop.

Of course, I didn't know that she was making our life humanly possible. But the books. Such caverns of endless exploration and delight. Size is such a relative factor when you are young. There seemed to be endless shelves reaching to the ceiling, confined, narrow, with that unmistakable smell of age and dust. The cheap bargains in racks outside, the piles of apparently neglected or discarded books, the remembered books, the mysterious names of former owners.

I knew all the second-hand bookshops for miles around, but I bought very few books from Mr Gallop. Perhaps it seemed unnatural to buy a book, even for sixpence, from a man who employed my mother. But I had a sort of lust for books and, bit by bit, during my teens, built up my own personal library.

The first book I ever bought entirely because I wanted it for myself, and not at the suggestion of anyone else, was Thoreau's *Walden*. I wonder now what appealed to me about it, why I felt I'd got to have *that* book. Of that first collection of books, few are still about me – just one or two. Others are in a forgotten bookcase with my sister – a life of Ariosto (what on earth attracted me to that? Perhaps it was the price, because it was obviously a bargain), a ragged collection of various editions of Dickens, Burton's *Anatomy of Melancholy*, a marvellous edition of Rabelais with illustrations by Gustav Dore.

When I joined the Brothers in Cambridge, I made the gesture of bringing the best of my books – Hakluyts *Voyages*, Ibsen, Shaw, Chekhov. When the house was disbanded, they just disappeared. Brother Lothian, whose attitude to poverty had been influenced by affluence, and who, as a consequence, was a genuinely ascetic and simple man, always getting rid of things, got rid of some of mine as well. Not long ago, I happened to open a tattered book of verse in the Hilfield Friary library, which somehow had a familiar look, and there, inside, was my old name, "Roy Fisher".

Back to Clapham.

The High Road was, no doubt, part of the history of Clapham. But, when I knew it, a transformation had already taken place. In some ways, it typifies part of the social history of the first half of this century. Certainly, its unconscious impression on me was indelible. It sloped up fairly steadily from "Clapham North" to "Clapham Common", two stations on the Underground. It had widened and become a major thoroughfare from what had once been a main road to the coast – in fact, to

Brighton, which was, in my childhood, the other end of my
life.

It had cinemas at either end. The "Pavilion", where I was first
entranced – there is no other word – by the marvels of the cinema,
and, at the other, the "Majestic". The first film I ever saw at The
Pavilion was *"The Murder in the Red Barn"*. It cost fourpence to
get in. Films have remained for me an ultimate art form, and the
perfect escape. At The Pavilion, there was a little organ, to accom-
pany the films. At The Majestic – which cost more, and had a
balcony – they sometimes had a sort of string quartette, as well as
an organ. Later, of course, there were talkies. I vividly remember,
and can still recall, the songs of the early musicals – *"A Bench in
the Park"* from a Broadway extravaganza, and all that.

Not far from The Pavilion was a Temperance Billiards Hall,
symbol of Victorian rectitude, now, alas, mostly gone. At the
time, they were all over London. They must have been built about
1890, and reflected a rather distinctive art nouveau style. I tended
to slide in much as I wandered unnoticed into the art school. My
father played billiards there, and, later, so did I. The great dark
room, the rows of large green baize tables with their hooded lights,
seemed another sort of esoteric world to discover. Higher up the
road was a small shop which I could never resist. It sold tea! Tea in
large bowls, tea of all kinds, tea that suggested an oriental and, alas,
unattainable world. That sort of shop has long since gone, though
when I went to work in Fleet Street I bought my tea from Twining's
where, at that time, they first weighed it out and then tied it into
a little paper parcel with string. Another list of magical names –
"Lapsang Souchong", '"Orange Pekoe", "Darjeeling", "Assam".

Farther up still was the tram depot. All Londoners of a certain
age rave about trams. There was a special sort of splendour about
them. Great big, rattling, swaying, clanking double-decker trams.
The ping-ping of the driver to warn that he was coming; the adroit
conductors with their racks of tickets; the seats that were reversible
for the return journey; the single-decker from Clapham Common
that took me all the way to South Kensington, to the museums, the
galleries, the endless and effortless extension of my education. We
were given two pence; a halfpenny for the tram each way, a halfpenny for sweets, and a halfpenny for anything else that we could
spend it on. With sandwiches, it was a day out, peering at pictures,
staring at skeletons, pressing knobs, and marvelling at science.

Later, the tram was the journey to school, to the Old Vic, or on
to Sadler's Wells. It seems, in retrospect and certainly exaggerated,
that every adventure out of Clapham began on a tram. Yet oddly

enough, as I recall the High Road, it is nearly always the horses that I remember as well. The great drays, toiling up the hill, a long haul, and, at the end, the big horse trough. Their large and heavy heads, relieved of harness, dropping slowly into the water, coming up after a while, hair still streaming, looking slowly round, snorting a little, a slight shake, then back into the trough. And, after that, the sack of oats. I loved to look at them, and, in a sense, shared their pleasure.

At the end of Edgeley Road was a haberdasher's shop of great respectability. Inside were counters with little chairs for ladies to sit on while they made their purchases. Money was flashed in a cylinder on an overhead cable to a central cashier. I suppose it was a great innovation in its day. When, at sixteen, I first earned some money, I longed to buy something there for my mother. There was a sale on, and I saw some plates decorated, as I thought, rather splendidly in bright orange and yellow flowers. I *had* to get them. The minute she saw them I knew that she didn't like them, though she was glad that I wanted to give them to her. I suppose it was all part of being, as she thought, "artistic". At any rate, we took them back and changed them for something more sober.

I knew the haberdasher's for another reason. They employed a number of assistants who lived on the premises and were presided over by a formidable housekeeper. When I was twelve, I got a job with a rather nasty man who had a grocer's shop close to my home. Among other duties, I had to deliver large baskets of food to the housekeeper. She always gave me a tip, which was just as well. Mr Barston, whose wife was even more unpleasant than he was, paid me two shillings (10p) a week for which I delivered groceries every lunchtime and every evening. If there were no groceries to deliver, I was sent to work in a dank cellar, weighing up soda and packing it into bags. I think he even begrudged me the bag of broken biscuits he gave me to go home with. Of course, he knew how much we needed the two shillings, which went to my mother. So the tips were handy.

One really big event with the trams was the General Strike in 1926. I was eight, and had just moved into another class. My mother – at, I expect, some sacrifice – bought me a school cap, so that I could be like the other boys. We all congregated at the tram depot. I had no idea what it was all about, but there was a lot of shouting, jeering, and some stone-throwing. Of course, I joined in. Trams came out. Trams turned back. Men got angry, waved their fists, cheered, or shouted. I was in a little crowd outside a tea-shop (a few years later, I was to go there and, for the first time, all by

myself, order some China tea — a moment of delightful sophistication, coupled with just a little apprehension). In the end, I
returned home. "Roy, where's your cap?" Where indeed? I went
back and searched in vain. It was a terrible moment. Mother was
in tears. Only now, I realise that the cap was perhaps a day's
drudgery at Mrs Gallop's.

Half way up the High Street was Clapham Manor Street and
"The Two Brewers", with, behind it, St Peter's Church, a red-
brick, Victorian building, of little architectural worth, but with
a certain Tractarian splendour within. There is a fine Kemp East
window, a set of beautiful carved Stations of the Cross from Ober-
ammergau, a Spanish censer with an interesting history, and, at the
time that I went there, a saintly Canon Noel Tower as vicar, who
had enough private means to employ curates. By the side of the
church were two large halls, a vestry, and other rooms. It was all
intended as both a refuge for Anglo-Catholics, who came, some of
them, from a distance and treated it knowingly as High Church; and
as a "mission" for the poorer people who lived in the locality. With
few of the other alternatives now on offer, it was for many a social
centre, as well as a spiritual resource. It had never succumbed to the
more Baroque excesses, and retained a "sound" Tractarian tradition
of beauty in service, recognition of the Prayer Book, Sacramental
teaching, and a strong social conscience. The church was full for
services, and so were the Choir, Scout troop, Sunday Schools, and
all the other organisations.

It was the custom in many working-class homes for Sunday dinner
to be just after 2 pm, for the simple reason that Dad, and sometimes Mum as well, always went to the pubs in the morning, and
they closed at 2 o'clock. After dinner they liked to go to bed —
and the children were sent to Sunday School. And that is how I
first went to St Peter's.

By the age of five, I had been taught how to help by holding a
boat of incense. From that, I graduated to all the other duties of a
server. I sang, briefly, in the Choir, encountering Plainsong for the
first time; became a Cub, and then a Scout. At times, it seemed as
if all my evenings and weekends were taken up with St Peter's.

Since becoming a Bishop, I have been back there to preach, sixty
years on, and the few remaining friends have produced pictures of
me at that time, and when my mother died, a lot more came to
light. In an odd way, I recognise myself — almost too well. To
say that I was lonely would certainly be wrong; yet I never quite
felt that I belonged. I realise now that I tended always to use the
language of an adult, without knowing its significance, never quite

fitting in with other boys and girls, who resented the way in which I was usually picked on as a sort of favourite by those in authority. They mocked my adult attitudes, and I don't blame them. It must have seemed insufferable, though they probably merely resented the rogue elephant. I was the art master's pet, the Scoutmaster's favourite, the curate's hope for the Ministry. So I was taken for treats, granted little favours.

The curate, Fr Helby Chambers, eventually became the Vicar of St Bartholomew's, Brighton, where I had been taken by my grandfather. He once asked me, at the age of eleven, just after he'd prepared me for Confirmation and heard my first Confession (he was very new, and I was among his first group), "And what do you want to be when you grow up, Roy" And I dutifully answered as he had hoped, "A priest, like you, Father." Certainly, very early in life, the desire, almost the need, to please other people became second nature, and still remains a significant factor in the decisions I make. To say what I really feel without regard for what it might mean for someone else, is very difficult. I prefer to please, sometimes at the expense of my integrity, and working out what I feel is a costly business of trial-and-error for which others, as well, pay a price. Only very recently, when on one or two occasions I have had very publicly to make a stand alone, have I found my real self and, surprisingly, discovered genuine approval from others, not least from those who disagreed with me. How long it takes – fifty or sixty years. Yet, at the time, I *did* want to be a priest, even if all the motives were wrong. Helby Chambers, the curate, did all he could, talked to my headmaster, and offered to pay for all my education, an offer which my parents were too proud to accept, or perhaps too fearful. At any rate it did not happen, and, by the time I was fifteen I had left his church.

The Scouts "Rover Mate" at St Peter's was Hugh Waters, a man in his early twenties, and an ordinand at King's, London. He, too, was a working-class boy, who had become unexpectedly wealthy through the patronage of a widow who sponsored him. He had a home movie camera. Sixty years ago, in Clapham, that was rather rare.

He proposed making a film of the Scout troop in the vicarage garden. By some odd chance, that film came to light recently, and I was given a private showing of it. There we all were – in 1932. All the old faces, many now dead. I saw myself as the precocious little Scout, cooking sausages over a fire, pretending to be "an accident" and given First Aid, singing Scout songs. He took me under his wing and encouraged me. He was also beginning the sad sickness of multiple sclerosis, and, at fourteen, I became his almost constant companion, reading to him, writing for him, playing his gramophone. His influence on me was, no doubt, very great. He encouraged me to read very widely, listen to music, and I took him to concerts and plays.

At the age of eleven, I left my elementary school and moved on to Clapham Central School. The Central Schools, which no longer exist, were something of a precursor to the Comprehensive School. They were designed to give some of those who had failed the eleven plus — or what corresponded to it — another chance, and I think that I was very fortunate to go there.

From all that I have discovered, Clapham Central was not alone in attracting able and dedicated men to its staff. In retrospect, I recognise the outstanding ability of one or two of them in particular. The French master didn't get much French into me, but he taught me to box! The Art master not only shared his enthusiasm for drawing, but his love of paintings. He taught me really to look and see. As one of a small group he coached for scholarships, I was sent all over London to look at paintings as, much later in Fleet Street, another enthusiastic teacher sent us out to look at buildings.

I was at this school for three years, and there won scholarships which might have given me the sort of education some of my older friends wanted for me. Unfortunately my father was still intermittently out of work. I had, in some way, to become less of a financial liability, so my next school had a practical purpose, a school of printing and allied crafts, in Bolt Court, Fleet Street. Jane accompanied me for interviews, together with my small portfolio of drawings, and afterwards we walked along the Embankment while she questioned me about my answers. That school has also gone. Though I left prematurely at sixteen, it laid more foundations for an informal education than many people get.

O'Shaughnessy, a craggy Irishman, taught us History and Science. He loved London, and communicated his love. Every spare moment was spent enjoying the luxury of living where it had all happened for two thousand years. It is an enthusiasm I have never lost. Then there were the theatres and films — best of all, the gallery at the Old Vic and Sadler's Wells.

From 1932, I saw literally every production at both places, some of them repeatedly. Olivier, Edith Evans, Maurice Evans (the most moving Richard II of them all), Gielgud, Peggy Ashcroft, all in the springtime of their careers — all for four pence (late doors) in the gallery. Held back to the last minute by a fierce doorkeeper, and then a mad dash up the stone stairs, like any tenement dwelling, to find a place on bare wooden steps in the "Gods". The delight of seeing the people you knew, making new friends, comparing notes, cheering madly on the last night until Lilian Bayliss came on for *her* curtain call, knowing all the actors and most of the lines of many of the plays.

Then, one wet Saturday on my way to a football match in North London, I passed by Sadler's Wells, and saw that there was a Saturday matinee of Ballet. I went, and was hooked. Oh, the magic of it! A little later, I saw some of the very great dancers, Riabouchinska, Markova, but nothing could replace that first love — Fonteyn, who was just emerging and dancing marvellously with Robert Helpman. There seemed nothing they could not do. I have never been swept off my feet by Opera in the same way, though I find it enormously enjoyable. The only comparable excitement was the Proms, not as they are now, but the cosy intimacy of the old Queen's Hall and Sir Henry Wood. The predictable nights for Wagner, Bach, or Beethoven, the luxury of a season ticket and thirty-five concerts in a row. To be saturated with so much music, so many paintings, so many plays. And all the buildings, and all the people who shared the excitement. That was one part of my years in London, before the Second War put an end to it.

Chapter Three

A Young Communist – in the Army

When I left school at sixteen in 1934, I was considered fortunate to get an apprenticeship with Lascelles & Co. in Essex Street, just off The Strand, near Fleet Street. They helped to produce *The Illustrated London News* and a whole range of high-quality magazines including *The Tatler, The Sketch,* and several others. I still have the Indentures – portentously signed by the big man in a rather over-awesome ceremony: testimony to a world now long gone. I was put into the retouching department, preparing magazines for production. It was still very much a family business, and one quite old man had been with the firm since he joined it as a boy learning how to engrave illustrations on wooden blocks.

In the evening, I continued at the school in the art classes, drawing from casts or from life, but more often wasting time in delightful indolence, talking all night, in pubs, cafes or clubs.

I had abandoned the church but a new and absorbing interest was Politics and the Trades Union movement. There were several enthusiasts among the men, who encouraged the apprentices to attend Chapel meetings. The idea had been mooted that the apprentices should have their own Chapel. (In the printing trade in general, all branch meetings are called Chapel meetings, and the Chairman is called the Father of the Chapel; a peculiarity said to have its origins in the setting up of the first printing press in a disused chapel at Westminster in the early 16th century.)

An enthusiast for the apprentices' chapel was a man who worked in Watford, Bill Budd. By Christian convictions he was a Methodist, and an earnest Trades Unionist who spent all his spare time at meetings. A remarkably caring man, we all learnt far more from him than we realised, as he drew about a dozen of us together; taught us how to conduct meetings; coached and coaxed us so that we thought that we were doing it all ourselves. We began meeting in 'The Three Tuns', a pub off Fleet Street, and in 1936 the first "Combined Apprentices' Chapel" was born, with Charlie Arben, my friend from Bolt Court, as Secretary and me as Chairman.

18

We seemed to recruit rapidly, and the following year had our first Annual Dinner. I presided in a suit which was one that had been cut down — and didn't feel very comfortable. Bill helped me to write my speech, and over ninety sat down to a meal which included steak-and-kidney pudding. We were all so pleased with ourselves. We little realised that only Bill had made it possible, and that our knowledge of what we were doing was pathetically small. That was my first 'big' speech. The following year, the party was much bigger, and Sir Walter Citrine came as our guest. People were taking note.

I went to art classes less, and political meetings more. One evening, I went to a meeting as a representative of the Apprentices' Chapel, against Bill's advice. I no longer recollect the reason for his objection, though I think that he regarded it as too revolutionary and critical of the movement. He was always a moderate man, short and stocky in build, earnest in attitude, not smiling much, and by nature cautious.

The vast hall was almost empty, and the speeches echoed around, lacking the conviction that only a crowd might have given them. I sat alone, with seats all round me, until a girl came to keep me company. She appeared about my own age, had a lovely smile, and a head that seemed, very slightly, too large for her body. The meeting came to its final unconvincing harangue, and, as we left together, she suggested a drink. And so I met Joan. She lived, to my surprise, not far from me, at Clapham Junction, close to Wandsworth Common. She was, apparently, just as keen on the cinema as I was, and together we began regular visits to the little picture houses showing continental films. Our favourite was one under the arches close by Charing Cross station, with the distant rumble of trains overhead competing with the sound track of *"The Battle Ship Potemkin"*, and the greatly daring *"Bed and Sofa"*. Life was getting hectic, and sleep short. Chapel meetings, art classes, Hugh, whose M.S. was getting worse, to visit, and now Joan, who I wanted to see as often as she would let me. But her time was taken up by another boy-friend and political meetings in Lambeth. So, inevitably, I went along with her. It was my introduction to the Young Communist League. Poor Bill. He warned me against it, but I was hopelessly ignorant, though learning fast, and longing to be enticed.

The South Lambeth branch of the YCL was not very large, but very active. "Intellectuals", students from Cambridge or the LSE, came from time to time to encourage us, preach or teach about Marxism-Leninism, and give me a chance to talk, talk, talk, which I always enjoyed. So we argued into the night, every night, and

Joan and I would loiter on Wandsworth Common or Clapham Common with Joan on the way home while a different sort of education developed. I discovered all the new jargon; delighted in the conspiratorial world; and genuinely believed that a brave new world would come with the revolution, as we sang;

> "I am the worker; he's the boss,
> And the boss's day is done,
> And the worker's day is coming
> With the rising of the sun."

There were three million unemployed, and none of the Social Services that we have now. The rise of Nazism, the Blackshirts, skirmishes in the East End, and, supremely, the Spanish Civil War, all gave a point and urgency to our lives. Collecting money for ambulances for Spain, rubbing shoulders with those who were going; pinning up a poster in my bedroom, and longing to go there myself. I knew so little of the real squalor and horror of it, and only came to appreciate all that it meant to my generation years later, when the men whom I had known did not come back, some of them disappearing altogether: the vivid pictures; the painful poetry; the heroic longing for a creation greater than the romantic illusion that sent so many to a disillusioning and desolate end.

When I first went to live in Cambridge, in 1942, I came to know Frances Cornford and, through her, Stephen Spender and others who had a different view on Spain. Frances lost her youngest son, John, in that war and, through her, we adopted a Spanish refugee, Gerardo Tomé, just a boy, and one of a large family that came to live in Cambridge. Through their eyes, I began to see it all differently. Yet I have never lost the sense that through the Young Communist League and my very ignorant identification with the Civil War, I came face-to-face for the first time in my life, with the sort of heroism, the real "not-to-count-the-cost", which can relate sacrifice of any kind to the perfect Sacrifice of Christ on the Cross. In spite of the mixed motives, the betrayals, the cynicism and selfishness, the brutalities and the hopeless inadequacies, something was there, like the desperate shrieking cry of pain in Picasso's *"Guernica",* that protested the integrity of the human spirit, the living flower of human dignity and the rights of man which Jesus Himself came to affirm. The people of Spain were defeated by all the new powers that were coming into the world.

It was about then that I made a more prominent appearance as a public speaker. It was in Poplar Town Hall on a Sunday afternoon.

I was there on the platform representing the "younger generation". The hall was crowded, noisy, and somewhat belligerent. There was a tram strike at the time, and probably a few Fascist infiltrators there to stir up trouble. The first two speakers were much older men, well-seasoned, with the somewhat ranting style that I had come to accept as normal – and, of course, the party jargon. They got a rough reception. Then it was my turn. There were some shouts and catcalls as I went to the microphone. Someone bellowed, "Give the lad a chance!" I was determined to make my point quickly, loudly, and clearly, and started straight in, hands flying. What I didn't know was that someone, either as a joke or because they thought I'd be nervous, had turned the volume up full! My voice came resounding back from the walls and ceiling, just a vast inde-cipherable noise. The audience loved it, shouted, laughed, booed. The Chairman tried to call for order. I tried to carry on with my speech and ignore the noise, while looking round desperately for someone to tell me what to do. A scuffle broke out at the back of the hall, more of the men were standing up and shouting, and the Chairman finally admitted defeat. The platform party left by a back door; the police cleared the hall; and that was the end of my first big public meeting. Joan wasn't there.

My father, knew where I had been, though he vastly disapproved. The Civil War poster had been the last straw: "Either that poster comes down off the wall, or you leave this house!" When I got home he asked me how I'd got on. I gave a very non-committal reply, and he just carried on with his supper. Later, I learnt from my mother that, in spite of his objections, he couldn't resist finding out how I would manage. He *had* been there.

I remained a member of the YCL and Chairman of the Appren-tices' Chapel until the war broke out. In that time, I learnt a lot more about speaking in public, and all my subsequent experience as a preacher owes a great debt to The Party.

My relationship with Joan became more intense. But I had also started an affair with someone else, another evening commitment, and joined the Territorial Army, which took up my weekends as well.

Joining the Territorials was an odd business. We really did believe that the Communist Party could change the world, and, with a war coming, the party line included infiltration of the armed forces, so I was ordered to join. With our pathetically few members, that must seem comic, but it wasn't to us. (It is interesting to note that there are, at present, seven thousand soldiers of various kinds in Northern Ireland to hold down a Provisional IRA of terrorists that number no more than three hundred.) I first tried to join the Navy, but there was a waiting list; and then the London Scottish, because another new friend, Fred Ashford, was already in it.

Fred knew none of my YCL or TU friends. He was a typical public school Tory, whose parents were professional actors. We met in a pub, and our mutual enthusiasm was the stage. Fred and I had a plan to go to Ireland with a travelling company to learn the ropes of acting. His friendship was enormously important to me because it existed for its own sake, without any ideological commitment. He hated my political attitudes, disliked Joan, was amused by my artistic pretensions, competed with all my other friends for time, and taught me how to love someone for his own sake alone, without false demands or expectations. He thought that I was mad to get involved with the nurses when I went to a military hospital, and even madder when I eventually told him that I intended to become a friar. His religion was as necessary to him as anything else, but he thought it just an exaggeration for me to be a monk − or a Communist!

In the second year of the war, when an appeal went out, he transferred to the Air Force and, all too rapidly, became the pilot of a Lancaster. He disappeared with his plane over the Channel on St George's day. The pain that I felt then, I have felt for a few others since, and it doesn't diminish. He gave me part of the person that I am still becoming.

However, the London Scottish was also full. So, on impulse, and because the son of our next-door-neighbour was doing so, I joined the 5th East Surreys, a local regiment, which shortly after became an anti-tank unit. When the war broke out, we were mustered in Streatham, and then taken to a hall in Epsom. It was there, one day, that about the most unpleasant person in the unit, someone whom I had barely noticed and certainly avoided, indicated that he wanted a private word with me. He was my "Contact", instructed by the Party to get in touch with me. What a contact! The whole idea of being associated with such a miserable creep repelled me. It was the beginning of the end so far as Communism was concerned, though my reasons for finally leaving had more to it than that.

I *had* done my homework. The laboured hours with the 'Little Lenin Library' had been sincere. I may not have read the whole of *Das Kapital,* but I'd read an awful lot of it, and Engels as well. So much commitment could not be easily dismissed. And there were the Comrades. People have always mattered most, and distinguishing between political commitment and personal affection was always difficult.

Then, I think God took a hand. At least, there seems no other way of explaining it, even if it sounds prosaic and pious. Church Parade! It was early in the war, and everyone was still learning "how to do it". Church Parade meant the whole unit marching to a rather evangelical parish church for Mattins, a service which was a complete mystery to me, having been brought up upon nothing but the Mass. Conducted by a hearty parson, it was all too much. I looked for an escape. One was to ask to go to the Anglo-Catholic church in Epsom, where we were stationed. Unfortunately an NCO would have had to go with me (to see that I attended) and a parade of two was not permitted, so – request refused. I then realised that a small but exclusive parade *was* permitted – the RCs, complete with a Roman Catholic sergeant to make sure that they got there. My request to join them was allowed. The Mass was early, and we were all sitting comfortably in a cafe afterwards to watch the others march by! I began to feel serious about it and the local priest encouraged me. A quick instruction, in the circumstances, would be possible.

The Army intervened. Change your religion? Forms must be filled in to make sure that you're buried properly when you get killed. The Anglican chaplain admonished me, and a sub-altern, with whom I had struck up a close friendship, pleaded. He was a Baptist who felt that such a conversion was much worse than death.

Then suddenly the unit got moved from Epsom. Driving through the night, gas masks at the alert and with full equipment, we hunched up in the back of the trucks and said "This is it – France". We ended up at another race course – Lingfield! Here, I was selected for a cadre course for potential officers, taught to ride a motor-bike, and then everything got bogged down in the coldest of winters while we guarded prisoners of war on the race course. I began feeling ill, and finally collapsed and was taken, unconscious, back to Epsom, where I was briefly nursed, and nearly killed, on the race course there. And so to Epsom County Hospital with acute pleurisy and pneumonia. I didn't know it, but that was the end of my engagement, my army career, my political excursions, and the beginning of another sort of life.

When I finally left the Young Communist League I wrote to my closest friends and tried to explain, but they could not hear. Many years later, when I encountered extreme evangelicalism in Cambridge I found that defectors were treated with the same blind rejection.

Joan returned to the boyfriend I had apparently taken her from, married him, and later became a consistently unsuccessful Communist Party Candidate for Parliament. It took me a long time to discover that the whole thing had been planned. I had been spotted as someone it might be worthwhile to recruit, encouraged to attend the abortive meeting in the empty hall, and Joan had been instructed to bring me in! Well, in a certain way she did.

Chapter Four

Papworth Sanatorium – Care in a Community

So my army career came to an abrupt end in the middle of the night on Lingfield racecourse. It had been turned into a POW camp, and we had been assigned to guard it. Security was high as enterprising German sailors had managed to dig long tunnels and create a diversion to escape. It was a terrible winter, and we were ill-equipped and undermanned. The guard huts were desolate, suffocating traps for coke fumes and soldiers' sweat. Each night, a nauseating dixie of soup, with a thick scum of fat floating on it, was kept on the stove to add its own particular odour. To come into the hut made you feel sick, but outside it was so cold that you could build up icicles of spit on your rifle as a diversion.

The officer in charge that night discovered me with my clothes all loosened and my rifle propped up against the barbed wire. When he tried to put me on a charge, I collapsed at his feet. And that was that. I don't remember much of the next few days, but I came to in the County Hospital at Epsom on February 2nd 1940, and was there until June when I was transferred to the Military Hospital in Epsom. From there, on November 11th, I was sent to the sanatorium at Papworth near Cambridge where I remained for almost a year.

The ward in the County Hospital was bossed over by a little tyrant in gold-rimmed glasses. She was an easy object of hatred, and unfairly disliked. But what a regime it was! She was convinced that we were all out to make her life difficult, and that some of us, including me, were in alliance with the other nurses against her.

My illness was finally diagnosed as TB. In those days Tuberculosis was still thought of as a killer. On a table, not far from my bed was a jar full of syringes with very long needles – rather sinister. It was with mild horror that I found myself on the receiving end. Screens were drawn round; the Sister talked to me in a "calming voice", but, in fact, as the doctor put it into the back of my lung, I didn't see it go in, or feel very much. But my imagination was active and, afterwards, Sister prescribed brandy – a teaspoonful!

Her attitude changed a lot. I suppose she assumed, as my parents did, that I would die. Sister told me the diagnosis with the same solemn, calming voice. There had been a case conference round my bed. Two doctors, two nurses, two students. After much examining of X-rays, tapping, listening with stethoscopes, they all went outside the screen, leaving me alone. But, of course, I could hear the discussion. Finally, the doctor's voice came through the screen. "Well, will you tell him? Or shall I?" And Sister replied, calmly, "I will." So she came in and, with her special voice, said, "I want you to be brave. You are a soldier. There is something I have to tell you." She paused, and I broke in rather too brightly, "You are going to tell me I've got TB." Poor woman! Had I been kinder, I wouldn't have stolen her lines.

Later on, a young nurse came to hold my hand and look sorrowful, which I rather liked, and when the news got round the ward, those who were able tried to cheer me up. The difficulty was that I really could not feel particularly sorry for myself. Since I had been admitted to the hospital, I had seen some sad sights. A few days after I arrived, a young Welshman in the next bed had died of a tumour on the brain. I had liked him, and felt acutely the distress of his little wife. I had never been so close to death before. Even now, I fear something like that happening to me. Yet I didn't feel pain from the TB, only weakness; it was sometimes boring in bed but I had a chance to read and read, sometimes two short books a day.

I was put out in the open, together with another lad of my age who also had TB, and we became friends. We were given better food and more milk. I almost felt that I was letting other people down when I didn't feel frightened.

Something else happened at the County Hospital. I received Communion again after many years. The Chaplain, a pale, indecisive, rather diffident young man, came round looking for likely candidates for Easter Communion. I had already said an uncertain "No" when he came to my bed − and so had almost everyone else. I suddenly felt an awful discomfort for him − so as he was leaving us I looked again in his direction, caught his eye, and impetuously said, "All right. I'll take it too."

Something, although I was not certain what, had happened. This was different from the superficial return to Church in Epsom. I looked round the ward, but the one or two men that I had got to know kept their heads down in slight embarrassment. I had put up a small barrier. The following morning, I found the Crucifix which Jane had given me and put it on my locker. The Chaplain came and celebrated in the ward. Two or three of us received the Sacrament. I didn't feel very different apart from the persistent sense that something had changed a bit.

Of course, the Chaplain came again, and commented on the Crucifix, but then, I had put it there to please him more than God. He didn't say much, only enough to establish my identity as a Christian. He left me feeling that it might get difficult to reverse the trend. *But I didn't want to. That* was the unexpected thing.

Not long after that, I was moved to a military hospital just outside Epsom. It was really an old mental hospital, with the majority of patients moved elsewhere to prepare for the expected influx of casualties.

They certainly came after Dunkirk, in horrifying numbers, but, when I arrived, it was almost empty. I was driven there by a well-meaning lady from the WVS. On the way, she asked if I had any relations near, so I gave her the address of my mother, and she promised to let her know of my move. She was as good as her word, and turned up at home. Jane came to the door.

"Mrs Fisher?"

"Yes, that is right."

"I have come to give you information about your son. May I come in?"

Jane, shocked though probably not showing it, took her in and offered her tea. Formalities over, the good lady, ignorant of the hospital situation, continued in a solemn "understanding" voice: "My dear, you must prepare yourself for a shock. Of course, I am sure he will be all right in the end. They can do wonders these days. But I have just taken your son from the County Hospital to be admitted to Horton Mental Hospital."

Poor Mother. She knew that I had TB, a killer complaint; Brownie was away in the army, Sybil had been in a surface shelter which received a direct hit, and was one of the few who survived; and now I, presumably, had gone mad. Later in the day she rushed to the hospital with Reg, and there I was, sitting up in bed and wondering what all the fuss was about! In fact, what interested me more that day was Edith.

Edith was the nurse from King's College Hospital who had admitted me, taken my pulse, noted my respiration, and put a thermometer into my mouth. Making up my chart, she suddenly looked up. No make-up, lovely eyes, an oval face, and hair in a tidy bun at the back of her head. Unusual, and not as prim as it sounds. I caught her eye and she smiled, "Do you ever say your prayers?" She took the thermometer out and, while she read it and shook it

down, I replied, "What on earth has that to do with you?" "Well",
she said, "Your papers say that you are Church of England − how
do you expect to get well if you don't pray?"

So we started talking about religion. Eventually, she lent me
books, *"The Imitation of Christ", "Brother Laurence",* wheeled me
to the Chapel for a Service, or to the Hall for concerts, talked about
God a lot. My best friend from the Young Communist League, Stan
Segal, came to see me once, but he never came again. Later in the
war, a gun carriage rolled back on him, and he was crushed to death.
I always wanted to make it right with him and it hurt intensely that
I hadn't. Finally, I wrote my letter resigning from the Party, and
Edith put the pressure on for the priesthood. She was engaged to
an ordinand, but he was in India. I discovered that they were both
something called Tertiaries, associated with the Franciscans, and
knew a monk with the unlikely name of Algy, whom they had met
in St Ives, but it meant nothing to me. There was another soldier
on the ward who became very fond of her, and of me, and the three
of us fell mildly in love. So my Christianity got caught in a rather
human romantic web.

Dunkirk put an end to it. The hospital was suddenly overwhelmed
with men who cried fearfully in the night, gasping horrifying
sounds. In a short while the whole place had an air of wartime
emergency, and remarkable efficiency. I was allowed up, and helped
with the bed-making, fetching and carrying. Wearing the old army
blue uniform with white shirt and red tie I would walk into Epsom,
and be treated like a hero − an undeserved embarrassment. We
watched the Battle of Britain by day, planes circling and wheeling
overhead, and were entertained in the evening by Evelyn Laye and
other stars. Summer turned to Autumn and my stay there seemed
endless. Then I was suddenly posted to Papworth Sanatorium, near
Cambridge.

Papworth Village Settlement was started by Pendril Verrier Jones
in a village near Cambridge, and intended entirely for men and
women suffering from T.B. The village was dominated by a small
country house, which was his first hospital. Verrier Jones really
believed in the healing and acceptance of the whole person and the
creation of an environment in which that could be made possible.
Men and women came there, often with quite advanced TB (and
before all the modern medicine), as a last hope. Many who came
to die stayed to live, and to live fulfilled family lives with their
wives and children, working in the industries he had established
in the village, living in one of the cottages, and with hospital facil-
ities available if they were ever ill. They knew that illness would

not lose them their jobs; that they would have immediate treatment from doctors (some of whom also had been TB patients) who knew their case histories, and that they would not be shunned by their workmates or neighbours, all of whom were in the same boat.

People outside Papworth were sometimes frightened of it. We heard of those who always closed all the windows and drove through the village as quickly as possible in case they caught something. The settlement was a self-contained place, outwardly ordinary, with village shops, schools, post office, church. The village hall was popular for dances, WEA classes (how much I owe to them and, because of the proximity of Cambridge, the remarkable and talented tutors we had for everything from Saxon settlements to bee-keeping). The factories produced high-quality furniture, leatherwork, and printing, and the hospital became a centre for research. Some of the same spirit continues now that the place is used for heart and chest diseases and transplants.

I lived in a community of fifty patients, each with a little canvas hut. Fresh air and "building" food were still almost the only treatment – apart from some radical ways of collapsing lungs!

When I started work, I had the pleasant option of assisting in the pathological laboratories. Part of the process of giving men and women a sense of worth and dignity was encouraging them to work, to do something. At first, one worked for only an hour a day but gradually this was increased if possible. For this work we were paid. Only a token, perhaps, but it meant that we still felt of use to others. I have spent a lot of time going to hospitals ever since, for regular checks on my chest and, much later, for a couple of operations. At both the military hospital and Papworth Sanatorium I was taught to look after my health, and, though I suspect that I am sometimes mocked for being a hypochondriac, the fact is that I've lived a very full and fairly arduous life; been many times round the world, on safaris in central Africa and Papua New Guinea, with one lung doing the work of two. I owe it largely to Papworth.

I believe in healing. Healing of all kinds. Healing, for me, begins by knowing what is wrong, trusting the experts, believing that God uses doctors, nurses, psychiatrists, physiotherapists, and all the rest. By trusting their knowledge, and, as far as they will let me, sharing it, I know that I am trusting God who is the source of health, whether the doctors believe it or not! My concern for health and healing began with Hugh and multiple sclerosis and I have had many friends since with that disease. As President of the Multiple Sclerosis Society in Cornwall, I found myself caught up in my own life with something that I could share with them, which is part of a healing ministry. Through the TB, I know what it is like to feel frustrated, but also aware of the new opportunities that acceptance of *any* handicap can give us. More recently, for the past ten years I have had to adjust to glaucoma and cataract. That was a bit of a shock at first. But my over-reaction settled down and, though I cannot do quite what I did, fresh avenues and opportunities have appeared.

One result of inadequate vision has been broken bones – when I don't see steps, wires, or road levels. I also suspect that these accidents occurred at times when I was already emotionally vulnerable. They have certainly all, so far, been related to events which I found challenging or fearful. I broke my wrist – my left, my writing wrist – in the first week of a sabbatical at Cambridge. And my ankle just as I was about to cover the interregnum in Truro diocese when the Bishop, Graham Leonard, was translated to London.

It was a new experience – crutches and wheelchairs. I attended a General Synod in York in a wheel chair and Archbishop Runcie announced to the Synod that I had joined the "Year of the Disabled" (which was then being kept), but only temporarily. On the other hand, did I have the accidents as a defence? The one thing of which I am fairly certain is that they were not merely "accidental" – a conclusion which I draw not from my experience alone, but the observing of others.

Healing of the whole man; body, mind, spirit, and emotion, seem to me to go together. Beginning with any one of those elements, you can be led on to take the other three into account. Spiritual Healers, and all those who seem to isolate one element at the expense of the rest, are always a little suspect to me. The first, and most important thing, in my eyes, is to be concerned with the person, to love them and share their life. This, after all, was the approach of Jesus. I don't think He ever saw anyone as a "client" or "patient", but always as a person, and as such, unique. When people come to see me, I want always to create the possibility of knowing them and, to that end, of letting them know me.

Papworth gave me a basis for learning to look after myself; to rely on the expertise of specialists, to believe that I could always give something which was of value to others, that I was worth something. It taught me the value of sharing – "bearing one another's burdens"; of knowing that the whole world is a hospital ward, and all mankind handicapped. That God is the Great Healer, whether we know it or not.

It was at Papworth that I decided for the second time that I might try to become a priest. I also heard again of the Franciscans – but felt sure that they weren't for me.

Chapter Five

A slow train to Dorset – and The Society of St. Francis

I was finally discharged from the army on a pension in 1941. I was twenty-three, and the Papworth Village Settlement pressed me to "colonise", settle down as a resident. It was attractive, but I knew that it was also not what I wanted. But what did I want? To return to Lascelles and *The Illustrated London News* would be easy, but dull. An old friend, Walter Humphries, who had some sort of connection with The Old Vic and knew everyone in the theatre, felt certain that I could be taken on at the Liverpool Rep, a career, which I had frequently found attractive. That pipe dream reached the point of a contract, which just needed signing. Another friend suggested that I join a large and distinguished store in London. In the end, I doubted the seriousness of the jobs which I was being offered. At any rate, I hung fire.

In any case, there was still the nagging sense that I might "go into the Church", the infinitely more flattering idea of being ordained. Then I met Norah Everis. A mutual friend had assured me we would enjoy each others company. Norah was a moral welfare worker, living in a flat at the top of a bicycle shop on the corner of Jesus Lane in Cambridge. I called late one wet and cold afternoon. The stairway seemed dusty and dark – and when she finally came to the door I felt a moment of disappointment; she so much looked the part – that blouse and skirt, those sensible shoes.

Norah was one of the loveliest people in my life. She later married a probation officer, and eventually died of cancer. I owe her much. One winter evening, over tea and toast, she said, "And what will you do when you leave Papworth?" So I told her that I couldn't escape a persistent sense of wanting to be a priest. When she asked me why, I tried to explain about a sense of calling, of gratitude for my recovery from TB, of wanting to help others, of beginning again. What I didn't say, though I vaguely knew it to be true, was that I had a romantic attachment to the idea, had found all the emotional enthusiasm of my boyhood aroused at Papworth, where the Church and ceremonial was so much like St Peter's, Clapham; that I enjoyed the close company of clergymen, was unconsciously looking for a costume part in life, and the whole clerical idea appealed; but then, I had not said as much to myself. Perhaps I was also looking for a way out of Papworth and an attachment I had made to someone there whom I didn't really love.

Weeks passed, and suddenly, out of the blue, I had a letter from a Father Denis in Cambridge, apparently a Franciscan. I knew that there must be Franciscan Brothers there; I had once seen one in the street. But this was an invitation to supper! "Could I come? I would be saving him from losing a friend if I would say 'Yes'." Norah Everis had given him my name.

Much later, I heard the story. Norah was sitting behind Denis at a meeting of Moral Welfare Workers, priests and others. Before the meeting started, she leant forward, tapped Denis on the shoulder, and said, "Dear Denis, there is a young man, a friend of mine. I would like you to invite for tea or supper. I think you could help him over his future."

Denis, always impetuous, impatient, nervous, and, as a result, sometimes spontaneously negative, turned round abruptly and said, "Really, Norah, I'm far too busy to see any casual young man you send round."

Then the meeting started, and William Temple gave a brilliant address on Charity as the basis of Social Service. At the end of it, there was applause and, when it had died down, Denis slowly turned his head and humbly said, "When is he coming?". There are many Denis stories and that, as I was to discover, was typical.

So, one evening I presented myself at St Francis House, Lady Margaret Road, and rang the bell. After what seemed an interminable time, the door abruptly opened, and there was the tall, romantic figure of a Friar, swathed in the many folds of a big brown cloak. So far as he was concerned, I discovered, it was only protection from a cold in the head.

We sat in a badly-lit room, in long cane student chairs, which creaked as we moved, in front of a bubbling and inadequate gas fire, surrounded by faded photographs of Tractarian worthies. He asked me all about myself. (How many times was I to be confronted with the question — "And now tell me all about yourself." I try to avoid it but, only a day or two ago, a young man the same age as I was then sat down to talk, and I nearly said it.)

So we went over all the ground, and he, wrapped up to the eyes, listened and observed, his handsome face and chestnut hair were already enough to lull me into acquiescence in any plan he suggested. Finally, he asked whether I would care to come and live there for a while to sort out what I might do. Would I like to – I could hardly wait.

So I left Papworth in the summer of 1941 and went to live in St Francis House in Cambridge with a group of friars I hardly knew. Ronald was there, a Pacifist in the novitiate, a musician, conjurer, preacher, an exciting and very hard-working young man, digging for victory in the lovely lawn behind the house. Gilbert, a bearded priest with a beautiful baritone voice and a sad face. He too, was a powerful preacher. In the end, he died, alone on a hillside in France, his breviary and a bottle of wine beside him. Arthur, the elderly eccentric ex-missionary. Denis, the best of the preachers, striding or cycling around Cambridge, attracting students to the house and St Edward's Church, where the brethren worshipped in those days. Given to bouts of moodiness, flashes of anger, uncertain and insecure, relying on his charm, and quite considerable gift of acting to get him through; loving, caring, but erratic and temperamental. Without knowing it, I had embarked on a friendship which, though it was never mentioned except in the objective language of spiritual enquiry, or in concern for other people, and never expressed in letter, nevertheless began to change my attitude to all other friendships.

I learnt a lot from Denis, though I didn't know it at the time. A lot about the way in which God uses our vulnerability, our weaknesses, fears and fantasies, even more than our strengths.

I was shattered when, after a few months, it seemed as if the TB was coming back and I had to go home for a while. Ronald, too, was ill with a disease in his eye. I came back to Cambridge and we were both anointed. I rapidly recovered, while Ronald lost his eye, and we were both faced with mystery.

Then Fred Ashford was killed, and it seemed like a chapter closing in my life. Denis tried to help me over that. I made new friends among the students, though it embarrassed me to admit that I had no academic ability or future.

One week, there appeared a little poem by Frances Cornford in the *New Statesman*. We both read it, and liked it so much that I persuaded Denis to write to her and say so. She lived just down the road at Conduit Head. A few days later, in the middle of a fearful storm, the doorbell rang, and there stood a bedraggled figure, short, with sharp eyes and an instant smile, assuming that we would take her in. Through that encounter, she gradually came back to the Church, and was the only Darwin to take up religion. Her friendship meant meeting her friends. For a while, Francis, her husband, tried to teach me Greek, but it was a disaster! He knew too much, and I too little. So instead of going for the classes which I dreaded, I went for supper which I loved. Frances often came to St Francis House.

Inevitably, I began to feel that I was meant to be a Franciscan. My health appeared to be a hazard, but there were very few Brothers then, twelve or fourteen at the most, and some of the new ones were even less fit than I. Almost anyone was recruited it seemed. I didn't know that of course. I knew little or nothing about the Church, or the Faith, or the Religious Life. The sense of wartime emergency also played a part. I had already been in one uniform; so why not another

My parents came to Cambridge for the day, and were warned by Gilbert, but encouraged by Denis. I talked it over with the saintly Fr. Edward Wynn, a member of the Oratory of the Good Shepherd, who was to become the Bishop of Ely, and would ordain me many years later. "Tell me all about yourself.": he, too, warned me of being carried away with a romantic notion, and of the possibility of great loneliness (which I did not understand, though I do now), and suggested a little caution. Of course, Cambridge itself cast a certain spell. There were hardly any cars, a still city of ancient buildings, warm tradition, sophisticated, understated, infinitely and danger- ously charming, as were so many of the people whom I met.

So it was decided that I should go to Cerne Abbas in Dorset and meet Algy Robertson, the Father Guardian, and find out if I had a vocation, and if he would have me.

I remember the journey as if it were yesterday. Such little country towns and villages were new to me. Of course, I had been to Sussex, and Scotland, but the unchanged life of Dorset was new. The slow train to Yeovil Junction, the shuttle train to Yeovil Town, a walk through the streets, and then on to Yeovil Pen Mill. The little steam train seemed to amble through the countryside, almost pushing aside the branches to make its way. We sat in a carriage the like of which I'd never seen before: with seats around the edge, making country conversation possible (in a dialect I could barely under- stand) between men who talked of pigs and sheep, women of cakes. From Evershot station there was the walk, up hill and along a ridge of the downs, opening up endless views of Blackmoor Vale, and so after three miles to a steep hill, down through an almost covered lane − with at the end of it "The Friary".

Chapter Six

Encounter with Algy

"The Parlour", like the rest of the Friary, seemed designed to pre-serve my sense of romantic illusion. A small, low room, a rough stone floor, latticed windows, and walls crowded with books. Two long tables had the rugged irregularity of what had once been car-penters' benches, but now, brilliantly polished, reflected a bowl of marigolds.

Somewhere, I'd seen a notice which bluntly said, "Silence", so, as I was shown in, I said nothing, but sat down uneasily, and, accepting a mug of tea with a slight smile, was left alone.

A lazy fly droned somewhere. The sunshine streamed in. I'd been told to wait, so, having finished my tea, I considered the backs of the nearest books. The silence became a heavy stillness. I was sitting right opposite a clock. Now I could hear it. Waiting and – fear? No, not fear, but a sort of prickling apprehension.

Then, suddenly, the sound of steps squeaking on stairs; like someone creeping down, trying too hard to be quiet. A silent pause outside the door. The old-fashioned latch rattled, and I instinctively looked up as the door opened, while a head looked sharply round the room through gold-rimmed glasses. I went back to staring intently at my empty mug, and a little man, having apparently accepted the room as empty, came in. He was *such* a little man, with shoes that seemed too large. A friar's habit, held together with a white rope that trailed a bit behind, cov-ered him bulkily, like a squat bear that had been uncertainly stuffed.

There was a large, flat book under his arm, and, reaching a chair in the far corner of the room, he opened it on the table. I tried to watch him without being seen. Suddenly, plunging his hand into a fold of his habit, he brought out a bundle of picture postcards. These he sorted into piles, occasionally holding one at arm's length, looking at it, head cocked to one side like a critical bird. Intent on his scrapbook, I came to accept that being ignored was just part of the "Silence", and gazed out of the window. The fly continued to search it with lazy indifference, and the only other sound came from the steady tick of the clock.

Then, suddenly, I knew − but how do we know such things? − with a prickling sense of curiosity, almost of excitement, I *knew* that I was under observation. A quick glance − each time he looked at a card!

I'd only just arrived at this idea when he suddenly put them all together again in a neat pile, pushed them back inside his habit, picked up the book and, without any sort of recognition, went out. His steps receded up the stairs with the same exaggerated caution, and I was alone again.

Another twenty minutes crawled slowly past the face of the clock. Another rattle of the latch. Another brother.

"Father Algy would like to see you now. I'm sorry you've had to wait." Father Algy. I'd heard so much, but had no idea what to expect. In my mind, he had become a tall, powerful man, the Head of the Community. From the endless stories about him, I found the prospect a bit fearful. I was led up the stairs to a narrow corridor. There were various doors, one of which had a crooked notice hanging on it which said, "Engaged". We tapped, and waited until a rather high-pitched voice cried, *"Do* come in!" As it opened, we seemed to crowd the entrance, bumping into yet another brother who was leaving.

But then the whole room was crowded. Books everywhere: on shelves, on tables, piled on the floor, crowded on a bed which took up most of the space. And in the bed, hunched up − the same little man! "Do come along. I think you'd better sit on the end of the bed." He acted as if he'd never seen me before, and stretched out a hand, small, delicate, cold. My mind was so full of the image which I had created − the big, powerful, masterful leader, that it just could not feel anything in response to his obvious warmth except an instant sense of being cheated or tricked.

I did as I was told. There was, in any case, nothing else to do, as there was no other place to sit. It would have been difficult even to walk out.

By the side of the bed, and behind it, were tables piled with prayer books, hymn books, and bottles. On the table beside the bed, on the floor and on two chairs, were a bundle of little mapping pens, bottles of ink and bottles of ink eraser. Oh, the complication of all the erasing! Two bottles with dippers or droppers. A bottle of ammoniated quinine ("*quite* the best thing for a cold!"), bottles of medicine ...

One whole shelf had musical editions of every imaginable hymn book, another a large pile of Bibles. The window had a deep recess, with half-open drawers stuffed with papers and books, more books on top.

A tall, melancholy, lean, and apparently frightened man towered in the middle of it, his black cassock held, here and there, with safety pins. He was reading out loud in a monotonous, powerful voice, quite oblivious, it seemed, of another figure in black who, when he spoke, had the lilting vitality of Welsh in his voice. Algy was dictating a letter to him, periodically waiting for him to catch up, and meantime addressing a word or two to the reader. "Dear Charles, *do* read that again." – "Yes, Vincent, I know I'm keeping you waiting." – this to the secretary.

Hunched in the middle of the bed, he seemed almost invisible. The bedclothes and blankets were covered by a large brown cloak, with a tartan rug slipping out from under it. The pillows were piled high and, on all sides, there were towels. Sometimes, he seemed to roll one up and tuck it behind his head; later, it became a sort of turban; while another he held across his face, so that only his penetrating eyes behind the gold rims peered out, missing nothing. Of course, there were books open all around him on the bed, from which he would read, occasionally writing a comment in the margin with the mapping pens, or putting a note in another. At intervals, he would suddenly remember a letter that need writing and his hand would go searching for a writing pad. The letter would then be done while he carried on listening to the book that was being read to him, a letter was being dictated, and he was making notes – possibly for a lecture!

At the same time, I might add, he was also interviewing me – and the rest of my life might hang on it. In the event our meeting seemed brief, and little to the point. An enquiry about the journey, my health and a *"Do* make yourself at home – and I will see you later." It was indeed, very much later that day before I saw him again. I left Algy's room late at night – or, more accurately, in the early hours of the morning. He seemed to thrive on such hours, and be most alive and alert when everyone else had gone to bed.

While reading a description of William Wilberforce, the great Evangelical reformer and abolitionist of the slave trade, I was struck by the way in which it seemed also to be an apt description of Algy, who, after all, came from a similar background of wealthy upper middle-class "trade", and Evangelistic zeal.

He wasn't ugly – and, if the pictures are accurate, neither was Wilberforce – but he was, like him, very short, and his

bright piercing eyes and rather high-pitched sweet voice, sometimes speaking rather rapidly, were instantly captivating. Asleep
or resting, the lines of pain were more clearly marked on his face,
which was, to me, strangely compelling.

He was born in 1894. Baptised William Strowan Amhurst
Robinson, he was given the name "Algy" by his friends at Cambridge and it stuck for the rest of his life. He was short, slight and
dapper in those days. An energetic person, always on the move,
with a life-style that was always too crowded, dominated by his
love of people, his inability to say "No", his enthusiasms which he
persuaded his friends to share and whose lives he organised with
greater success than he did his own. His generosity and impetuosity together with an unusually developed power of persuasion
made him the centre of a whirl of activity erupting in the lives of
men and women, organisations and individuals, like a tiny human
tornado. It was irresistible.

After Westminster School came Cambridge, where he read English
and won a prize for poetry. He had a light and eloquent voice, and
later became a powerful preacher: no doubt it was also a part of
his ability to persuade, certainly there were few who ever found
the way to say 'No' to him, and those who did frequently found
themselves confronted with such disarming courtesy that they came
to regret it.

His countless friends of all kinds have always found it difficult to
say just what it was that made him the unique centre of love that he
became. Once in Glasgow cathedral he was leading a service and, as
often was the case, operating a shade louder than anyone else. As
his voice seemed to ring out in the psalms "I am small and of no
reputation", Outram Walsh, a life-long friend of his, sitting next to
me said under his breath "Oh no you're not, Algy!"

He then taught in India for a while before returning to Cambridge to prepare for ordination at Westcott House under B.K.
Cunningham. His curacy at St George's, Cullercoats, in Northumberland is still part of the folk memory of the parish. He
instantly embraced the world of the Geordies and was laughed
at but never mocked, loved, for his witty, somewhat dandified
ways.

In 1924 he returned to the student world, where he always felt
instantly at home, and as the Secretary of Theological Colleges for
the Student Christian Movement had the whole country to travel
in, communicate his love for God and men, his enthusiasm for the
Gospel, his passionate belief in his countless friends, and his love
of organisation.

His next enthusiasm involved a return to India. Captured by the imaginative vision of Jack Winslow, himself also something of a religious Pied Piper, Algy recognised the possibility of appealing to the Indian people, whom he already loved, to recognise Christ through the devotion and example of St Francis. The ideal of renunciation, of deliberately embraced poverty, of sharing their life, seeing Jesus through Indian eyes and in an Indian life-style, all found a total response in him. Algy, like Francis, was in the best sense a romantic.

So in 1927 he went with some of his friends to India, where he made a strong impact on the Franciscan Ashram near Poona, the community started by Winslow in 1922 and called Christa Seva Sangha. For nearly twenty years that experiment in the Religious Life made a striking and unique witness in India. But the price paid by Algy was a severe one, and in 1930 he returned to England with a sickness from which he never recovered. He became Vicar of St Ives in Huntingdonshire, and turned his vicarage into a friary to recruit and train men for India.

Among those who joined him was Francis Tyndale-Briscoe. His family included notable missionaries in India, and it was Francis who encouraged Algy to consider merging his small group of Franciscans in St Ives with those of Bro Douglas Downes in *his* Friary in Dorset – The Brotherhood of St Francis of Assisi. After a trial year Algy took his brothers there in 1937, and the two groups became the "Society of St Francis".

Brother Douglas, with Kenneth and Arthur, and a little later, Charles, had started there in 1922, caring for homeless unemployed vagrants and generally supervising twelve other Homes of St Francis for wayfarers all over the country, tramping the road themselves and preaching as well as sharing the lives of the men they met. It was a hard life and few of the recruits who came to join the brothers stayed for long. Douglas was a great contrast to Algy. Tall, shy, a little diffident, though absolutely convinced and determined in his care for the men: an old-fashioned sacramental evangelical rather than an eclectic Anglo-Catholic, which was the mark of Algy's spirituality. They both came from Free Church backgrounds and shared that sort of evangelical freedom.

My first visit to the Friary was in the second year of the war, and by then Douglas had moved to London and taken up a ministry to the troops (he was a Chaplain in the 1914-18 war). Charles was helping to run a parish in South London, and Arthur was in the house in Cambridge which had been the "headquarters" of the Oratory of the Good Shepherd, a fellowship of celibate priests. The

Oratory had a big influence on Algy as a young man, and many of its members were his intimate friends and part of the Cambridge connection which so influenced his life, and mine. It was in that house that he was admitted as a prospective member of the Indian community just before he sailed with his friends for Bombay and Poona. When I first met him in the Friary in Dorset in 1941 I knew nothing of this: or that he, more than anyone else, would be the paramount influence in my life, as in the lives of so many. During that first visit, I "made a retreat" - something I'd never done before. The great idea was that it would give me time to make up my mind about becoming a friar. Father Algy talked as if it were a forgone conclusion, but then that was his manner with most men.

No doubt I wanted to be persuaded, and he was a powerful persuader. There were three other men who would also be "going into retreat", and he said, "I shall conduct it myself!" The jargon of religion, so obvious to the initiated, so incomprehensible to the ignorant, was also beginning to acquire the glamour of a very new world into which I had only recently been drawn. When I finally became a novice, one of my newly-found priestly friends wrote, "You are probably entering the finest school of sanctity in the Church of England at the present time." It was a very perceptive remark, for, in fact, there were precious few signs of the existence of such a school, though, of course, I didn't know that. The School of Sanctity was Algy himself, a latter-day Aelred of Rievaulx, who had already attracted to himself, and, through himself, to God, a small group of men as foundation stones for the Franciscan Society.

Algy believed passionately in the Religious Life as an instrument of God in the establishment of the Kingdom of Heaven on earth. His enthusiasm and integrity gave him an almost uncanny ability to communicate that love to others. His overwhelming care for people was a reflection of his absolute surrender to the love of God, human and divine. It was enormously and irresistibly attractive – as Francis of Assisi must have been. Francis too was a little man with a hint of the dandy in his youth. This comparison cannot, of course, be too closely drawn – but from the same sort of middle-class affluence they came to an indifference towards wealth and a love of man which sprang from a deep and clear acceptance of the incarnate Christ from crib to cross, in a single-minded commitment to preaching the Gospel, and in a profound awareness of prayer and the contemplation of God. They both died prematurely from sicknesses incurred in the service of a Master to whom they gave unswerving, eccentric, romantic and costly obedience.

By the end of the retreat the die was cast, and one by one we all told Algy we wanted to join. Of the four of us I was the first to return to Cerne Abbas, after a few more months in Cambridge, going there in August 1942 and being made a Novice on St Francis' Day, October 4th, that same year. The others? also became monks, and came to the Friary, though only one other, Geoffrey, stayed. He finished his degree at Cambridge, was ordained and served a title before coming. Ultimately he took over the parish and work of the old S.D.C. at Plaistow in East London and rebuilt the Church which had been bombed, building up an impressively large ministry. Later he founded all the work in the Pacific which now has a flourishing Province of brothers who are almost entirely Melanesian, as well as houses in Australia and New Zealand. Eventually he became the Minister General and my immediate predecessor.

The other two also came, but ultimately left. Both became Roman Catholic monks, one a Benedictine, the other a Carthusian.

Algy's retreat might seem to have been worth the energy he put into it.

Chapter Seven

"I think it might be right for you to Help me"

The first Franciscan at Hilfield was Br Giles, who had once been a friar of the S.D.C.- Society of Divine Compassion – the first Franciscan Brotherhood in East London. He went there in 1921, but his health collapsed after a year and he was obliged to leave. Br Douglas followed in 1922, and eventually attracted the support of three others: Br Charles, a young priest, Br Kenneth, a young artisan who had been trained as a printer, and Br Arthur. In those days they were called the Brotherhood of St Francis of Assisi. Arthur I already knew from the Cambridge House. A splendid period piece if ever there was one! He came from a Welsh family. In fact, his old home had become one of the Homes of St Francis for Wayfarers. Large, with a straggling beard, an enormous nose, and the enthusiasm of a boy for God – and cricket. He'd sit in the Chapel at the old St Francis House in Cambridge on a sultry afternoon, with the distant sounds of a game on John's Cricket ground in the background. Once, the lesson at Evensong was mildly interrupted by a burst of applause, and Arthur, one ear on the game, exclaimed, "He's out!" His room was a Victorian jumble of endless bric-a-brac, pots, pictures, scrapbooks. Priceless editions from his home would have picture postcards pasted into them. All that remains from it is a sloping desk – which I still use. Arthur had been a missionary in Africa, and liked to talk of great days there. He belonged to the same affluent world of gentle gentlemen who could afford to give up everything, and did so with generous dignity and charm.

To understand the early days of the Franciscan Movement in the Church of England, it is necessary to recapture, if it is at all possible, the flavour of the world from which so many of its founders were drawn, and of which Arthur was a typical example: James Adderley and Father Andrew in the SDC;[1] George Potter in the BHC[2]; Douglas and Charles and Arthur in the BSFA[3]; Jack Winslow, Leonard Schiff, Outram Walsh, Bill Lash, Verrier Elwin in the CPSS; [4] Algy, Francis, Denis, Owen, Stephen and many more in the SSF[5] – all had characteristics in common. The security of the settled world of Victorian or Edwardian England; a public school education, Oxford or Cambridge for University, Westcott House or Cuddesdon or their equivalent for Theological College. A heroic curacy in the north of England or, at any rate, in a slum parish. A longing to go abroad to India or Africa; a generous concern for the underprivileged, as we now call them; a genuine sense of dedication to God, and a simple love for His people. It still, in recollection, has slight overtones of quite unintended condescension, the enthusiastic sharing in "hop picking missions" or "fruiting campaigns", a sort of "slumming" among the poor. Not that they saw it in that way. In fact, they were loved for being the eccentric gents that they were. Loved for a charm that came from a freedom to move, talk, just exist, because the restraints of real penury have never been felt. They had a freedom which could easily have been directed into other channels, and often the naturally assumed confidence that went without question. Instinctively, they knew that something was wrong with society and tried to correct it. In the eyes of their parents and peers they were either noble or slightly ridiculous, to be tolerated and loved for their eccentric determination to be monks. The "High Church", tradition in Tory families, was a respected one. After all, James Adderley the founder of the first Franciscan Order was the son of a Peer. Algy's family, less exalted, could nevertheless be respected for having become rich and established. Algy's excuse, whenever we had a meal in a hotel, "My dear mother will pay for it" was an exact excuse. The gap between the truly poor and the really rich was never quite bridged. Except that, with some of them, the integrity of personality won through. Douglas was deeply loved because he had the mentality and attitude of the trenches in the 1914-18 war. Under him, all men really were equal, and the fire still blazed even when the all clear was sounded. They embraced the incipient socialism, that had very little to do with politics, but had much to do with their uncensorious solidarity in love of men and women made in the image of God.

Even Algy, who, I think, could never entirely enter into the life of what, for want of better words, we called a "working man", nevertheless could attract *any* man or woman by reason of this clear love for people. Actual poverty, or what he took to be poverty, embarrassed and distressed him. In the early days of our friendship, I would sometimes stay at, or go for a meal to, his home in Ealing. It was a remarkable experience for me of life on "the other side of the Common". A very large house in its own grounds, 22 Ealing Common. Not, in fact, as large as his Aunt's nearby, but still a house with a big basement in which, though rarely seen, was a cook. A housemaid opened the door and, in the background, a chauffeur-cum-gardener. I rather fancy that there was another maid as well. I think the servants came from a "Home", one of those charities which Mrs Robertson supported with lavish and generous gifts. Algy still had a room in the house, and so had "Monkey", his brother, who had been a soldier, though both had long since left home. In fact, the whole place was kept going just for the old lady. The drawing room extended through the house, with long windows and two fireplaces, each with burnished steel.

In the dining room, Mrs Robertson, a very little lady, always sat upright, never allowing her back to touch the back of the chair. She had a remarkably adroit way of flicking her chair forward to sit on, almost like magic. There was always a bowl of beautiful shining apples, but I do not recall that she ever ate one, and Lucozade to drink. If it was tea, then that would be taken in the small drawing room, and came in on a large silver tray. If she knew we were coming, there would always be water cress and Marmite sandwiches tiny, frail, wafer-thin for Algy, and rock cakes for me. The house had an uncanny quiet, and never quite seemed "home".

From time to time, Algy would retreat there, just to recover from his most recent bout of illness. The chemist on Ealing Common had a prescription for his medicine, as had chemists all over the country; bottles and bottles accumulated everywhere. After the first Mission on which I ever went with him, at St Alban's Holborn, we went back to Ealing, and he dictated an outline of all the Mission addresses, with full instructions on how to give them, and illustrate them, suggesting prayers and, as it was one of his great concerns, the hymns.

Which was as well. Algy soon discovered how little I knew when I arrived at Cerne Abbas and became a novice. Algy recruited recklessly, and travelled incessantly to make the Society known. Regular visits to Scotland, always returning to the North-East, convinced that they were the best people in the world; to the Universities – well, to Oxford and Cambridge – preaching, teaching, counselling, confessing, cajoling, with the same irresistible charm. Denis's mother had once said to me before I joined, "Don't go near him. He'll charm you as he did Denis!" But wasn't it all for the Kingdom of Heaven, to build up the Community?

We novices were an odd lot. Charles Martineau I have already mentioned, the one with the cassock held up by a safety-pin. Cecil, who became a novice with me ("You two will be the most difficult novices I will ever have to manage," Algy said one day after a mild escapade.) Robert, who came because he was a Pacifist, and combined being a Brother with working on the land, as did Hugh. Alan was partially blind. Wilfred, almost completely so. Peter had been in a bit of trouble, and also had physical problems. Harold was another pacifist, and a brilliant organist. And so on. Of course, there were others, a few, and, as time went on, more and more, some with real gifts, as he drove himself to build. There was a crisis, and I nearly left. Instead I moved into the room beside his. Room! It was little more than a large cupboard. And so began a most precious friendship.

He took me in hand, as he did everyone, with the same tireless, ruthless determination. Eventually he asked me to be his secretary and travelling companion. Or rather, he *didn't* ask, but sent for me and said "Dear man, I think it might be right for you to help me." "I think it might be right" was his invariable, and maddeningly oblique way of telling anyone what he firmly intended them to do! And so for the next six years — and many more after — my life was entirely determined by his. It was another more exacting apprenticeship than I ever could have imagined.

Notes

1 Society of Divine Compassion, founded in Plaistow, E. London 1893
2 Brotherhood of the Holy Cross. Peckham 1921
3 Brotherhood of St Francis of Assisi. Cerne Abbas 1921
4 Christa Seva Sangha. Poona 1922
5 Society of St Francis — finally established as such in 1942.

Chapter Eight

Life with Algy Robertson

Algy knew he hadn't long to live. He came back from India in 1930 with a mixture of tropical complaints, and a lethal medicine to dose them with. I never knew him as anything but a sick man, with a driving force inside him, and a determination to succeed, that gave him the power to carry on long after other men would have given in to pain, frustration, and sheer weariness. He would sometimes set his mouth in a thin, grim smile, his eyes fiercely bright behind his glasses, skull cap askew, and beads of sweat on his face, just before embarking on a lengthy mission service, a journey, or a long session of Confessions and interviews. How often people complained that he was late. How rarely they knew the miracle of his appearance at all!

At some point, after his return from India, while he was Vicar of St Ives in Huntingdonshire, he knew with absolute certainty that God had called him to be the founder of a Franciscan Order in England. In fact, he did something rather more remarkable, and refounded two orders, the one already established by Brother Douglas in Dorset, which had almost collapsed; and the other the Indian Community, the Christa Prema Seva Sengha of which he had been a part in Poona. When I visited Poona in 1958, I was very moved to celebrate Holy Communion, together with Bill Lash, at that time Bishop of Bombay, and one of the few remaining members of the C.P.S.S. We used the chalice which Algy had used, and his own Altar Book, the back of it absolutely broken from the inevitable hard treatment which he gave all books. In the Hostel there, Algy looked down from the wall in a faded and mottled photograph, surrounded by the students from the University for whom he founded it. It was the Indian Rule, still used by the Society of St Francis, that Algy brought to Dorset, together with a small handful of men, including Denis (the one whom I first met in Cambridge) and Francis, to join Douglas and *his* handful. It was in 1937, not long before the war, which, when it came, almost immediately put the whole project in jeopardy.

Early in 1940 Douglas went to London, living as chaplain at the evacuated old Westminster Hospital opposite the Abbey. It had become a hostel for service men, and Douglas felt completely at home in a world he had known in the First War.

In 1939 the house owned by the Oratory of the Good Shepherd (a community of Anglican celibate priests) became available in Cambridge, and Algy snatched the chance of having a foothold in "his" university, so Denis was sent there, together with three other Brothers, to begin a ministry in the undergraduate world. He could ill afford to send them, yet it left him free to impose his own stamp on the Friary at Hilfield, in those days called Cerne Abbas. (The name has changed with the redrawing of boundaries or the demands of postal or local authorities. "Batcombe", "Cerne Abbas", "Hilfield".)

At the outbreak of war Algy was tempted to retreat to Cambridge — but finally remained at Cerne Abbas where he pursued his determined course of turning a rather haphazard and apparently casual and disorganised group of brothers into a conventional religious order. It wasn't always welcomed. Algy's style was very different to that of Douglas.

Douglas had evolved a very simple, if arduous, pattern of life which gave prominence and priority to the wayfarers, as he called the homeless unemployed. Prayer was said at regular intervals, and the Holy Communion celebrated. He was a truly devout Evangelical who valued the sacraments, and had his mind set on the conversion of souls. He loved and deeply respected the men who came to live with him off the roads; and they responded to that respect with clear devotion. They had to be fed and housed. So the prayer life jostled with making jam, or digging in the fields, mission preaching in local towns and villages, and regular travelling "on the roads" himself. Some men came and stayed, but the majority were birds of passage — and *all* were called 'Brother'.

Algy recognised the value of this, and saw in it a true reflection of the Franciscan spirit: but he was also bitten with a conviction that it could better be supported by the ordered and structured life of the kind already being tried in the other Anglican Orders for men.

By the time I got there in 1942, he had already established his own eclectic routine, borrowed from every medieval or modern source. His enthusiasms ranged from a vigorous belief in the Second Coming to the Devotion to the Sacred Heart and the hymns of Wesley and Watts! He was impressed by the Quakers; admired the Jesuits; and was a passionate devotee of the Tractarians. During his time at St Ives he was for a short time deeply influenced by Frank

Buchman and the Oxford Group Movement. Nothing escaped him, and everything was absorbed and communicated to the rest of us at breakneck speed. He was a very demanding man.

Douglas paid rare visits to the Friary where he was bewildered by bells, confused by Chasubles, and overwhelmed by a variety of piety which, though he was no simpleton, went well beyond his own simple "Bible Religion". Yet despite these differences the two men respected each other deeply. On the occasion of one visit, Algy decided that we should all show our respect to the Minister by dropping on one knee and kissing his hand. Algy would lead the way. So we all reluctantly hung around in the drive, waiting for this most modest and mildly quiet and great man to arrive. A car drew up, and Douglas got out, looked around with vague surprise at Brothers lurking in corners, when suddenly Algy almost hurled himself at him, plunged on to one knee, his skull cap all askew, and snatched his hand. Poor Douglas! He just wasn't used to being kissed on the hand, or treated (as he might think) like the Pope. It clearly hadn't worked very well, and though one or two tried to follow suit, the gesture petered out into hearty handshakes.

Soon the seven-fold office was established, times of prayer and meditation, bells and silences ("greater" and "lesser"), readings at meals and a pecking order of procedure in and out of Chapels and refectory. All had to be taught, discussed, explained – and above all directed by him! Unless he said beforehand that he was not going to be present, Offices and meals waited for his arrival – and he was not infrequently late, carried away by a lecture, a letter, or a captivating visitor. It was maddening to those impatiently sitting it out in the Chapel, but it would have been worse if we'd started without him; then the eyes behind the gold-rimmed glasses would flash displeasure "But of course, dear man, you know I *always* come to None." At four in the afternoon, None was in some ways the biggest trial. It was not just the Office but the interminable prayer and intercessions which followed, not only then but, it seemed, every time we entered the chapel. There was a whole row of little books, all devised by Algy, with prayers for every conceivable occasion and concern. Prayers after None were for overseas missionaries, and seemed to go on for ever. When, working our way round the world we got to India, we knew that the end was in sight and the bell for tea near. (There were of course bells, different bells, for getting up and going to bed, food, prayer, recreation and any other movement in the Friary.) The list droned on with the slightly improbable names of missionaries known mostly only to Algy himself: "Dundas Battersby-Herford, Tyndale-Biscoe,

Pakenham-Walsh...", the names still come to mind of these wonderful men and women who gave their lives to the mission fields in
far off places.

He leaped with equal enthusiasm on the seasons of the Church
year to add yet more devotions, more prayers in Chapel and at
table, as meals got cold, in the refectory. Advent involved little
dissertations on the Advent Antiphons, the Second Coming, the
anticipation of Christmas. Lent meant extra sermons on Sundays
and weekdays, special readings, extra silences and preparations for
Holy Week and Easter and of course the sermons that had to be
written for the additional preaching of Lent courses outside the
Friary, in fact all over the country. In the end virtually everything
was prepared by him, and in retrospect I marvel. At the time it
was exhausting, but as I knew nothing else it didn't surprise me. I
did wonder at the wide compass of his interests and his unflagging
enthusiasm for everything. I could get exasperated at his impatience
and envied his rapid grasp of the essentials of anything. So far as
preaching and talking were concerned, his orderly mind could plan
the whole thing and deliver it without notes. What a pace! Whenever
he left the Friary the whole place sank back into a state of recovery
and counted the time as precious until his return. As I was nearly
always with him, I didn't enjoy this as the others did; in fact for me
it was sometimes a relief when we left, though the dictating went on
in the car and train, oblivious to the presence of other passengers.

Departures were always a combination of triumph and near disaster. He would be on his bed until the last minute, a car and
impatient driver waiting, constantly looking at his watch, sending
messages to say we'd miss the train, getting angry. Then the mad
rush to stuff things into bags, shoes, bottles of medicine, books.
He must change his rope, find a scarf, a new bottle of ammoniated
quinine, a special Bible, send a message to Vincent, make a quick
telephone call, have a word with Sydney (the Brother who ran the
garden), and so on, all at once, with the constant hooting of the car
in the background! Then the final dash down the path, his cloak
over his shoulder and the new rope, already come loose, trailing
behind him. A small entourage of brothers following, being given
yet more instructions. The drive to the station inevitably became a
trial of nerves, at any rate for me, as we skirted other cars, splashed
through a farm yard, and squeezed along Dorset lanes. He hated to
be early for a train and delighted to get there just before it pulled
out, so that the whole platform became involved in the last minute
wrenching open of a door, the bags bundled in and seats captured
as a sort of triumph. We took up a lot of room but somehow the

other passengers would succumb to his smile, as would the porters, ticket collectors and dining-car. attendants, as inevitably we went for tea, charging and recharging the pot with hot water to make the whole thing last almost all the way to Waterloo, while I, of course, would "just take down a few letters" or he made some notes for the sermon he was to preach that evening.

Astonishingly, he also found time to treat everyone in the Friary as a personal concern, and as someone of infinite importance. His delight in all the preaching and teaching, the communicating of everything verbally to God or man was almost an indulgence. He spent a lot of time in prayer, but the evangelical enthusiasm for words meant *saying* prayers. Even more important for him, however, were the people. He was a remarkably good listener, and could wait with endless patience for the right moment, the right word: could pick up the most obliquely stated need, a mere nuance, and recognising it as a clue, slowly and with infinite care, draw it out, render it painless or at any rate possible. His power with people was truly remarkable and the price he paid for it enormous.

We had a little ramshackle and scruffy guest house which I with Peter, a fellow novice, looked after. It was often full of half-frozen guests living in a slightly squalid discomfort. Yet this did not stop them coming. Nearly always it was to see him, waiting, as we all did, for hours, even for days to get their turn. The friendships he made lasted for ever, and some of them he shared with me. I also shared some of the consequent pain, the sheer weariness and exhaustion, as I made tea and then read to him for an hour or two as he retreated under the pile of blankets, pillows, towels, cloaks and rugs, and it got dark. Then suddenly there would be a minor eruption and he would emerge from it all to clatter down the stairs to give an address at Evensong, or preside at Supper.

As his secretary my day was dictated by his, and usually began the night before. It was always impossible to predict when Algy would decide that the day was over. Often he would carry on until 1 or 2 am and only then would he set a time for saying Mass, and a time for getting up. He rarely said Mass later than eight, in the little, holy, untidy, Chapel of St Clare which was the larger room beneath his. Sometimes, my day began with a knock on the wall which divided his room from mine. "Dear man, I'm sure we ought to go down now." So I served his Mass. Even that could have unpredictable moments, though it was always very carefully prepared, with an Anglican Missal, strung with endless ribbons, carried down as a captive under his arm.

I'm not sure that he ever took off any clothes in order to sleep. He *did* put lots more on when he got up, stuffing them all under his habit, the whole lot held together by his rope. A little ditty from a Sherborne schoolboy said:

> "Algy met a bear.
> The bear was bulgy,
> The bulge was Algy!"

Algy *was* bulgy! And sometimes the bulge would become loose. He hurled himself into Mass with the same enthusiasm as he did everything. "Through *my* fault, my *own* fault, my own *most* grievous fault." At each phrase, his arm would swing round, narrowly miss the server, and land with a resounding *thump* on his breast. The altar was a shaky contraption of wood, that barely stood up to Algy's genuflections. And he meant it. For him, faith was one with a total devotion to and giving of himself, in the Sacraments.

Underneath the vestments which were always a little askew, bits of clothing would come loose; the leg of a pair of long pants would appear beneath his alb. Clearly, at the last minute before leaving his room, he had feared the cold and stuffed the nearest thing he could find under his habit. As the Mass went on, more and more of it appeared, while he, quite unconscious of this source of fascination, moved about with those trailing "long Johns".

Oh, but we were wrong. He *had* known. The moment came when the pants finally became loose and dropped to the floor in front of the altar. What would he do about that? With an adroit flick of his foot, that would not have shamed a ballet dancer or a centre-forward, the offending garment was suddenly kicked beneath the altar frontal, to be rescued later by a discreet Sacristan.

After the Mass, I'd go to the kitchen for our breakfast. This was always the same. A large pot of strong tea, bread, cheese, mustard. It never varied. Once, during the war, a friend in the Canadian Air Force made a secret landing in occupied France. When he got back, he appeared at Hilfield — with a Camembert cheese for Algy's breakfast.

After breakfast, indeed often during it, he would retreat beneath his blankets, towels, pillows, until sometimes there was only an untidy lump in the bed, and a voice. I read to him. There were, of course, interruptions, the phone, the door, but I dealt with them as well. Until *The Times* came, I read for perhaps an hour, sometimes two. Poetry: Browning, Swinburne, all the metaphysical poets, Wordsworth, Milton. I recall immense commentaries on the Epistle to the Hebrews, Romans, and the sermons of famous Scottish Divines. Later, there would be leading articles from *The Times, The New Statesman,* or anything else that captured his imagination.

Sometimes, the mound on the bed remained immovable for so long that I thought he had gone to sleep. But no: "Dear man, you can't possibly mean what you have just read. Of course, you read *brilliantly*. In fact, no-one can read *quite* like you. But really, I think you must read it again." Of course, he was right, and I knew it. He barely realised that I had done it all many years before with Hugh and his M.S. It was all part of my education. He took over a lot of my life. After the reading, the post came, and the dictating of answers. I did the letters while he was interviewing. And then there was the arranging. He dominated everything; the library, which was being rearranged; the garden, which was looked after by a saintly Brother Sidney, a real expert from Kent — but that didn't deter Algy; arrangements for services, for meals, preaching, outings; "The Home" in which we looked after a number of men; the Office — and, of course, the Novices.

He was also Novice Master. We all saw him regularly, some once a week, and he took most of our lectures. Algy had a remarkable knack of getting hold of the essence of an idea and communicating it to us. We met each afternoon in the same parlour in which he'd first met me. Sitting round the polished tables, sometimes with a large iron kettle quietly simmering on the stove for tea. He was invariably late, and clattered down the stairs apologising profusely. He was brilliant, really brilliant, at making the Bible or the Psalms come alive, or Church History a living reality. When I finally did the GOE exams, I passed, I am sure, largely on the strength of Algy's lectures.

Then he dictated the notes of the lecture he had just given. Nothing left to chance. He told us where to put in commas and full stops, parentheses, and footnotes. The main notes were on one side of the page, meticulously laid out with paragraph headings, subsections, numbers. On the opposite side were illustrations — quotations, from hymns, psalms, stories, anecdotes. In his mind it was all going to be delivered *in a sermon*. One day, we would need it as preachers. It was a goal he had for us all.

Then there were sermon classes, with an outline for three sermons posted for every Sunday, — Morning Prayer, Eucharist, Evening Prayer, in case we had to go out to a local village, as indeed we often did.

His own preaching was of a kind which we hear rather less now. In content, it combined rather traditional Catholic theology with very solid Biblical authority, and evangelical fervour. He always "preached for conversions". At his best, he was brilliant, captivating, and deeply moving. He was also very long.

I've watched him lying on his bed, or sitting swathed in pillows, getting it all clear in his mind. Then a consulting of the Bible – "There *must* be a text, dear man!" – and, finally, the back of an envelope and, with his spidery mapping-pen, the main points put in the middle, and the other chief clues all round. Sometimes, he would fill it out on several sheets with a few lines to each page.

He loved planning courses of sermons or addresses, retreats, missions, and conferences. It was for him, in some ways, a sophisticated game or pastime. And all was passed on to the novices in endless note-taking. It was a wonderful indoctrination in public speaking, the organising of material, and all the rest. I had the advantage of my Y.C.L. days. Algy knew it, and built on it.

Hymns were the most compelling passion of his life. He nearly drove us mad with it. His knowledge of hymns, hymn writers, the composers, and all the tunes, was phenomenal. In his room the rows of reference books, and the endless editions of all the hymn books had prior place. When he died, there were dozens of little books with lists of hymns in them, arranged for every Sunday or Feast Day; hymns for special occasions or celebrations. Re-arranging hymns, deciding on the most suitable tunes, never tired him, and he always worked lying on his bed, using his little mapping-pen. At a service, a faulty or unsuitable tune would be stopped and the service would have to wait while the right book, or the right tune, was found.

Rehearsals were frequent and, seemingly, endless. The three Masses for Christmas morning would involve about twenty hymns, and at all festivals the sequences were sung. After six years, I knew the *English Hymnal* backwards, and a good many others as well, and must admit I loved it all, or almost all. Only once did I rebel, in the middle of a choir practice in which he had been more pedantically trying than usual, with many additions, repetitions and alterations, I just cracked, ripped up a Carol book and threw it at him! The others agreed that I had acted on their behalf, but the personal trauma was awful.

From time to time, we would go off together, travelling all over the country, but especially, each term, to Cambridge and Oxford, and regularly to Durham and Newcastle, sharing his love of the Geordies, preaching, talking, recruiting.

Each summer, he took retreats at a splendidly antique Victorian retreat house called "Sunnybrae", near Walkerburn in the Scottish borders. The retreat house was run by impeccably holy nuns, and the retreatants were mostly solid Scottish ladies, Episcopalian, "landed", devout, and rather formidable. They loved the Victorian courtesies, and spoiled him when they could. In between retreats, we took sedate (there is no other word) drives in an elderly car to St Mary's Loch, or Tibbie Shiels, Moffat, or just to Peebles for a light meal – "Of course, Mother will pay." But it had to be planned, the guides read, the background studied, nothing must be left to ignorance. In Edinburgh, he stayed at the Theological College, while I sometimes stayed with a beloved family in a housing estate where I had once been with Algy for a mission. He revelled in Edinburgh, and so did I. Drinking tea in the old-fashioned club-like tearooms on Prince's Street, and enjoying the spaciousness of one of the most beautiful cities in Europe – as it was then. And more excursions.

We once went to North Berwick, where he insisted on sitting by the sea to dictate some letters. I did point out that we appeared to be sitting on a golf course, but he brushed it aside. A few minutes later, there was a sudden gasp and he collapsed backwards, unconscious, hit on the head by a golf ball. The lad who ran up, full of apologies, was startled to find that he had knocked out a rather fat monk! Algy was helped to the club house and given brandy. I unwisely told Charles Gillet, Principal of the Theological College, and he never allowed Algy to forget!

After three years, in October 1945, I was professed in the three vows of poverty, chastity and obedience together with Cecil. Again it was St Francis Day. Three years later, in 1948, I was due to take my vows for life. So much that had happened seemed logical, inevitable. I knew so little about the Christian Faith or the Church when I first went to Cerne Abbas, and absolutely nothing about the Religious Life, that it didn't occur to me to question what I was doing, or what Algy was doing to me. In some ways I took God for granted, at least I didn't question him. I had friends but little realised how alienated I was becoming from some of my brothers, and isolated, by my life with Algy.

I went into retreat to prepare myself for this final step. The effect was disastrous. I felt ill, disorientated, confused and desperately unhappy. The one clear thing that seemed obvious was that I couldn't go through with it. I must marry, see the world, somehow break loose, be myself. God just didn't want me as a friar, and the thought of an eternity in Cerne Abbas seemed condemnation to something rather worse than prison. My mind raced around, my prayers were too painful.

So I asked to see Algy and tell him. But, of course he was busy. "I *will* be seeing you, dear man, but not just now. Of course, we must have a rehearsal for the profession, and *you* must choose the hymns". So I was sent away. I tried again the following day, but he said he would send for me when he was ready.

So I wrote it all down at great length, horrified in some ways at what I was doing, wondering how I could ever face him after saying so much. I marked it "Private", sealed it, and poked it under the door. There was no response. Strangely enough, I began to feel better, more relaxed, able to pray, I even ate a better meal. I also began to go over in my mind all I had said. It was true − I did want to marry, I must leave. Yet I also began to see what I was leaving, the part of me that had first come to live there, the changing person I had become. I did what I had done before in retreat, went through my intercession lists, read *The Confessions* of St Augustine and other books I already knew well and had supported me in the past. God himself was by no means remote, but there was no clear "voice" or guidance, nothing to urge me forward − or encourage my departure. It was, I think, confusing; in a remote way it still is.

He finally sent for me the night before the profession. What was there to say? I said nothing.

A few days later I was clearing his bed, trying to bring a little order to the jumble of bedclothes, books, hot water bottles that had accumulated, and there suddenly among the crumpled towels was my letter. Unopened.

So I was professed in Life Vows on October 23rd 1948 and Charlie Arben my one remaining friend from my school days in Bolt Court came, and also a fellow Scout from St Peter's Clapham who cycled down from London for the occasion, and I settled down in my role as Algy's secretary, though a good many other jobs came my way as well.

Undergraduates, ordinands, schoolboys, and others began coming in larger numbers for visits, and Algy, who was, of course, the Guestmaster, appointed me his assistant. I began preaching in schools: Sherborne, Bryanston, Christ's Hospital, Marlborough, and others much farther afield; and I discovered that the boys were sometimes glad to talk to a complete stranger who would leave after a day or two, so there began a new ministry which has persisted. My delight is that many of the boys that I knew then are still my friends, and so are their wives and children. Many became priests, some of them distinguished in the world of art or letters, the press or politics: all came as boys, many to become Algy's penitents.

Bryanston School, in particular, became important to me. It had as its Chaplain the unusually brilliant Jack Winslow, who had returned from India as Algy had, but in Jack's case for reasons which Algy really regarded as base. He had joined the Oxford Group, while he was still the leader of the Christa Seva Sangha. 'Guided' by the Group Movement he gave up his leadership, the Sangha, and India.

He invited me to preach, and I found the experience different from any other. I went back the following term and, for a few years, this became a regular practice. The school gave me a little room, and boys were able to come to me, virtually *"incognito"*, during any free period. Bryanston, with its liberal, artistic, and sophisticated attitude to education, appealed to me. I made an enormous number of friends, heard a good many emotional confessions, and learnt something of the art of counselling. When Jack suddenly left, I had the place to myself during a lengthy interregnum. The clue to the place was Thor – Thorold Coade – the headmaster, a slight, grey man, pottering about the place looking vaguely like a gardener who had wandered accidentally into the huge, Edwardian building that housed his school.

One evening, sitting in front of his study fire, he quietly encouraged me to talk. I was still conscious that Bryanston was a Public School, conspicuously dependent on wealth, and far from my background. I felt an interloper, and, for once, I said so. It was an enormous relief. I can't remember his reply. I *do* very well remember that he gently led me to a degree of self-acceptance which I had never known before. It was his way with everyone: staff, boys, parents. He never missed the Daily Mass in his little chapel in the crypt. He had the instincts, time, courtesy, the shy confidence, the lack of exaggeration, of a Quaker. He was by any standard a great headmaster, a great and a good man. He counted a lot in my life.

The Society already had a "Third Order" which was part of our heritage from India – men and women who strictly followed the Franciscan ideal and discipline in secular life. Now Algy turned to the establishment of a Second Order, following the Franciscan tradition of Sisters, who lived an enclosed life of contemplative prayer and work, after the example of St Clare. We travelled round looking at properties, interviewing ladies who might join them. He had come into touch with a number of women whose spiritual lives he directed, all of whom hoped to test their vocations as Sisters of St Clare. They met together for the first time at a Church at Kennington in South London, together with a nun from Wantage who was to be their mentor. It was, for them, a momentous occasion, and one full of hope as well as, perhaps, anxiety, not helped by the very late arrival of Algy. I had stayed with him at his mother's home, and we drove there from Ealing in his mother's rather splendid but elderly car. So they met together for the first time. It was the beginning of what became the "Freeland Sisters", the Community of St Clare.

In 1947, the Society was offered a small monastery in Worcestershire for the brothers. We went to look at that as well and finally lived there for six months while it was opened up again. Algy of course was often absent, going backwards and forwards to Cerne Abbas, preaching and visiting all over the place, but he usually went alone. There was just a small group of us, re-establishing the monastery which had been occupied only by temporary residents since its founder Father William ("William of Glasshampton") had died there and been buried in the garth several years before. During the war it had become somewhat run-down and derelict.

The building itself is beautiful – a large courtyard open on one side with accommodation at each corner. A corridor runs round the inside with cells for brothers in what were once spacious horseboxes. William had been an architect, and his transformation of these splendid Georgian stables had been sensitive. Glasshampton is a place where I sense, instinctively, the sort of numinous presence which is difficult to describe. Others do too, though not everyone agrees and I have heard it spoken of with something corresponding to fear. At any rate, we settled into a routine. Algy, of course, was in his element, planning prayer, offices, vigils, readings and all the rest. Bro Stephen came to get the garden in order and to start growing some vegetables. Poor Stephen, the day Algy came back from a trip to Worcester to discover he'd cut down the Wisteria all hell broke loose, and we all suffered for it. My job, in addition to my usual secretarial work, was cooking. We went in early June. Some guests and visitors inevitably turned up to see Algy, but I mostly remember it as a summer when it never rained, a summer of warmth and flowers, silence and a sort of improvised holiness and seclusion.

It was soon after the reopening of Glasshampton that I discovered that Algy had been working something out in his mind.

"Darling man" – the phrase was used when he spoke to many of us, and usually as a prelude to disaster – "they seem to need another brother in Cambridge. I really can't think what Denis has been up to." (He had in fact done a fine job in establishing a Franciscan presence in Cambridge.) "But of course Lothian is *splendid.*" Lothian was indeed splendid, but I hardly knew him. He was shy and not very communicative, or so he had seemed when we once worked in the garden together, a plan, I later discovered, so that he could find out whether he could put up with me in Cambridge where he was now in charge.

A return to Cambridge: I was both attracted and appalled, but the attraction won, and in any case, I had no real choice, even though the proposal was made as if I had. Life without Algy however — that was a new idea.

Chapter Nine

Return to Cambridge

The first time I went to Cambridge in 1940, I knew nothing of Franciscans. I was still a soldier. Jane and I sat in the buffet on Liverpool Street station sipping Guinness. (She had great faith in its ability to warm and strengthen.) The old station with its clouds of steam and its smell, was war-time dim and dark, with the dank feel of a drizzling day in London. The whole uncertainty of the future lay solidly upon us. There were young soldiers, heavy with serge, kit bags and respirators; a group of hearty airmen returning to East Anglian airfields were nearby, and, in fact, I too was travelling on an army pass, though not far from my discharge. My destination, Papworth Sanatorium, had been described to me by inmates from the army hospital, from which I was being transferred, in lurid details: in the depths of the country; spartan; cold; with a ruthless regime. I was a bit fearful. It was also November, and the prospect of sleeping in the open air was hardly attractive.

That was the first of many farewells at Liverpool Street – and I grew to love the station and "collected it" as some men and boys collect train numbers. Stations in England were part of the inventiveness of the Victorians and were to me, a source of endless fascination. Until very recently, even the smallest "halt" might have a little detail, a lamp or bracket, a table in the waiting room, a splendid notice in cast iron or an old bench with L.N.E.R. stamped on it, or what you will. Until recently there were also still some ceramic tiles in brilliant peacock colours at Worcester, some old L.N.E.R. glass at Berwick-on-Tweed – and it's worth missing a train to enjoy the classical portico of Newcastle on Tyne or the great curved sweep of the track.

Well, Liverpool Street has its own charms. It also, for me, always seems to be raining! Raining on this first day, and raining when I arrived in Cambridge. Always raining when I arrive there. On that first occasion my instructions were to go to Bene't Street to be picked up by the 'Colony' bus from Papworth, waiting in a yard just close to the church – the same church

59

that was later to be the spiritual centre of my life for many years.

Eight years later I was again sitting with Jane and a Guinness, returning to take up my life in Cambridge and to join the household at St Francis House, Lady Margaret Road, the place where it had all started for me. Denis was no longer there, and the gentle, diffident, but infinitely discerning Lothian was in charge. Over many years, he gradually won the love and admiration of countless women, and a great many men. He could swear like a trooper. I once heard a voice say, "I was watching a rugger match at Grange Road, and someone behind me was turning the air blue. When I looked round to see who it was — it was that monk!" Watching rugger, tramping over Wicken Fen, that was rare relaxation for him. I think his mind, at least, was always searching for a suitable way to express his certainties about God and salvation. He read English as an undergraduate, and developed a longing to find always the exact word for what he wanted to say. His gentle voice could quietly mock the merely trite. Wodehouse, Saki, writers of the lightly cynical not only pleased him, but reflected his own personality not a little. But such lightness was a thin disguise for a spiritual depth, exceptional by any standard. He knew the great traditions of classic spiritual writing with a knowledge that reflected a painful determination to profit in his day-to-day living by what he read. He appeared not to suffer fools gladly, particularly pretentious fools, and yet he did suffer all kinds of people very readily indeed.

Drawing unconsciously from the depths of his own experience, he was always wary of the superficial. He could sometimes prick a pretension with a word, hardly aware that he was doing it. In that sense, he seemed, at first meeting, a somewhat formidable figure. His way of saying, "*Well,* my friend.." became a warning that something rather devastating was in the offing. Yet he was kind to me and certainly gave me my head.

The rest of the household included: Cecil, with whom I had been made a novice; Nicholas, who was reading theology; Barnabas, who had returned to take up his career as a theologian (I had first met him in 1941 when he had just come up as an undergraduate and I was paying my first exploratory visit), and David, a priest who had joined the Society more recently and was eventually to become the Minister, and then first Minister General. In various ways it was a "family" of intimate friends with very varied backgrounds and abilities. There were also several men with various needs to whom we had given a home, and become very much part of the family.

In retrospect, I recognise the hand of Algy, like a wily alchemist, creating a team of brothers who would offset each other, providing an apparent strength that would always be greater than its parts. As far as we were concerned, by some sort of holy accident, we were just Franciscans, living in, what seemed to me, a spacious house with a big garden, committed to a church, St Bene't's, and seemed a ministry. It was useful that we all seemed to speak or preach, (except dear Cecil, who was horrified at the thought), and I was delighted that one principal means of achieving our mission was doing what I always liked doing, meeting people, talking, attending or organising meetings, parties, gatherings. Politically, there was the interest of promoting Catholic thought and action without being too Anglo-Catholic or offensively "High Church", with the added interest of trying to come to terms with the rigid evangelicalism of the CICCU – Cambridge Inter Collegiate Christian Union – in the University.

Lothian was remarkably sensitive to the needs of the nurses from Addenbrooke's, young women from Girton, and all the women dons and teachers; indeed a recent Reverend Mother of our Poor Clares was one of them. Barnabas was beginning to find acceptance in the strictly academic world, particularly among the theologians, and it was a great moment, some years later, when I opened the door and found Charlie Moule, the Lady Margaret Professor, on the doorstep delivering the manuscript of Barnabas's Commentary on St John which he had just finished reading and wouldn't trust to anyone else to return. "Look after this carefully, Michael," he said as he handed it over, "it's very good." And so it is, and eventually he followed his father by being awarded a Doctorate. Later, in 1978, he became Rylands Professor of Divinity at Manchester.

The very first undergraduate I was sent to visit by Lothian was Michael Apps, a rather sincere Evangelical who had just arrived at Pembroke from the army. He was friendly, courteous, and seemed a little alarmed to find a monk at the door, but he gave me some tea, talked about his mother, who was an invalid, accepted an invitation to tea with us, kept his word, and we became friends. In fact, his friendship over the next four years, while he was in Cambridge, was a considerable factor in my life. In the course of time he became Brother Bernard, and many years later he, Barnabas and I met regularly as members of the General Synod – Barnabas representing the Northern Universities, Bernard the Religious Orders and I as a member of the House of Bishops.

Looking at my diaries from this time, I see that, day after day, I was talking to groups on every subject under the sun, leading Bible studies in colleges, organising meetings, attending services, preaching in chapels. There was also a stream of students finding their way to Lady Margaret Road for what nowadays is called "counselling".

I was discovering how important it is to learn to listen. I was not always good at it, and still make mistakes, but *really* to listen is to hold yourself open to hear what is not being said, to pick up the inarticulate voice as it only hints at what *might* be said if there were words, or courage, enough to say it. To hear what people don't know *how* to say, or even what they are quite unaware of saying.

Sometimes − rarely, but occasionally of necessity − to risk putting a word into their mouths, or a thought into their minds. Sometimes, to say what they find impossible to say, through fear or doubt, reticence or embarrassment. They could be amazed that I had seemed to read their minds, when, perhaps, all that I had done was to describe some of my own feelings in a similar situation, without disclosing the source of my information.

In the end, this became, and has remained for me, the most significant and, I would like to think, valuable part of my ministry. All this I owe to Algy as well, both for his care for me, and what I saw of his care for others. It also could be dangerous. You cannot fail to care very deeply for the people who trust their lives to you with an intimacy that transcends human friendship, but inevitably contains it. If, at times, I fear the consequences in pain, there has always been a remembrance of all the other older spiritual friends and guides who seemed to lead in just the same way; bold in love, often very direct in speech, ready always to speak the unspeakable if it has to be spoken, sensitively teasing out the truth so that it was made possible to say it in your own words, infinitely patient, and always establishing unbreakable bonds of friendship. If I learnt it from Algy, I saw it as clearly in Charlie Gillet, Ken Carey, Eric Abbott, Sam Wylie, and other intimate friends in the Lord.

It was easy to be attracted by so much eager response, trust and willingness to share, and I was, again and again. And, always in the background, the percipient, gentle but sometimes astringent voice of Lothian would say with dry affection, *"Well, my friend ..."* Many of those I counselled I later married, and my little regiment of Godsons and Goddaughters is permanent witness to the enlargement of their love as they included husbands and wives in our common bond.

Algy would visit us two or three times a year, to be resident while he interviewed all manner of people. What a business that was. The preparation of his room, bottles of medicine from Coulsons, his late arrival and almost invariably, immediate retirement to bed. Having arrived there he would need hot water bottles, soda water, arrowroot, pots of tea and glucose "D" to put in it. One by one we would be sent for until the room took on the proper sense of confused disorder and a certain expectancy, even slight tension. Books were searched for, urgent telephone calls put through. Arrangements were made to meet Dons, Chaplains, Students and old friends who happened to be passing through. Comments had to be passed on about the food, the Offices, the timetable, until finally, with everyone organised, and slightly exhausted and confused with the effort and all the reins in his hands, he could sink once again behind the usual piles of pillows, blankets, towels until all that was left to be seen were a pair of gold rimmed glasses and behind them the bright eyes that twinkled with amused and slightly mischievous satisfaction.

He also encouraged us to begin our own movement of Companions of St Francis, an association of students who kept a rule of life and some commitment to the Franciscan ideal. They, of course, had *their* secretary, meetings and services, all centred on the house. A big event each week was "Thursday Teas". Tea and buns from 3.45 to 4.15. A talk or Bible Study for about twenty minutes, discussion, and all was over by 4.50 for the sake of those who felt committed to a lecture! At its peak, as many as a hundred crowded into our common room. The object was instruction in the Faith and commitment to it, but it was also a chance for a quick cup of tea and an opportunity to meet others. The other meetings each week were a Sunday service at St Bene't's, with a theme of sermons each term, always given by "The Franciscans", and a Sunday Tea meeting from 4.0. to 6.0. These were serious and sometimes exciting occasions, even if a little unpredictable! Lothian invited the speakers, frequently very distinguished (they liked coming to Cambridge perhaps), but would the students turn up? Sometimes they did, in huge crowds, so that we ran out of tea and space, as when Rose Macaulay and C.S. Lewis engaged in a dialogue with Frances Cornford in the Chair. But when Nicholas Pevsner came to talk about Masaccio it was a different story, and the sparsity of the meeting was painful. The Sunday teas had a way of attracting undergraduates who were far from Christian and who were surprised at not being "got at". My list of friends grew and, from time to time, Lothian had to remind me not to burn the candle at both ends.

The Thursday teas, in particular, were a recruiting ground for help with evangelistic activities elsewhere, out of term, and particularly in the north of England. Algy had been a curate at St George's, Cullercoats, on the coast in Northumberland, where he had made an indelible mark on the parish. He then became the Theological Colleges Secretary for the SCM, and began his endless travels all over England, all of which he wanted me to share. He also wanted me to share his abiding love for everything to do with the North East, the "Geordies". His passion became mine, and has remained so.

Chapter 10

Finding my feet in
the North East

My association with the North East began in South Shields in 1945, several years before I went to live in Cambridge.

The Methodist Board of Mission had promoted a form of Mission in towns, which they called a "Commando Campaign" and, towards the end of the war, invited Algy to send Brothers to South Shields on such an enterprise. He thought that it would be a good experience for me, and introduce me to that type of evangelism, so I went for two weeks, with Father Gilbert. I was terribly raw.

For preparation, Algy helped me to write two addresses, a short one and a long one, which I might find useful, according to opportunity. In the event, I used neither of them.

To staff the campaign all the Churches and Chapels of South Shields formed a team of minister, priest and helpers, to be joined later by a visiting team of priests and ministers, lay teachers, etc., making together about a hundred.

The home team prepared by visiting all the schools, hospitals, factories, shops, clubs, *any* gathering place for work or leisure, and asking the authority in charge to let three or four representatives from the team address them in the lunch break, dinner time, before or after work, just for about ten minutes. The technique was to keep this meeting brief so that you were invited back again. This was supported by a full team meeting every morning for prayers and Bible study, to report back our successes, and be given our assignments for the day. The Campaign concluded with mass meetings in a local cinema.

As a campaigner, I nearly came to a sticky end on my first outing. I had no idea what to expect, felt self-conscious in my habit, couldn't understand the dialect, and was daunted at being thrust among the all-too-eloquent Methodists who predominated.

Gilbert and I were met at Newcastle station by one of the leaders, a very self-assured Methodist Minister with a really insistent smile, a sheaf of official-looking papers in his hand, and a terribly confident voice. We sat down in the buffet for a cup of tea while waiting for the train to South Shields.

"So you are Brother Michael. Welcome!" Big handshake, bigger smile. He ran his pencil down the list of names with a big display of efficiency, "Ah, yes. Your first assignment is tomorrow morning, six o'clock, at Bolden Colliery. Talk to the men in the canteen, probably coming off shift. You'll like that!" My heart sank. What on earth could I say? My carefully prepared little speech seemed desperately inappropriate. Would anyone, coming off a coal face (about which I knew nothing), be interested in anything except going home to bed?

The following morning, I was picked up by three Methodists who were the other members of the team. At five in the morning, the streets seemed dark and cold and my footsteps echoed on cobbles. The others were all rather older than I, and obviously a bit startled by the sight of my habit, rather a contrast to their conventional dog collars, and over-reacting with a degree of hearty welcome that did nothing to overcome the bleakness of the morning, the dim, irregular lighting of the streets which echoed to our clattering footsteps, or my own interior gloom. We were taken to the pit, a place I'd never seen before, and knew only from the romantic stories of hunger marches in the thirties, and eventually were ushered into the pit canteen, where our guide made himself scarce. A very few men were sitting at tables, who looked up briefly as we came in, took us in at a glance, and looked down again quickly. Nobody noticed me any more. No-one spoke. I looked to our leader, and even he seemed uncertain.

So we stood there, three men in sombre clerical black, and a nervous, slightly frightened friar. After what seemed an interminable time, the leader of the team gathered us into a little huddle to plan our "campaign". We'd wait until some more men came in, and then he would speak and introduce the other two. But not me. Relief struggled briefly with disappointment, and won easily. As a newcomer to campaigns I was just to stand and listen, learn from them how it was done and, of course, pray. They now looked confident campaigners, with serious looks on their faces.

More men arrived, collecting tea from somewhere, and giving us the same brief, ignoring glance as we stood in our little huddle at one end of the canteen. Finally, our leader was suddenly galvanised into action. Jumping on to a form, he launched into his introduction. He had a fine voice that must have filled many a large chapel – it certainly filled this canteen! Briefly he told them about the Commando Campaign, "front line troops" – "making sudden, hidden attacks on the power of evil" — "taking the devil by surprise" and so on. Good stuff, and it left me feeling not only how brave he was, but how inadequate I was! Then he introduced the two speakers, whom, he assured us, would be brief, and got down from the bench in a heavy, unresponsive silence.

The first speaker got off to a good start. "Men, my father also worked in a pit . . ."So it was obvious why he had been regarded as suitable. Then he seemed to reduce his advantage, and I couldn't help feeling sorry for the man. I'm sure he didn't mean to do it, but it sounded as if he had rather improved his lot by becoming a Min- ister! After about five minutes, he got down to an equally sepulchral silence. So the next man went in. He had an even better advantage. "Men," he began, "I'm glad to tell you that I, too, have worked in a mine. I began as a boy in . . . . mine, and then God called me." Well, he told us how God called him, and ended with an appeal.

The appeal was a great feature, and still is, of some evangelical preaching. It gives an opportunity for many hearers to make a personal commitment; and, on this Campaign, when we reported back in the morning, one way of assessing the success of a visit was by recording the number of people who had responded to the appeal and come forward to take a commitment card. A very lit- eral counting of heads.

This kind of evangelism has always been a part of Evangelical Christianity, practised as much by famous Catholic preachers as well, relying on an appeal to the conscience, a recognition of guilt, and the answer of faith to the example of Jesus. Conviction of sin, compunction, confession, and finally Conversion. But to squeeze all that into five minutes was a tall order! Sometimes it really worked; sometimes there were those who had some compassion on the speaker and "came forward"; and, since then, the huge cam- paigns of men like Billy Graham have suggested that it is a valid way of leading men and women to God. Yet it is difficult to avoid the sense of it being a simplistic interpretation of the Gospel, liable to result in a sharp reversal at a later date in those who reacted emotionally to an appeal, which, in the cooler reality of daily life, was insufficient in the face of the hard world of daily living.

At any rate, on this occasion the place and purpose seemed sadly inappropriate. The second speaker also drew blank. Sud- denly, I found the leader whispering to me, "Go on, you must speak too. You'll have to start some time." Well, as a teenager, I was for a while an "all-the-year-round" swimmer at our local open-air swimming pool; splendid in the summer, but desperate in the winter, when a small group would turn up, break the ice at one end of the bath, and plunge in. Only bravado and fear of looking a coward ever got me in. How often I dreaded it — and glowed with pride afterwards!

In much the same mood, I jumped on to a bench to say my piece. Of course, I was wholly unprepared, saying the first thing that came into my head. "Brothers, I've never worked in a mine. My father never worked in a mine. I've never been in a mine before today — and, at present, I hope never to come to a mine again!" I was a bit scared and, as usual, spoke too loudly. Well, it woke the place up. "I can't think why I am here, interrupting you when you want to go home — so do I — but, before I go, I had better say that I am here because, in the end, I am convinced that there is more in life than just working in the way that you do..." Words to that effect, and a brief account of how I became a friar. It wasn't tremendous, but at least they clapped — a little. I didn't make an appeal, or ask them to take a card.

One or two of them shook hands when I got down, and we finally left.

To my astonishment, when we assembled later for the team meeting to report back on our activities, my leader told the assembly of my great "testimony", and the response of the miners. A success! The awful result was that I was included in team after team, at canteens, class meetings, clubs, to repeat my testimony. I don't think I was taken in, but I did it.

Two other recollections of that Campaign have always remained with me. We went to another local mine, where it was suggested that we should talk to the men when they came off the pit face, before they went up in the lifts to the surface. We travelled down in a sickening, sudden descent, huddled in a cage which suddenly seemed to drop so that my stomach shot up to my mouth, an old trick played on the uninitiated. Down below, there was a wide, poorly lit tunnel. As the men came off the pit faces from passages which led to this wide one, they squatted on their haunches, waiting to be taken up. It was strangely silent. Their black faces were expressionless. I was told that I had no more than five minutes. The men gathered, squatted, said nothing. I had a little speech about God into which I launched. There was no way of telling how they reacted — until suddenly, after a minute or two, when I was just beginning to get to the point, a bell rang behind me. Without a glance in my direction the men got up and walked away to the lift. I was left alone, in full flood. Then a lot more men came and squatted, so I started again, trying to keep it shorter. But again, much too soon, the bell rang. I tried several times. But I never got the timing right.

That evening, rather breaking ranks, I managed to get myself invited to the local working men's club. There seemed considerable surprise when I was offered a drink — and asked for a pint! One of the men said, "I saw you earlier today." "Did you?" I replied, "There was no way I could recognise *you*. Well, what did you think of it?" "Oh, it was all right." "Go on," I said, "what did you really think?" "I think it was proper daft!" How I agreed with him.

We came back from another mine late at night, travelling in a pit train. It had no windows, hardly any seats or doors, a sort of derelict train, chunting along, rattling and clattering. There were about twenty of the team mixed up with the miners. In the dark, some sort of camaraderie was just possible. Suddenly, far down the clattering train, some of the men started singing, "The Lord's my Shepherd" to Crimond. It sounded distant and, for once, strangely beautiful and "right". Bit by bit, other carriages took it up. After a while, in a warm night, unable to see each other, yet feeling the security of anonymity, the whole train, jolting, swaying, lurching along, sang the familiar words, the sentimental tune, in a way that seemed solemn, moving, an echo of some sort of emotional truth. I've heard it, of course, many times since; and sometimes remembered that moment. Perhaps it is for others, as well, the one valid memory of a Campaign in which I learned many lessons.

That was my first experience of "going North", of which I had heard so much from Algy. It was the beginning of a romantic infatuation with all things "Northern", Tyneside, Wearside, shipyards, pit villages, the wild and beautiful moorland beyond Rothbury, the largely deserted coastline, the border country. But even more than these things I was drawn by the characteristic warmth and directness of the people; their long historical roots, craggy independence, directness of speech, great warmth of love and acceptance, betraying the powerful sentiment of men and women who were born close to the earth and the sea, worked and lived with hardship, poverty, the imminence of death; roused to sentiments of anger or joy, sharing pain or happiness with a simple unqualified directness that I have not found in quite the same way anywhere else. They are very practical people, and the steady stream of men and women who have joined the Society from there invariably bring with them invaluable gifts of practical experience.

There's a shyness about "Geordies"; they don't wear their hearts on their sleeves, but from the first I not only found myself loved, but discovered I moved among people who understood my love.

Spiritually I also discovered the Northern Saints. In the earliest days of Christianity in Britain the North of England was converted by missionaries from Iona, where Columba came from Ireland. The saintly King Oswald sent to Iona for help and the man who came was Aidan. He established missions up and down the coast, and finally died and was buried in Bamburgh. As he died so Cuthbert came, a shepherd lad from Melrose, to the newly founded monastery on Lindisfarne, the island, one of a group, off the coast above Bamburgh.

Cuthbert eventually died on the most remote of the group – the Inner Farne, and was buried on Lindisfarne. When the Vikings attacked, the monks fled with Cuthbert's body in its Saxon coffin of wood, bold with carvings, the head of Oswald, and the Lindisfarne Gospels, one of the greatest of our Saxon manuscripts, only outshone by the Book of Kells. After much wandering the monks finally settled in Durham, where Cuthbert is buried behind the high altar. The coffin and Cuthbert's vestments are all to be seen in the treasury there. The book of the Gospels is now in the British Museum. I don't know about Oswald's head.

What cannot be denied is that the Venerable Bede, another "Northern" saint, who lived in Jarrow, produced the first major historical work in European Literature. In it he tells us in detail not only about Cuthbert but about all the other holy men and women who shaped the pattern of Christianity in the northern counties. There is so much remaining to fire our imagination and help us recapture that great age of faith and those heroes. I'd read all about it, and now began a love affair which tinged every visit to the North East with the excitement of exploration and discovery.

To stand on the windy and bare slope where Oswald raised the Cross and won a famous victory against Penda – he called it "Heavenfield' – to pray in Bamburgh Church at the simple shrine which marks the spot where Aidan died, to spend a week or two alone on the remote and sometimes storm-bound small island where Cuthbert lived and died, with only the seabirds and black rabbits for company, undisturbed since the last monks left at the Reformation. Northumberland in particular is one of the few comparatively unspoiled counties in England: the spiritual air is "thin" and the breakthrough to transcendence and glory can happen without violence. I came to "know" Cuthbert in particular as a friend at Court, and some of the places associated with him became my familiar haunts.

A year after the South Shields Campaign I went north again, this time for what was to become an annual event for several years. In 1946 I travelled to Newcastle with Brother John for Holy Week. He was bound for Ashington. I was to pay my first visit to Newcastle.

As usual we had been given a thorough "briefing" from Algy about our sermons and addresses. By now I'd been through the whole experience at Cerne Abbas several times, so we were armed with sermon notes, and over succeeding years I was to amass a series of different addresses suitable for Palm Sunday and Holy Week. For the "Three Hours" on Good Friday I stuck, for many years, to the "Seven Words from the Cross" − entering the pulpit at twelve noon, and standing there until 3 pm exactly with my seven addresses interspersed with hymns, prayers, psalms and silences. There were plenty of stories going around of brothers who had forgotten the time or had a watch that broke down and went on to 4 pm − others who dried up by 1.30 pm or collapsed before it was over! In those days it was assumed it would all be done fasting from the night before and in the more catholic churches there would have been a Mass of the pre-Sanctified and other services earlier in the morning.

The Diocese of Newcastle is one of those industrial centres where Anglo-Catholic parishes sprang up in the latter part of the last century, and young men from the south were sent for their curacies after Cuddesdon, Wells, Westcott House or some such theological college. My destination was just like that. I'd been told to take a tram from outside the station and ask for Stanhope Street. Forty years ago the present cleaning, rebuilding and general distortion of the city had not taken place. The centre of Newcastle was an early example of town planning; not perhaps on anything like the same scale as Bath, but in its limited way it had something of the same grandeur. Neglect and vandalism has destroyed some of it. Latter-day planning and preservation has destroyed even more, including the whole of Eldon Square. Grey Street remains very grand, wide and with a sweeping curve up from the river, and the great shopping thoroughfare of Grainger Street and Dobson Street, through which my tram clattered, had not entirely lost their dignity. Once free from the centre it was a different story. The tram reached the football ground and then changed gear to sweep up the steep slope of Stanhope Street. It was wide enough, as wide as Grainger Street, but on either side were row after row of the mean terraced houses, stretching it seemed endlessly which were the hallmark of industrial Britain. Cramped accommodation for large families, with at the heart of each house a kitchen table, a big coal fire range, a sense of heavy heat as you came in, and a short walk in icy wind or wet to the lavatory, in the little yard outside.

There were two churches for that area: St Philip's and the Holy Spirit Mission, where the Vicar, David Siller, lived with the Curate, and where I stayed. They were proud that among other distinguished curates in the past had been Conrad Noel who became known later as the "notorious" socialist vicar of Thaxted in Essex. I arrived to find the Vicar ill, the curate only just ordained, and neither of them very confident in getting a Franciscan Brother who had never preached for Holy Week before. The parishioners however were marvellous, asked me for meals which, in spite of rationing, seemed enormous, and the church was well attended. Then there was the organist, Honor. She was a bit older than me, a big woman with striking blond hair who sometimes wore a cloak. She was not only the organist, but seemed to run most things, and was certainly capable of taking an inexperienced friar in hand ! What the curate and I didn't know she quickly told us, modestly, courteously, and very firmly. After the first, service we were invited to her home for supper. She lived on a corner half way up Stanhope Street where her parents ran an "off licence" for Newcastle Breweries, and, unbelievably, for this pillar of the church, it was called "The Mitre"! We usually went in a side door as the living accommodation was mostly overhead, but if I went into the shop, then I would be privileged to have a flap in the counter opened up so that I could "go through to the back" where eventually a bottle would always appear. The back room was inevitably a big kitchen and in no time the table would be covered in pies, scones, cakes, cold meat and tea. Honor Tyndall was a mine of information about the diocese. Many of the clergy shopped there and often stayed for a chat and perhaps something in the back room to warm them on their way. She was portentously discreet and to the end preserved an almost regal dignity – but she also loved a story and was expert in prising the latest news from the clerics who enjoyed her hospitality. She would speak in a personally possessive way of *"My* Vicar" or *"My* Provost" or *"My* Bishop" and I discovered later that I had joined the clerical entourage with which she had chosen to surround herself. Her parents died, her sisters and brothers all married, and in the end she was running "The Mitre" alone, very successfully, but a terror to the breweries, and a bit of a tyrant to the clergy, but retaining her dignity to neighbours and customers. As I travelled north more and more, I often used the night train, and it became my invariable custom to go to Stanhope Street for breakfast and a rest at Honor's. On one occasion she nursed me through a severe throat infection and always sent me off with sandwiches, chocolate and sometimes a bottle of something. What a very generous person – she certainly helped a lot in that first Holy Week.

During that week I sometimes found the people in the parish calling me "Father Ernest". When I asked about this I discovered that there had recently been a Father Ernest as curate — Ernest Marsh. He had gone on from there to be Precentor at the Cathedral but had died suddenly. We apparently looked very much alike. The coincidence didn't stop there.

Ernest Marsh had been a boy at St George's, Cullercoats, where Algy was curate. Later, when Algy returned from India, he joined him at St Ives, was ordained, and intended going to India himself. He became Algy's secretary and went with him to Cerne Abbas when he linked up with Brother Douglas, but was not happy with that development, so returned to Northumberland and the curacy at St Philip's. Honor had hoped he might marry her, but I wonder. She took me to meet his mother, who gave me the typewriter Algy had given Ernest. That all seemed a little strange.

So year after year I went to a parish in the North East for Holy Week — Ashington, Seaton Hurst, St John's, St Michael's, and in many of the churches in Sunderland, and South Shields as well as small pit villages. But rarely to a country parish. In the past forty years I have not often failed to preach in Holy Week and on Good Friday, though to my regret the Three Hour Devotions has been largely replaced with liturgical services.

The next annual event was the revival of "The Wooler Camp". Algy as a young curate was full of ideas for encouraging the young men and women who came from the fishing villages or the mining towns. He was an enthusiast for camping — about which he knew little! So together with Bill Wright, a priest from Sunderland, and several others he found a farmer prepared to let them camp on a site in Skirlnaked Valley near Wooler. The valley is wide and dramatic with a stream running through it and the Cheviot hills rugged and bare in the background. The camps, a week for boys followed by a week for girls, were a huge success from the start, the one opportunity to get away from the soot and squalor into the sunlight. Algy's friends from the university came to help and the young curates joined in all the games. Though Algy left Cullercoats, he always remained in touch with "the Wooler Camp." Only the war could stop it — and once the war looked like finishing he began a plan for its revival.

He hardly accepted that things might be different when the war was over, and he himself now lived in the depth of Dorset. But he organised a meeting in Sunderland at St Luke's, which had a Vicar he much admired, Gordon Hopkins.

As a result, in 1946 the camp began again, without Algy, and with Denis in charge and me as his assistant. Algy tried to plan it all from Dorset, as if he were going to be there himself! The time-table, services, meals, programme – the lot. About a hundred boys came, with a contingent from the South, which included students from Oxford and Cambridge and boys from Sherborne, Hailebury and other schools. Some of us assembled in Newcastle, and were driven up on the back of a lorry, picking up others as we went, eyeing one another with suspicion, a little awkward and uncertain – but gradually losing our latent fears so that by the time we were tumbling out on the camp site we were all roaring the same songs, though mastering the Tyneside accents and local ditties was going to take longer. "Cushy Butterfield" and the "Lambton Worm" and "Keep yer feet still Geordie Hinie" sung with gusto probably need a pint or two of "Newcastle Brown" to help them along – but it's wonderful how well they can go on strong tea! Camp, games, swimming in the pools, climbing Cheviot and all the rest was given a particular character. There was a big marquee for recreation pur-poses, and the rain; and another used exclusively as a chapel. A daily Mass, which was voluntary, prayers and Bible study, and an evening 'sing-song' followed by a talk and night prayer. It sounds like a lot of religion for a holiday, but nobody stayed away, and the camp went on increasing in size each year as the regulars came again and again. How it acquired its unique atmosphere of spontaneous commitment to friendship with one another and to God can only be part of that mystery of Being which is God himself. The openness of the moors, the prevailing power of beauty, the accepted intimacy and freedom to express feelings which were customarily buttoned up tight, all played a part. Most of all there seemed a nearness to God given us by the natural world that led us by its own nature into the supernatural.

The boys had all been brought up in an atmosphere of Catholic worship; candles, bells, incense, ceremonial, some of it aestheti-cally awful, though a church like Algy's at Cullercoats was of its kind very beautiful. Yet to discover God waiting for them in the natural world of their own countryside was new, and unconsciously exciting because for them not easily articulated. Awareness also of the beauty and holiness they found in one another – though *that* could never be stated except very rarely and privately. You could say things at camp you couldn't say anywhere else.

There was a lot of laughter, boisterous horse-play and jokes at the expense of others. We were often at the camp for the Feast of the Transfiguration, and "'Tis good Lord to be here" became a sort of anthem, and as we sang it at the last Mass before we left. I've seen men in tears for fear, I think, that this precious sense of the numinous could not be taken with them, a new insight that might be lost.

I have met "Wooler Campers" all over the world. Elderly men and women who speak with nostalgia of a discovery they once made in the mist, the subtle colouring, the clean and open world of the Northumberland moors, and the human love and unexpected friendships made there that lasted a life time.

Algy, who was not really a natural camper and never quite adapted himself to "roughing it", nevertheless had the insight to recognise that any thing which gives us an opportunity to live "provisionally" as pilgrims might, or like Arabs or nomads, can as a consequence discover an intimacy of being with God, with one another, and with the world around us. The camp for families we started at Hilfield in the sixties depended on many of the same factors for its success.

As the camp at Wooler involved, for me, bringing a party of young men from "the South", it seemed a great opportunity to do what the "Compagnons de S. François", a Roman Catholic ecumenical movement, had been doing since before the war; organising an actual pilgrimage. The idea was to visit places associated with St Cuthbert − who else − ending in Durham Cathedral where he is buried, praying and evangelising as we went. During the camp we learnt, more or less, one of the *Little Plays of St Francis* by Lawrence Housman: "Sister Gold." Denis was the producer and also played St Francis. He was quite brilliant, not least at improvising the lines which he and other members of the cast forgot. His enthusiasm, like his laugh, was infectious and by the last night of the camp we were ready with the first performance.

The following morning we set out. I'd borrowed an old scout treck cart from Durham and can see us now pushing and pulling it up the hill out of the valley. Each day we celebrated Communion, then after breakfast walked for the first half hour in silence, hopefully meditating.

We performed our play in the open air, attracting a good crowd of visitors and holiday makers. At the end of it Denis made a stirring appeal. At Kelso the following day we slept in the Roman Catholic Church hall, and the priest joined us for Compline − quite a step forward for those pre-Vatican II days, and then on to Melrose, the starting place for Cuthbert, Jedburgh and on to Hexham: all of them with the ruins of ancient monasteries. From Hexham it was a bus to Chester le Street, where Cuthbert's body rested for over a hundred years, and finally on foot to Durham, via Finchale Abbey.

Entering Durham, on tired and blistered feet, dragging the treck cart up the cobbled streets, the great cathedral towering above us and in the shadow of the castle, we felt very truly the pilgrims we had set out to be. We had been invited to stay in the house of Michael Ramsey, the Van Mildert Professor, another Cambridge connection. Until then my only encounter with him had been the rather remote one of hearing him preach in Oxford, but this was to be the beginning of a close and caring friendship between him and the Society of St Francis. "Big Michael", my friends called him, and that was right, big in every way. Somehow he found room for us all in his home just by the cathedral. Soon after our arrival I was going up the stairs and met a girl coming down. She smiled and I said "It's very kind of your father to have us all here like this" — but she just smiled a little more and said "Oh not at all", or words to that effect. When I got to the top and told one of the others I'd met her he roared with laughter. "You idiot — that's not his daughter, its his *wife*!", and so it was. Some bricks can never be picked up.

Dean Wild had agreed we could do the play in the Galilee chapel. It went better than ever before, and we then headed a procession, barefoot, from the tomb of the Venerable Bede right down the length of the cathedral with its great Norman pillars to the tomb of St Cuthbert, and having prayed there returned to the screen before the High Altar to sing "'Tis good Lord to be here!"

Parting from one another after all that was not easy. The pilgrimage took place annually for another ten years and the camp, transferred finally to Budle Bay, has continued, with one or two interruptions, to the present day.

After two years the girls' camp was disastrously "washed out" by a terrific flood of water during a raging storm; and a new site had to be found.

A Mrs Weller-Poley, later to be known as Sister Ursula, came to the rescue, as indeed she had done more than once already. She was a very devout person and a member of our Third Order. Hearing we needed someone to organise the cooks, a group of mothers who came camping with us, she volunteered. Originally she volunteered her own cook — but *she* was too much of a lady to go camping! Mrs W-P wasn't much of a cook, but a splendid and masterful organiser, who eventually started her own Franciscan Sisterhood at Low Fell in Co. Durham. She had a responsible post during the war, and, I think as a consequence, knew Lady Grey of Howick Hall in Northumberland. They had plenty of fields near the sea — and offered us one. So the camp moved there.

Lord and Lady Grey were devout High Church Anglicans, and it was a little daunting when the entire household, including all the children just home from school, turned up to attend the camp Mass. I was invited up to the Hall for a bath, and stayed to tea, and came to know them all. Their daughter Mary took great interest in the camp and the whole Franciscan idea. Her own connections were with Mirfield, but her enthusiasm for the friars, "Molly's Monks" as her family sometimes called them, began at the camp. As we came to know each other better, I discussed with her my hope that one day we might have a permanent home in Northumberland.

After a year or two at Howick we finally found a site at Budle Bay, further north, within sight of the Farnes, and right next to the sea. We also combined the boys' and girls' camps *("then* you'll have trouble", they said — but we didn't, or not much).

It took a lot of visits north to organise, and as I was being asked for preaching or teaching missions more and more I gradually came to know the clergy and people of the North East better than any part of England — almost a naturalised "Geordie".

Chapter Eleven

"The Noblest Employment of Man"

There has been a long tradition of Parish Missions in our church. I was interested to discover in the parish church of Pendeen at the most remote end of Cornwall a plaque commemorating a former Vicar who is said to have been the first to promote them. Certainly in the S.S.F. they constitute a major part of our evangelistic outreach. At any one time in Britain there can be as many as a hundred or so Parish Missions under consideration, being prepared for, or being conducted.

My first experience was at St Alban's Holborn in London during the war. Algy was the Chief Missioner and two priest Brothers, Owen and Charles, supported him. I was joined by Bro Harold (who had also recently joined S.S.F.) as the Children's Missioners. Algy told us what to do and say, planning the services with us, and our course of talks and instruction. As a consequence I began to develop at first as a "Children's Missioner", sometimes as junior partner to one of the Cowley Fathers, Father Manson, in country villages in Cambridgeshire, at Horsham and later on at Wallsend in Northumberland.

I also began, after a year or two, planning my own Campaigns for Young People. The first, done with all the complications of bomb alerts and black outs – it was still wartime – was at a church in Coventry, and I took a "team" with me. This was a significant development. It wasn't large, just three or four young men and women I'd met preaching in Dorset, or on their visits to the Friary, but it established a pattern which became an invariable rule – and once I got going in Oxford and Cambridge with all the student resources available there, to the big Campaigns and Missions in the fifties.

It wasn't new, Algy had known it in his more evangelical days, and was eager to establish challenging catholic counterparts to the highly successful evangelical campaigns run by the Oxford and Cambridge Pastorates, and the Christian Union. On one occasion, just after the war, we actually combined with them in a memorable mission at Keighley in Yorkshire.

The Pastorate had been invited to take a team of students with clerical support organised from Oxford to all the parishes in the Keighley Deanery. Two of them which were "high church" rather resented the very low church approach and asked for students and priests that represented a more catholic attitude. Howard Guinness, a prominent Evangelical evangelist with whom I later struck up a warm friendship, approached Algy, and he promised to produce a team, led by himself and Br Charles, a veteran founder of the Community. I was to be his assistant at one of the Churches. Algy at the other had Br James, and together we enlisted the support of Oxford undergraduates, our headquarters for the purpose being Pusey House.

It was certainly a learning experience, Charles was a most lovable and saintly man, with a slightly ethereal, dreamy manner, a boyish, punning sense of humour and an ascetic Franciscan life style, who also played the fiddle. Hymn singing or hymn practising was a big part of the mission services, with Charles in the pulpit playing his violin, and me walking up and down the aisle waving my arms, reading the verses, and encouraging the congregation in the choruses. We used the Mirfield Mission Hymn Book when we could. The Community of the Resurrection at Mirfield in Yorkshire were pioneers in this form of mission service and its collection of old Moody and Sankey hymns, Anglo-Catholic sacramental devotion and sentimental Victorian tunes was enormously successful. The mood differed very little from the Methodist Chapels which was the more familiar ground of many in that Yorkshire Methodist stronghold.

The services themselves were of the simplest structure, hymns, prayers, hymns, some Bible Reading, a brief instruction on prayer, church going, confession etc., and a long sermon which included sometimes an appeal – and of course more hymns. The church was packed. All this was supported by tireless visiting of the parish, having meals in parishioners' homes, and a team meeting each morning. The Catholics had already been up for an early Mass and sometimes arrived for the meeting of all the teams from the various parishes in a bit of a rush. The meeting began with prayer and a chorus or two introduced by an earnest young minister with a wide dog collar, brushed back hair and a reedy voice. As he launched into the chorus he looked so much like the comic curate that chuckles broke out in our team, which became infectious.

I went on another mission with Charles, to Barrow in Furness, but soon began organising my own, recruiting mission helpers from the Universities: and devising my own system of Youth Campaigns as well as leading Parish Missions. In the North East one Mission led to another, and once I'd moved to Cambridge the autumn mission at the end of the Summer Vac became a regular feature, involving not only much preparation in Cambridge but many visits to the parish to make preparations there as well. All this preparatory work began two years ahead, so I always had two parishes to visit, one for remote preparation the other for something more immediate.

I continued to arrange missions of this kind all the time I was in Cambridge, the last of them being a real blockbuster at All Saints, Gosforth, Newcastle. Gosforth has a number of large houses, and I persuaded ten ladies in the parish to act as hostesses and invite thirty or forty neighbours for evening drinks etc. on four nights running. One of the team of clergy would also be present, introduced by the hostess. After a short talk he would answer questions. The atmosphere of the sort of social gathering they were accustomed to would, we hoped, make for ease of communication. In fact it succeeded far beyond our expectations – and each evening we could reckon on there being about three hundred people in the parish, many of whom had never darkened the door of the church, settling down to serious discussion over a fork supper or cocktails. On the following three nights we had events in the Church Hall, with local politicians or others taking part, and then for three nights we had "all out" mission services in church. It was all supported by several celebrations of the Eucharist each day, an hour of prayer and Bible study each morning, visiting in the afternoon, a household which bravely gave themselves to be the centre for the parallel Youth Mission – with the inevitable (in those days) rock and roll – and meetings for men, for women, demonstrations and publicity. I went back to that church many years later, and found the effect of the Mission still evident in the lives of people who had discovered a new way of recognising God.

I am convinced that nothing can replace the direct preaching and teaching of the Gospel. The many different forms of communication available to us now, television, radio, video, tapes, are obviously capable of being immensely effective. But in the end they are all "second hand". The recognised vulnerability of a preacher or teacher confronted with a congregation or audience is in itself a powerful ally in communication. Of course there are all the dangers as well. You can't go back and edit or revise what you say, and you can be the victim of a badly lit pulpit, a reading stand that scatters your notes, or a microphone or speakers that distort and blur your voice! You can have a severe cold on the day, a fierce headache, a sore throat or a bad attack of nerves. It can happen that you have far less time to prepare than you expected, panic and lose your way in your sermon – and it shows. Yet the immediate rapport possible in a "live" service or meeting can overcome all obstacles if the intention is sincere and there is a genuine belief in what you are doing.

Over the years I began to recognise the value of extempore preaching – and its pitfalls. The possibility of an immediate relationship between a congregation and a preacher built on personal appeal and understanding. I discovered that my own human experience could be a simple and direct way of attracting and holding attention. Most of all, I think I was confirmed in the notion, though not perhaps too consciously, that I had a good and strong voice which, in itself, people might listen to – though it was important to have something to say!

I have heard some fine preachers and splendid sermons. I have also heard sermons wrecked through dull or unconvincing delivery, jumbled or confused ideas, or just thin and trivial material depending for effect on slick language or unconvincing tricks of speech for effect. And I have not always lived up to my own ideals.

Soon after the war I shared in a series of University Missions in Oxford. As a consequence of regular visits with Algy, I had built up a circle of acquaintances among the undergraduates and we attended the Mission addresses in the Sheldonian, going as a party and returning to colleges afterwards to discuss the addresses over late drinks.

The Sheldonian – a very great building, Wren at his best – is a natural theatre where a real relationship between speaker and audience is possible. The two missions I remember best were preached by Stephen Neill and Michael Ramsey, both of whom I came to know well, even intimately – and knowing them can assert what should be a self-evident truth for preachers, that what they had to say sprang from their own deep personal conviction and was one with their own lives, surely one of the several secrets of great preaching, and must have been just as true for Wesley or Newman, even if their styles were different.

With one exception, I think Stephen Neill was the finest preacher I have heard. He had been the Bishop of Tinivelly in South India, and returned from there to be Chaplain of Trinity College, Cambridge. It was during that time that he preached the Oxford University Mission. Though he appeared to have hardly any notes he held the packed audience spellbound for about forty-five minutes each night. His subject was always clearly announced and beautifully laid out. Points were made in succession without fumbling, illustrations were occasionally witty, and always absolutely relevant to the argument. (Oh! those unnecessary stories included only to keep the congregation happy, amused or in suspense.) His voice and articulation clear, his timing superb. But above all he had something to say which combined theological insight with academic enquiry and deep personal conviction. All in clear uncluttered English. I can hear him quoting Browning even now – indeed I've quoted the same passages from *A Death in the Desert* or *Saul* myself. I know priests today, now well into their retirement, who trace their first complete conviction concerning the Christian Faith to hearing Stephen Neill, sitting on those hard seats in the Sheldonian, and recognising a truth that had to be explored.

He was a commanding man with a commanding personality. I later came to know that he was also a man whom some considered flawed, with personal weaknesses that had almost ruined his ministry: so he left India, and then could never quite be accepted by some in Britain. The first University Mission I ever conducted myself was at Trinity College Dublin in 1956 – and that was because Stephen Neill had first accepted, and then some mysterious authority had obliged him to withdraw.

His books included an expansion of those University addresses, and a masterly account of the Ecumenical Movement. So God used this great man – with his, in some ways apparently crippling weaknesses – to bring other men and women to Himself. His gifts of scholarship and powerful ability to communicate were not wasted. For me he is one among a group of men who helped me to understand the power of preaching and the economy of God, who uses the vulnerability of men. Perhaps it is one reason why he preached so well, he knew it was for himself also that he proclaimed forgiveness and reconciliation.

In the same way, with many of the same gifts but with a different voice and with innocence rather than weakness to make him vulnerable, Michael Ramsey proclaimed the Glory of God at Oxford. It is astonishing and rather wonderful, that the same message can sound so different, yet ultimately lead to the same goal. What Stephen Neill did just after the war, Michael Ramsey did a few years later in a Sheldonian once again packed to the ceiling. I was stationed as an assistant in one of the colleges, and there was a new collection of undergraduates to share it with.

I was also beginning to be invited for Missions in other Universities. One of them eventually took me to St Andrew's in Scotland and Dr. Archie Craig. As his assistant, I gave a series of lunch time talks on prayer in the University Church of St Salvatore. It must have been a bit surprising for that pulpit, once the stronghold of John Knox, to be occupied by a Franciscan Friar. Dr Craig gave the main addresses in the evening. He was at that time a Professor in Glasgow, one of the most prominent of Presbyterian Ministers and undoubtedly, for me, the most moving preacher I had ever heard. It was my first encounter with the Kirk at this level.

Archie Craig had a splendid voice and Scottish burr and used it with unconscious effect. What he had to say revealed a depth of understanding and profound Biblical awareness I had never quite met before. There was a sort of grandeur about it which I found enthralling. Here was a man who knew the truth of the Gospel could be communicated, man to man, who made the human voice and human language a channel for a divinity that led to transcendence. Yet it was a preaching singularly free from gimmicks or tricks. He used words and ideas which anyone could understand, but with a conviction, clarity and economy which was, as I was later to discover, all one with the man himself.

Algy knew what he was doing when he encouraged me to sit at the feet of such men, because like them he was absolutely convinced of the power of the spoken word, and regarded preaching as an essential and most significant element in our ministry, something to be taken very seriously and treated as a privilege. It was also, and must be expected to be, hard work. So far as he was concerned every brother should be equipped to preach to the extent of his ability. Not everyone agreed. It never occurred to me to question otherwise.

Quite early on in my time as his secretary I was instructed always to sit at the back of the church and take full notes of his sermon as he preached it. I still have them, hundreds of them I should think. I soon discovered a facility for writing rapidly almost verbatim, as he preached on the whole slowly. I sometimes wondered whether I was being used so that he might discipline himself. Certainly he was invariably clear if not always concise.

And now I find that, even if I have to preach at the shortest notice, I instinctively follow the pattern given to me by him which has changed little over the years. I need a text − preferably a short passage of scripture rather than a brief verse. I need striking or provocative words, something which *The New English Bible* frequently provides − at any rate it is the translation I use the most. Then in my mind's eye, I see it set out, three or four points I can make round a central idea. Then I try to find in my mind an anecdote, something from the radio, a film or book, an encounter, an event in the past few days, something human, immediate − but not an invention – which will help to introduce it all. Stick to the text and conclude with it.

Once you have come to believe in preaching the whole of life becomes a preparation for it. I sometimes recognise a poem or a newspaper story as an obvious illustration, more often it is only in the actual preparation and writing of a sermon that something jumps into my mind. You've got to believe in it, want it to happen and adopt a sort of recklessness in snatching ideas out of life to press into service for the sermons.

I write out all my sermons if there is time, but I can't begin to do that until I have an idea of what I want to preach about, and let it turn over in my mind for days, going to sleep with it, waking up with it, finding it a background during meals or prayer or conversation. Suddenly hitting on a phrase or an idea, then wondering how it will fit in. And always unconsciously saying to myself, "Where does this fit into the grand plan of God, which bit of the story of our creation and redemption am I trying to illustrate? Where is the Cross, where is the Resurrection, where is the Holy Spirit at work?" Of course you can't get it all in – only a bit. But sermons are not merely for edification and never just for entertainment. Somewhere in every sermon we should be led to an encounter with the living God, and be hoping to lead others to Him.

The choice of words matters enormously. I often find that a sermon to be delivered on Sunday morning is only finally written on Saturday afternoon or evening, not through slackness so much as a sheer inability to collect the thoughts and feelings and give them coherence. It means also that having been written so late on Saturday I should get up extra early on Sunday to give plenty of time to go through it carefully on Sunday morning, correct the language and if necessary write it out all over again.

Algy had vast respect for the English language, and led me to love poetry as much as he did. Poetry undoubtedly gives words power, the magic of the right word in the right place, and the love of such beauty for its own sake.

The co-operation of the congregation matters also. At St Bene't's Cambridge, where I live at present, the congregation really cooperates with the preachers and recognises what they are giving to them, making it a shared experience in which the Holy Spirit intervenes. Most of them really want a sermon, are intent, listen carefully and are constructively critical. It makes all the difference. The congregation there confirms my belief in the supreme importance of preaching, – the "Breaking of the Word" in the pulpit side by side with the "Breaking of the Bread" at the altar.

Alas, it is not, I think, a view that is held by all the Franciscans today, and I know there are other ways of making known the glory of the Gospel. In the study of the Principal of Westcott House there was, when I first went there, a small framed autograph of Spurgeon the great Victorian. It said "The preaching of the everlasting Gospel is the noblest employment of man". I just believe that is true.

Chapter Twelve

At Westcott House

For several years after I went to Cambridge I continued to spend some time with Algy at Hilfield and Glasshampton, and in the summer in Scotland. It was at Glasshampton one hot summer afternoon in 1950 after the time of solitude, that Algy sent for me and I turned up with a pad expecting to take down some letters. Without looking up from his writing he said *"Do* sit down," indicating the end of the bed which was, as so often, the only place to sit. "I have been wondering", he went on, "whether you have considered the possibility of ordination. Of course I couldn't possibly press it on you, it must be your own decision, – but would you like to let me know what you think Not now, of course, but in a day or two". I said, yes, I'd certainly think about it, and as that seemed all, I left, just catching a glimpse of the slight smile on his face behind his glasses.

Would I think about it! I knew him by now too well, there was no question what the answer *ought* to be. Of course I'd first thought of ordination at the age of twelve, mostly to please the curate, then there was the certain urge to be a priest at Papworth and all those hopeless Latin lessons with Fr Gilbert and Greek with Francis Cornford. But that was nearly ten years ago, and I was accustomed to being a lay brother in a Community in which they were much the majority. To be a Guardian, Novice Master or Minister it was necessary to be a priest, but such an ambition had never crossed my mind even though, with hindsight, I see now that it had occurred to Algy. In fact I really believed in the vocation of the Lay Brothers and was proud of the fact that in this respect S.S.F. was virtually unique in the Church of England. (It still is, with their position considerably enhanced by the possibility of all those roles of authority now being equally open to the unordained brother.)

I see now that it was all part of Algy's plan. He hadn't many more years to live and wanted to safeguard the future as far as he could. He once said to me, a year or two before he died – "It will be first Denis and then you." Well it almost worked out like that. So that hot afternoon had its place in the plan.

A few days later I brought the subject up. Again it was in the afternoon. The uncanny stillness of a monastery in the heat, doors and windows open, a warm smell of summer flowers on the air, silent movement and the reflection on the brilliantly polished dark red floor in the corridor. A soft tap on the door and the piping voice saying "Do come in. Ah dear Michael — sit *there*": a chair this time. So I told him, and he didn't look up at first but showed his pleasure with a smile. I was sent to get tea. Then out it all came; and once more, as several years before, I felt a little cheated. "Of course I am sure you should go to Westcott House", his own Theological College. "Ken Carey — such a nice man — says he will be glad to have you. Of course, my dear Mother will pay." She was in fact very generous.

So it seemed already planned, all set up. I'd thought and prayed about it in the past three days, indeed I'd thought about little else, and I suppose in a vague way I'd thought also that if he asked me I would at least want to suggest a theological college. Certainly the idea of Westcott was attractive, after all it was in Cambridge so I need not leave all my new-found friends, but it also had a reputation for being elitist. I rather wondered if I could compete with all that. Several friends were already there, others had only just left. I hadn't the slightest academic qualifications, and thought I'd be a fish out of water. But Algy had it all arranged. So I accepted it, almost as a matter of obedience, but also I suppose secretly flattered a little, and glad to be following in his footsteps.

However, before Algy's plan could be put into operation I first had to go before a selection board; and this, to Algy, presented problems. Normally all candidates for the Ministry were interviewed by C.A.C.T.M., a board set up by the Church to advise the Bishops as to the suitability of those wishing to be ordained. As I was not going into the ordinary parochial ministry this was not regarded as right for me. An approach was made to the Advisory Council for Religious Communities, and it was agreed that in future a separate board would be set up specifically for members of Religious Orders. I was to be the 'guinea pig'.

I was notified to present myself at St Edward's House, the London house of the Society of St John the Evangelist, the "Cowley Fathers", where I would be staying for three nights. During my time there I would have a series of interviews with the Board. I soon found the Board members were a rather formidable group! The Abbot of Nashdom, the Superior General of the Cowley Fathers and the

Bishop of Oxford, Kenneth Kirk. In between times I was expected to pray. I already knew the house and liked its air of solemn Tractarianism, heavy oak, highly polished floors, high and gloomy corridors and rooms, inadequate lighting. The library seemed huge, the monks of a severity to be found nowhere else. The food solid, unimaginative, filling. But always, and at all times, even with silence so profound, soft shoes and doors that never shut with a bang, the most instinctive and absolute courtesy, and generous kindness.

The same was true of the distinguished men who had the power to say whether I should be a priest or not. I seem to remember long silences in the conversation. The Abbot asked questions about the Society, the Superior discussed our life in general, and the Bishop began by saying "Can you tell me what you think I am supposed to be doing?" Of course he knew, and in the end we got on very well, and finally I was accepted. I don't think the experiment of a separate board lasted very long. I never seemed to hear of anyone else being put through it in that way. I still return to St Edward's House for a retreat from time to time: it has changed remarkably little, perhaps that is why I like it.

So I went to Westcott House.

I really only knew Ken Carey by name. The Principal I had heard most about was B.K. Cunningham who had been there in Algy's time, as had Reginald, Stephen, Francis, Lothian and other members of the Community. His was a name to conjure with, and there were endless stories about him. Ken had been there a bit later than Algy, and was a contemporary of Eric Abbott, my chief mentor and guide after Algy died. Indeed, it seemed as if all Algy's more intimate friends had been at Westcott House.

He himself went there in 1920 just after his first visit to India where he had been teaching in Scotch College, Calcutta. I suppose I gave him a chance to relive vicariously some of his undergraduate days, revive old Cambridge friendships, and generally enjoy again all the enthusiasm he had known as travelling secretary for Theological Colleges in the S.C.M. Friendship meant so much to him, and his most intimate friend Outram Walsh, who had also been in India, then at Westcott came half across Europe to meet him off the boat from India when Algy returned to go there himself.

Times had changed, and in Algy's eyes Ken Carey was not quite B.K. − too liberal, too vague, "not really a Catholic", or for that matter, an Evangelical. So he saw it rather in terms of making the best of a bad job. In fact he was wrong. Without knowing it, I went to Westcott House at the beginning of a most remarkable decade in the history of the Anglican Theological Colleges.

Ken Carey was no academic, and didn't pretend to be, in fact he almost overplayed the disarming modesty with which he accepted the fact. One or two biographies have seemed to me less than kind or just in their assessment of Ken, though in this I may be prejudiced by the fact that I liked him very much from the first. In some ways I see now he was rather limited by his background. Supremely conscious and proud of being one of the Careys, with brothers who were to distinguish themselves in teaching and law, he came from what was for him the familiar and restrictingly self-conscious world of the people who, it is sometimes said, really ran England. Politically Tory, public-spirited, "born to rule", and in his case educated at Marlborough. Perhaps he always expected to be a Bishop one day, or a distinguished Dean. He was sorry about being passed over for Westminster Abbey when Eric Abbott became Dean, and in his heart he may have he found it a bit second best when he was offered, and accepted, the Bishopric of Edinburgh.

Yet for ten years he exerted a most remarkable influence on the Church of England, and from the moment we first met I felt I had a new and intimate friend. His study was at the end of a short passage with a notice on the door which read either "free" or "busy". When I first went in he was standing by the fireplace which had a mantle shelf crowded with a variety of little animals. He was wearing a dog collar, but for the rest, baggy shapeless flannel trousers, a woolly pullover and an old blazer. He had a boyish wrinkled face with a mole, twinkling eyes, a shy uncertain smile, and a cigarette. I discovered afterwards that he had been a bit alarmed at interviewing a Friar; it was not a world with which he had much familiarity. I was a bit alarmed at meeting him. Soon after we got to know each other he seemed to adopt the habit with me (he may have done it with others) of talking in a throw away, rather deprecating style. It was a bit mannered in a sort of tired "Oh dear, what a bore" way, as if nothing should seem too enthusiastic but, because we always knew just how to do everything, inevitably right.

He was rather a sentimentalist and seemed to have very conventional ideas about what was most widely held as right in his world. In this sense he was rather conservative. At the Westcott House Concert in my first year his contribution, treated with acclaim by everyone present, was the singing in a rather quavering voice of a romantic and sentimental ballad "Trees". I thought at first it was a joke, and saw the funny side of it, but fortunately woke up in time to the fact that he was deadly serious!

He could be influenced in his choice of students for the college by their background or connections. At the time Westcott House started it was customary for all students to have University degrees, often in Theology or Classics and almost invariably from Oxford or Cambridge. Though this changed a great deal over the years, Ken wanted to keep it that way, and through his connections in both Universities and his personal conviction, perseverance and charm, he succeeded. Charm was there in abundance in him, and in the people who surrounded him, and it seemed so important. It smoothed paths, eased ways, broke down barriers. However, it sometimes also carefully raised barriers as well. This was done with the greatest subtlety so that you hardly knew it had happened. It could unfortunately seem sometimes to create something of a closed shop.

A lot of it depended on the network; the inter-related world of Public Schools, University Colleges and Clubs. One question, dropped gently into the conversation with a slightly interrogative voice and the merest flick of an eyebrow "Who do you know there?" could be enough: or, "Perhaps I might have a word with old So and So". The name or the connection was invariably all that was needed to establish the ground rules for future conversations or decisions. That appeared one way in which he built up the reputation of the House. At that time there were always many more applicants than places could be found for. If you had been to the right sort of school and the right sort of college, it was apparently assumed that if you were 'High Church' you would press on for theological training to Cuddesdon, and if less high or "just C of E" to Westcott House. When I got there it really did have a number of men with considerable academic ability, prowess in sport, or other distinctions. Not of course that such things were ever mentioned. *That* would have been bad form except – very rarely – as a throw away joke or in passing mockery.

The prevailing mood at times, and one which Ken I think rather fostered, was a closed world of "gifted amateurs". We were bound to get it right because we were born to get *everything* right – including running the country or running the Church. For some there was a sort of boyish enthusiasm of the "isn't it fun" kind, and for everyone, behind the facade of a gentleman's theological club, a very great deal of hard work. After all, the casual attitude would be tested by examination results. It was the best of its kind and as such very good indeed.

The Chapel was undoubtedly the heart of the matter, though here as elsewhere it was assumed that discipline would be self-imposed as far as attendance was concerned. It was fascinating to discover how many of the attitudes adopted by Algy in running S.S.F. had been acquired by him at Westcott House. Morning or Evening Prayer, a daily Eucharist, times of corporate meditation or private prayer, all were allowed for: what you chose to do was largely your affair, though conspicuously frequent absence from chapel would be noted by Ken who would find time to look a bit sad or say "What *are* we going to do with you?" or words to that effect.

The House had a way of transferring to itself the Public School habits of serious mockery and the creation of "traditions". A meeting of the house was called "The Moot", and the senior student "The Sheriff"', and all the other people with jobs had names – so the sacristan was "The Temple Keeper".

There was a quiet day each term with much portentous preparation, the shutting of the main gate, and an imported Church dignitary to instruct us. Ken read at the meals. At the last meal he would make play of reading a profound theological work – which turned out to be "Winnie the Pooh" – greeted with much banging on the table. It brought out all that was most sentimental in him, reducing him almost literally to tears.

During my two years there I was fortunate to be among some of the most exciting younger minds in the Church, and all I have said about the general mood in no way diminished the atmosphere of theological enquiry which they stimulated. When I got there Alan Webster was Vice Principal. He later went on to Lincoln Theological College as Principal, to Norwich as Dean, and then to be a distinguished Dean of St Paul's. He married Margaret, an associate from the S.C.M., and together they blazed many trails, not least that of the Ordination of Women (of which Ken certainly disapproved). The Chaplain was Bob Runcie. When Alan left Bob became Vice Principal and Hugh Montefiore the Chaplain. When I first became a member of the House of Bishops I was surprised at how many of them had been at Westcott House, including a few like Graham Leonard who probably didn't enjoy the experience very much. Whatever the motive, however inadequate, or even misplaced, some of the methods may have been in the fifties, Ken made a significant contribution to the episcopate in England of the seventies and eighties. If there is a common style, an attitude, even a theological and social perspective held by many Bishops today, which influences the way they think, speak and interpret the signs of the times, and which makes them bold to challenge some of the presuppositions which could destroy our spiritual and social life, then part of that common mind and solidarity could be said to spring from the way in which Ken provided a place in which it could germinate. Of course it *was* another sort of Club or network, but why not? The decisions which affect the lives of others cannot always be assessed or arrived at without some sort of personal human encounter, some subtle understanding of the unspoken word. So often it is what is *not* said that counts. It was a very good example of the proper use of the resources – human and divine – and a great achievement. Since then much has changed.

Ken was quite remarkably English and Anglican, as was revealed by his lectures on the Spiritual Life. He was a man of prayer of a certain kind, and a great lover of men and of God. He was often lonely and thought himself misunderstood. He seemed not to be at ease with women, and, in retrospect, perhaps treated the few Westcott wives we had in those days with a degree of insensitivity. During my second year he had an operation and was away for several weeks. He returned to a riotous welcoming concert – with a rousing chorus line in which I danced, but could never get the steps quite right!

I preached at his consecration in Edinburgh, a very grand affair in St Mary's Cathedral and at first, with his Scottish connections and a Scottish home, it seemed absolutely the right place for him, but it was a delusion. He lived in a large granite house near the cathedral which I would have loved – but he, I think, found gloomy and intimidating. His housekeeper was a splendid Scottish "body" who looked after him very well, yet he was frequently alone and lonely, though a succession of devoted Chaplains did their best to share his ministry.

He often drove himself and later on there were stories of his arriving late, and of one or two near misses that might have been serious accidents. By this time I was Guardian at Alnmouth in Northumberland, and could see him regularly and he would talk with me about the problems of the diocese and other things, particular and personal. His biggest disappointment was his failure with the press. Some Scottish newspapers seemed to have decided to find fault with him. There was, as would be expected, a lot of discussion about ecumenical affairs, and he rarely seemed to get it right in their eyes. I'm not sure he always handled it very well. He could be impulsive, and sometimes a bit angry, and that rarely helps with popular newspapers. He certainly suffered, found it very hard to be unpopular, and shrank from all the criticism.

I was saddened when some of my Scottish friends spoke critically of him, thought him "indecisive" or passed on gossip. George Martineau, the Dean, a lovely man and an old acquaintance from the days when he was at Jedburgh, was very supportive, as were many but not perhaps all of the clergy. The truth is, I suppose, that though his forbears were Scottish, many of his roots were in the South, and his way of doing things was markedly different from the cultivated world of the Scottish Divines, though he did establish some valuable ecumenical relationships.

He invited us to work on a housing estate bordering Edinburgh. Pilton is a huge area and was home for some of the most deprived people in Scotland. I saw a lot of Ken while it was being planned and from time to time when I visited the brothers there I would see him too. I saw also his gradual decline towards his retirement. I stayed with him once in his family home in the highlands, and it was a sad business. We walked a little, talked a lot, but he seemed in a reticent, restless mood. He knew that I regarded it as a mistake for him to live such a lonely cut-off life and he would have been far better accepting an invitation to live and do retirement work with Michael Hare-Duke, the Bishop of St Andrew's, one of his own Westcott men.

In the evening we sat and listened to an old and rather worn record of Harry Lauder singing Scottish songs. The record player wasn't very good but Ken insisted it was one of the finest records he had ever heard. Shortly after that he began seeing doctors in London. The last time I saw him was a day or two before he died in 1979. It was a bitter winter. Alistair Haggart, his successor rang to say he was in the hospice and might not have long to live. I went and stayed with the Pilton brothers and Alistair picked me up. His room only had a dim light and I thought at first he was asleep. I just stood still by his bed – and a little later he opened his eyes, saw who it was and smiled. After a few words I told him the news (still a secret at that time) that I was to be to be the Bishop of St Germans in Cornwall. Standing in the corner, Alistair lifted his head slightly in surprise as he overheard me. There was a long pause, and I began to wonder if Ken had heard, or just fallen asleep again. Then he opened his eyes, smiled his old ironic mocking smile and said in a small voice "Oh dear, Oh dear, what *is the* Church of England coming to?" – and then, after another pause "Dear man, I'm so glad."

So we said a prayer. I laid my hands on him and gave him a blessing.

I went back to London. The weather got steadily worse, and on the day I returned for his Requiem and funeral it was snowing heavily. I woke in Pilton to discover that there was no public transport, and during the night roads and rail between Edinburgh and Berwick had become impassable. We walked to his cathedral through banks of snow. Scott's great building has a certain splendour as a mass, seen from outside, but the inside always seems to me dark and a bit dank, a real "gloomy portal". The stone looks black and the lighting inadequate, and on that day it was very cold. The congregation was large, but many had been kept away by the snow and a number coming from the south who had relied on the night train told exciting tales of getting there, many of them almost too late. Michael Hare-Duke preached a sermon with references to Winnie the Pooh, but the service as a whole had a sense of Scottish solemnity.

The two years I spent at Westcott under Ken gave me far more than I could ever have expected. I went to a lot of lectures in the Divinity School and assiduously took notes. Michael Ramsey was Regius Professor and I attended his course on the Atonement. How wonderful it seemed to me then − and in retrospect still does. His lectures were always packed out, and his slightly sing-song voice, exaggerated mannerisms, fiercely moving eyebrows and apparently absent-minded style never interrupted the meticulous care with which he presented one theory after another in language which was always accessible and never dull.

For the last lecture in the course it was almost impossible for him to get to the rostrum for students crowded on the floor and window sills. Towards the end of it his voice rose as he quoted:

"Rex tremendae majestatis
Qui salvando salvas gratis,
Salva me, fons pietatis

Looking up at us with his beautiful and striking face, speaking with an unwavering voice of added power and total conviction. You knew it was all one with him. Oh what a great man. It was moving, unforgettable, converting, and Brooke Foss Westcott, who like Michael Ramsey was Bishop of Durham, would have understood and approved the emotion − both of them in the best tradition of Anglican Divines.

When I returned to Westcott for a sabbatical in 1977 Michael Ramsey took the retreat at the end of term. It was at Walsingham and he talked much of his familiar theme of "Glory". On the way back in the bus we sat together and I asked him why he had never published his lectures on the Atonement. "Well", he said, "you may remember that when I left Cambridge I was asked to do a little job in Durham. So I put them away in a drawer and there was never time to take them out. Then just as I thought I could do something about them I was asked to do another little job, another little job at York. So I had to put them back again. And after that, well, I went to Canterbury, to Canterbury, and then it was too late, too late."

There were other teachers I remember well, particularly John Burnaby, but I expect the chief value for me was that it gave an entry to a world of scholarship that had previously been closed to me. There had never been a Franciscan before at Westcott so I was sufficiently unusual in that respect to fit in. What seemed remarkable is that in a place where academic distinction really counted, I should be accepted without an O level to my name and, as I felt it, nothing much to commend me. Probably there was too much of fake modesty about that as well. I'd been fairly indoctrinated by Algy and knew the ground rules of the world he moved in. I already knew Cambridge, and a habit is a remarkable passport to acceptance almost anywhere. Perhaps I was just accepted and "joined the club", something which my former friends would have, possibly, with a little justification, despised. It is something in my life over which I have never felt completely comfortable.

I still saw a lot of undergraduates who enjoyed the novelty of tea in my rooms and talks into the night. Ken kept a benign eye on me and made remarks about the "wet stream from Selwyn". As a background for the rest of my life it has helped: but there *is* more than that. It put my vocation as a Friar in a new perspective and gave some theological substance to my spiritual life.

The ordination was in Ely cathedral by Bishop Edward Wynn. He had once warned me about the loneliness of the Religious Life, now he seemed glad to take me on as an ordinand in his diocese, but not serving a curacy in a parish. I had rather dug my toes in with a concern to be ordained as a Religious to my own Community, as would a Benedictine. Edward Wynn was understanding, but what would I do for a "Title"? His solution was to revive a custom which I assume must have been pre-reformation and now only found in the Roman Catholic church, and ordain me to the Title of "Poverty". So it was.

In fact there were four of us being ordained Deacon, and all of us a little unusual. One was Geoffrey Platt, a pleasant man from a very Evangelical background. He was going to St Paul's, Cambridge, and insisted that he could not be ordained with a stole because it was too Popish. The other two were: a College Chaplain, who had been refused ordination by the Bishop of Oxford for various practical reasons, and was about to become Dean of Emmanuel − Howard Root; and an older and most delightful man who, in 1953, was being ordained as a "worker priest" – quite progressive for those times. Within a few days he was back behind the till in the Trinity Street Midland Bank.

Edward Wynn was a great strength to me, and someone I could turn to easily for advice, help, or just to be reassured. For a time he was my confessor and I learnt much from his gentle, perceptive capacity to put his finger on the spot.

I said Mass for the first time in St Bene't's, having been meticulously instructed by Br Barnabas beforehand. He also steered me through the service on the day. My mother came, and a whole crowd of friends. I remembered just beforehand that it was customary to give your mother roses at the end of the Mass – and I'd left it too late to get any! Fortunately in the churchyard there were two splendid rose trees, full of scarlet blooms. Absolutely right, and I found some scissors!

It was the feast of St Barnabas, and Br Barnabas' birthday. I first met him during the time I spent in Cambridge with the brothers before joining the Society. I had just left Papworth Sanatorium, he was in his first term as an undergraduate, and we came to know each other well. I said to Denis one afternoon after he had been to tea, "I think Freddie Lindars will be a Franciscan one day" – and was torn off a strip by Denis for being so presumptuous. In fact we both became Oblates and eventually lived together in that same house for many years while he developed his outstanding academic career. We were last together, talking over the past, on the day of Brother Kenneth's funeral in 1991. The sudden and wholly unexpected death of Barnabas the following day was a great and lasting shock, just fifty years after our first meeting.

The day after my first Mass I went up to Northumberland with Michael Apps, to spend a few days on the Inner Farne Island. We stayed the night before in Bamburgh, then were taken out in the morning from Seahouses by a fisherman, Billy Sheils in his boat 'Glad Tidings'. He was to do this for me many times in the future.

The Inner Farne was the home of monks until the Reformation. Of their foundation only Prior Castell's tower remains. There is a small chapel nearby overcrowded with superb stalls from the time of Cosin which were once in Durham Cathedral – and the light house.

The rest is huge cliffs covered with kittywakes and other gulls, spongy turf in which puffins have their burrows along with black rabbits, and every conceivable kind of sea bird constantly wheeling and calling.

I said my second mass there – and Michael complained at the inordinate time I took.

So I returned to St. Francis House, Cambridge, the SCM, Missions, and a busier life than I had ever known.

Chapter Thirteen

"That they all may be one" – The Student World and S.C.M.

Algy had been a travelling secretary for the SCM (the Student Christian Movement), and hoped that I would follow in his footsteps. The SCM itself was a national organisation for students, with, at that time, a substantial headquarters on the outskirts of London, a large permanent staff, and travelling secretaries, divided into regions, who maintained contact and encouraged action in universities all over the country. It had a publishing house, active, distinguished and successful; and organised conferences, nationally, locally, and in universities, colleges and schools. It was also interdenominational, cerebral, and enthusiastic. It took Church Unity very seriously, and provided many of the leaders in the Ecumenical Movement today. It believed in intellectual enquiry and integrity, and attracted a wide range of scholars who were glad to talk at its gatherings. Through the SCM, I embarked on another educational process which seemed to help my development, and filled in some more gaps in my education.

The centre pieces of its annual activity were two conferences at Swanwick in Derbyshire each year, "General Swanwick" and "Study Swanwick", and for ten years, these were a focus of my activity with students. Algy had done it all before me. "I'm sure, dear Michael, you will gain *much* more from *Study* Swanwick – that is intellectually stretching!" And so it was. Divided into seminars which embraced theology, politics, mission, economics, art, world affairs, literature, drama and other disciplines, all in the sense of making a more aware understanding of Christian commitment, they were strong on intellectual honesty, wary of any easy answers to biblical criticism, faithful in obeying the ecclesiastical disciplines and authority when it came to liturgical practice and expression. Till then, I'd hardly heard of Barth, Brunner, Bonhoeffer, Tillich, and all the rest. Now they were made alive and exciting to students who were reading Engineering or Agriculture as well as Theology. The big Ecumenical services were moving, the price we pay for our divisions, sometimes painful beyond words.

Oxford and Cambridge had a full-time secretary to look after them, and when the place fell vacant in Cambridge for a year or two I took this on unofficially.

But it was the University Mission at St Andrew's in 1955 that drew me all the more to the attention of the Student Christian Movement. I became a member of the General Council, with particular concern for theological colleges. The St Andrews Mission was notable for me in another respect because for the first time I gave a talk in public on sex! That might seem in no sense unusual now, but thirty years ago, and in a Scottish University with inevitably somewhat puritan attitudes, it might be thought at any rate, greatly daring. In any case it was something I'd always avoided. It seemed to me then as now far better dealt with in a personal and private way than in public with all the possibility of misunderstanding. But this time I had no option. A doctor (it always had to be a doctor then) had been invited, but at the last minute couldn't come. The obvious substitute was the chaplain. So I went away to the home of a 'canny' and devout Scottish Episcopal lady, Lucy Menzies, who had been a friend of Evelyn Underhill as well as of Algy. She provided me with tea while I wrote my talk. Well, I warmed to the task − if I was going to talk about sex I wouldn't wrap it up, but try to tell it as it was.

The word went round that 'the monk' was going to talk about sex − what could he possibly know about *that*? Lectures were missed, another meeting was cancelled − and when I got to the hall I couldn't get to the rostrum for students sitting all over the floor as well as on the seats. I got a good-natured cheer as I came in and one or two pats on the back. By this time I'd been there long enough to make friends who turned out in force to support the occasion. I talked a lot about falling in and out of love, touched on the difficulties of sex before marriage, sounded sympathetic about the guilt associated with sexual experimenting and masturbation, and tried to diffuse fears about homosexuality. I put it all, as far as I could, in the context of God as a positive, loving creator and father, and, as far as I could in those days, used fairly straight forward language which made it clear that my experience of life in this respect was not merely theoretical.

It seemed to go down well, there was a barrage of questions, and for the remaining days I was being stopped in the street for more. However the most significant consequence lay in the private talks. I'd indicated where and when I could be found for private enquiry and conversation. It seemed to have met a need.

I already had experience in Oxford and Cambridge of the tangle students can get into. St Andrews was no exception and every available moment was taken up with the delicate business of quietly building up trust, giving people time to relax, lose their fear and find their own voice and words. Listening takes time and *can't* be rushed. To begin with they had to accept *me*. Then, when the awful truth was seen to be not nearly so awful as they thought, and they recognised the possibility of being relieved of the guilt for sins which perhaps were never sins in the first place, the relief had to be given time as well – and perhaps another visit or two.

The President of the S.C.M. in St Andrews was a theological student, Malcolm Duncan. He suggested I should visit the other Scottish Universities to talk about Sex and Religion, and so I did: the word got round – Liverpool, Manchester, Birmingham, Reading, Bristol. I was in danger of becoming an "expert" on the subject and I didn't want that label. I said "No more after Liverpool", but when I got to Liverpool a lad came to see me afterwards with so desperate a story that I wondered what might have happened to him if I had turned down that invitation. Indeed it was the private counselling which compelled me to go on longer. In the end I wrote articles for the magazines published in this country by the S.C.M. and worldwide for the World Student Christian Federation and left it at that.

The sixties were a time of great change in the student world. Students were liberated to be themselves, to speak without inhibition, and use prohibited language without anxiety. It probably led to a lot of neurosis just because they couldn't always handle their new found liberty without damaging themselves. Yet before the sixties it is surprising how constrained with convention they could be. This was particularly true of homosexuality. Before the sixties, and long before AIDS, or for that matter, the Wolfenden Report, it seemed to be a matter for astonishment as well as relief that they could talk about it to someone in "the Church" who wasn't shocked, didn't immediately condemn or accuse them of sin or throw the Bible at them. To help them, to recognise God lifting them up to stand upright on their own feet without fear and recognise the truth about themselves without shame, seemed to me then, as many times since, the greatest personal privilege. So many of those I first met under a cloud of despair became prominent members of the Church or State, teachers, politicians, journalists, doctors, artists and so on.

There have been tragedies as well. Like Don, a brilliant young Quaker I met in an American University, gentle, loving, generous with all the Quaker courtesy and refinement of manner, fastidious and wholly without guile. In him I could see nothing but goodness and real godliness. He graduated brilliantly from Brown University and went on to Yale. Finding the world a hostile and judgemental place, he felt himself rejected and in the end killed himself. He died under a train. Telling me about his death, Kit Urwin, a mutual friend, said "He found the world an unfriendly place, and took one quick leap from it into the arms of God".

Don introduced me to the American poets, Robert Frost in particular. Driving up to Cape Cod to stay with the chaplain, Sam Wylie, in his summer place, we got lost in a wood and quite literally found ourselves with the nose of the car up against a tree, and tracks on either side of it. So he just got out of the car and said in his gentle New England drawl, "Two paths diverged in a yellow wood..." Certainly his road was, in the end, one "less travelled by", but he is not the only one among the men and women I've met and known well who, finding the world too hard on them, have died by their own hands.

In some respects the position of homosexual men and women has become much easier since the legislation made it no longer a crime for consenting male adults to engage in sexual activity in private (it has never been illegal for women to act in this way), but the sexual revolution in general, and all the publicity which AIDS has given to homosexual men has in some ways made it harder for an objective attitude to be adopted either by them, or by the majority who recognise themselves as primarily heterosexual. There are so many exaggerated attitudes on all sides that it is almost impossible to say what is normal without a thousand explanations.

By fixing the age of consent for men in England at twenty-one (though you can marry at sixteen, vote or die for your country at eighteen) the way is opened for surreptitious sex, "rent boys", blackmail, queer bashing and other distorting consequences. Custom and our social system condition men and women from an early age to feel, quite genuinely, a profound distaste for homosexuals or anything to do with them. "I'm uncomfortable being in the same room, and can't bear to shake hands, even touch them." Men and women who are otherwise generous, courteous, socially conscious and unselfish, react like that because that is how they feel, it is natural to them, and to change this attitude is very difficult.

On the other hand there are homosexuals who are disciplined, conscientious, hard-working, and who make a significant contribution to the life of the world and the church, often at the highest level, and are both married and unmarried. Sadly they are also often on their guard, constantly wary lest the truth be betrayed, and dependent on secrecy to the point where it becomes second nature. Unmarried schoolteachers or priests now have to be even more wary of their public attitudes to other men or boys, as well as the way they dress or the sort of house in which they live.

The same has become increasingly true for women, and the high profile given to homosexuality has made it a good deal more difficult for such "ordinary" people to accept and acknowledge their homosexuality, often harbouring not only fear of discovery, but despair at their "incurable" condition. If they *do* have intimate friendships with their own sex, it is at the price of such vigilant and surreptitious planning that the very thing for which they long is destroyed. It is the married men and women with whom I have talked for whom I feel most deeply. So often what seemed a really possible "solution" to their problem turns out, years later, to be a trap, in which not only are they caught, but also an unsuspecting wife or husband and perhaps several teenage children. The lime-light has made it harder for them also.

So has the publicity given to more overt and undisguised homosexuality. "Coming out" creates its difficulties as well. I find it a little strange the way in which cinemas and theatres can be crowded with audiences, presumably predominantly heterosexual, who acclaim plays and films which are overtly homosexual, or have scenes which are explicitly homosexual. It seems almost as if we can be tolerant at second hand over something we would abhor at first hand — or is it just one more evidence of the confusion of mind which we all have? On the television 'camp' jokes are frequent, transvestite acts draw large crowds, and Dame Edna Everidge *is* sometimes very funny. But the huge success of the act depends on the skill with which the uncertain sexuality is portrayed.

Public acceptance of artists, writers, musicians and actors has led to a greater tolerance — but something of that has perhaps always existed. Yet intolerance remains and has been increased by the AIDS epidemic, as has the crude advantage taken for violence by "queer bashers" and the like.

And the Church? Well the Roman Catholic Church in the person of the Pope has made it very clear that the practice of homosexuality, like contraception, abortion, premarital intercourse and masturbation is mortal sin. The argument for this, as he and the Catholic Church gives it, is in their terms completely logical, and is still to be found spelled out in uncompromising terms in tracts at the back of Westminster Cathedral. It cannot be complained that the Roman Catholic Church doesn't give a lead, or does not say what it thinks. The problem is that a majority of Roman Catholics do not obey what their Church teaches, no matter how good it looks in print. A great many Roman Catholic priests, both in the Confessional — which is used much less than it used to be — and out of it, spend a lot of their time squaring the conscience both of their people and themselves as they face up to the reality of conduct which runs contrary to discipline and faith.

The Church of England tries to be honest in its own terms: which means inevitably a genuine effort to accommodate conduct to a variety of often conflicting views. Because of this the report on homosexuality could not become *the* official position of the Church of England as, in order to be published at all, it had to include a minority report which refuted certain crucial attitudes within it. Efforts to have that report revised since it was published have always failed because this same minority (which has if anything grown in strength) would still stand out for a view of the Bible and Church Doctrine which, in effect, is similar in many respects to the Roman Catholics, and supported by extreme Anglican Evangelicals as well as Anglican Catholics.

The Quakers, as would be expected, were among the first Christians to publish views which were regarded as liberal and sensitive to the reality of the homosexual state, but Methodists, Baptists and others have however run into the same difficulties as Anglicans.

In subsequent debates in the Anglican General Synod there have been genuine efforts made to find the language of understanding which will not destroy human dignity. Archbishop Runcie spoke of homosexuality as a "handicap", and in the same sense as a minority of black people are handicapped living in a community of white people who are in varying degrees hostile. This is perhaps the sort of language that does least to diminish them. Certainly in the ongoing debate about homosexual clergy, both men and women, all the latent fears have emerged.

It seems as if knowledge of homosexuality in practice (though that is fairly difficult to define), can be so concentrated on physical sexual intercourse — which is understandably aesthetically and physically distasteful to a majority of heterosexual men and women — that it totally distorts the reality of love and trust between people of the same sex which more often than not has no more physical sexual expression than with heterosexuals. There is a type of sexual conduct which is based on repeated sexual experience with several or many partners. This can be found as much among heterosexual as homosexual women and men. It is surely Difficult to accept that such promiscuity and loveless sex can ever be right in either case.

An effort on the part of one Anglican priest to project a supportive role by televising the "marriage" in Church of two men seemed regrettable, incongruous, and misleading. There must be many women and men who have lived with partners for many years, faithfully as friends in a deep and lasting relationship of love and trust. The Church should surely pray for them and ask God to bless them, encourage them to play a regular part in Church life and help them over the inevitable hurdles of disagreement, illness and all the other normal crises of life. To call that "marriage" would seem to diminish all we believe marriage to be, and all such friends and partners living in love and fidelity to be.

I certainly discovered very early in my life as a Franciscan that there can be a world of difference between the idealistic renunciation of married life in the vow of celibacy and the hard reality of using sexual vitality and emotional drive in a way which is creative and loving as well as disciplined.

The Society of St Francis has from the beginning been a religious order dedicated to living closely to the day-to-day lives of men and women who are seriously deprived or disturbed, as well as caring for those who are coping with the problems of living a Christian life in a world which has discarded many of the barriers which at one time conditioned and controlled social conduct. People express themselves more freely, discuss their lives more openly, are more explicit about their emotional feelings, failures and needs. That sort of openness was only beginning to appear when I joined the Society. The Sixties undoubtedly changed all that to a marked degree.

Long before that, Algy was remarkable in the degree of openness he encouraged among the brothers who were joining the community. His language had the restraints of his Victorian upbringing and social background, but I had long discussions with him, and he wrote letters setting out his opinions on sexuality in the service of God. His views had been formed, and were held with conviction, by his friendships in Cambridge and in India and were coloured by a romanticism which seems to have been typical of some of those in the University at the beginning of the century. It was certainly not indulgent or frivolous, and by the standards of today, remarkably disciplined, but he did believe that God accepts every man and woman as they are, made in His image, and equal in his eyes. That celibacy did not mean a freezing or denying of sexuality but a liberating of it to be used by God in his service. We should enjoy the beauty, charm, gifts and goodness of other people more and more, and give thanks for them. A capacity for men or women to love their own sex as well as the opposite sex deeply and emotionally was God-given, so that any tendency to coldness of heart or withdrawal from involvement with others would be wrong in either case.

Inevitably this led from time to time to brothers finding themselves out of depth in emotional entanglements, but he was good and sensitive at dealing with that as well. He had a remarkable and uncanny capacity for being aware of what was happening all round him, and of exerting a caring and disciplined control.

I have seen it stated that homosexuality could be one indication of a Religious vocation for men and women (it is a popular view that people become nuns or monks to live with their own sex) – an idea which is surely wrong. If the point of celibacy is the willing sanctification of sexual drive for the glory and service of God, it is unlikely to be any easier for the homosexual than the heterosexual. That it *is* easier, apparently, for some than others may be due to the possession of a highly-motivated and disciplined emotional drive, or a very low sexual drive, which after all is not unusual and can be found in men or women with other vocations.

According to Kinsey, it can be expected that there will be a higher percentage of homosexual women and men in the Religious life and the Priesthood as well as the Army, Police Force, Teaching, etc. It is therefore not surprising that throughout its history the Church has legislated for the conduct of Religious, usually in a crudely restrictive way. Until comparatively recent times *any* sort of sexuality was seen as sinful and the rules for Religious abounded with regulations to govern every aspect of daily living that might minister in any way to "the flesh". Bodies were sinful – and so were minds if they deviated from a very strict line of purity or eyes that might see anything that could in the slightest degree tempt to sexuality.

So the mind had to be filled with other thoughts, the hands kept occupied, the eyes cast down (quite literally) and the body kept under with cold baths, long hours, unexciting food and fasting. At one Anglican monastery the students slept three to a room, and were moved around every few months to prevent anyone forming an attachment, and so on.

When Algy first took on the formation of the Society, a good deal of his teaching was based on these traditions, as well as his own natural courtesy and sense of what is right. We were expected always to stand up as he entered the room, but perhaps we would have done that in any case. It certainly doesn't happen now. We were also told always to take the hardest and least comfortable chair. "Particular friendships" were frowned on. His restrained attitudes in no way prevented the emergence of a new Community in Christian love.

Chapter 14

Finding Common Ground – Algy and Ecumenism

Sex was not by any means the only issue I was faced with through my work with S.C.M. The Ecumenical Movement also became an increasingly important issue as I realised more and more that disunity was the biggest stumbling block to the Mission of the Church. How can we preach the Gospel of Jesus Christ when we can't agree amongst ourselves about the Church itself. I was appalled at the intransigence of the Roman Church, but equally dismayed at the aggressively antagonistic attitude often adopted by the "Catholic" and "Evangelical" wings of the Anglican church towards each other.

Algy had long ago introduced me in a living way to the treasures of the other branches of Christendom. From the background of his own deep concern for unity and absorbing interest and understanding of all they did and said, I grew to appreciate the richness of the Free Churches, and, through the hymns of Charles Wesley, of Methodism in particular. (I found an early edition of *The Methodist Hymn Book* on a stall in Leather Lane in London and got it for sixpence. It has a fine copperplate illustration of John Wesley, and is beautifully printed. Inspired by a friendship with Dr Newton Flew I resolved to read from it one hymn a day – and did so for a long time, taking it with me on my first tour round the world.) From time to time I also began to attend the Quaker Meeting in Jesus Lane and it gave me something I could find nowhere else, a quality of waiting on God which invaded not only the Meeting for Worship but their whole lives. Algy also admired the Quakers, but I could never imagine that restless little man being still for long enough.

His enthusiasms, together with a widening understanding and interest in other Churches given me by the S.C.M., and most of all, the people I began meeting, sparked off a worldwide commitment. The S.C.M. Conference at Swanwick was an opportunity to meet articulate and knowledgeable men and women from other churches, and opened up the way to discover a deep unity in love and service of God through the personal exchanges of mutual concern and loving encounter with one another. We were, I discovered, already one in Christ, because we had committed ourselves to Him absolutely, and had the same ultimate goals.

Of course there were differences. At one of the first Study Conferences I attended I opted for a seminar on the Ecumenical Movement (more jargon to delight in!) which made an abiding impact on me. Not only did we examine the whole history of the divisions of the Church and the moves towards unity, but we considered as far as we could the theological and non-theological factors which continue to divide us. That was in 1953. Forty years later it is astonishing to recognise how vastly the situation has changed and how many of the things we longed for then have been achieved. It was the Student Christian Movement and the World Student Christian Federation (WSCF) which produced and encouraged a great many of the Church Leaders who in the seventies and eighties have helped us towards this position.

I knew that I would never be able to make much of a contribution on the theological front. That was for the academic theologians.

Non-theological barriers however are another matter and sometimes higher and more impenetrable. There is a mass of suspicion and prejudice, a sheer determination not to give ground, based as much as anything on fear and blindness. This takes a very long time and endless patience to overcome. It is to be found in all Churches – and *within* Churches as well.

Finding common ground, giving the time to discover some mutual basis for respect, establishing the ground rules of friendship and trust; above all just discovering at first hand the real facts about how other Churches see their own history as well as ours, their own worship (how many Anglicans criticise Methodist or Roman Catholic worship without ever having shared it), their understanding of God's relationship with them and with other Christians, takes time and patience. It is very difficult to admit to being wrong, narrow-minded or deeply prejudiced. Harder still to having likes or dislikes that are irrational and the product of upbringing or indoctrination. It took me a long time to realise how deeply the barriers between the Church of England and the Roman Catholic Church were affected by the history of the Catholic Martyrs at the Reformation, the enormous influence of our relationship with Ireland and the large number of Irish priests and Religious in Catholic parishes and schools. The unconscious assumptions adopted by unthinking and ignorant Anglican members of the Established Church do not help either.

I discovered, because the S.C.M. gave me a forum to do so, a means of learning, meeting, talking, understanding and loving beyond our differences. Not pretending that they do not exist, but by learning to live with them, and in a sense above them. If I couldn't make much contribution theologically, at least the pulpit was still my platform, and meeting people a way of unity which could be catching. I also discovered that it helped to be a Franciscan, at any rate one of our sort. To the vast majority of people outside, Franciscans were a completely new idea, and once I had made it plain I was not a Roman Catholic, there were no other preconceived ideas to be swept away. Friars were jolly and, in folk memory, sometimes fat; objects of fun, good for a laugh – human. That they pray and preach is not as often realised. That really is a great advantage. So is the habit. All the brothers develop their own "patter" to explain it. Until comparatively recently we wore it almost all the time – which presented problems once I started going abroad.

At that time most Roman Catholic friars in England, with few exceptions, still considered us to be interlopers. On the continent it was not quite the same because the subtleties of Anglicanism were almost totally incomprehensible to them. In their view (this is hardly an exaggeration) all England was Protestant except the heroic Catholics who, in the Catholic Mission, fought a winning battle against heresy. When Br Patrick visited Assisi in the fifties wearing his habit, he met a Conventual Friar, Father Max Mizzi, a Maltese who naturally spoke excellent English. He was astonished to discover that there was such a thing as an Anglican Franciscan. That meeting became the basis of Fr Mizzi's own concern for the Ecumenical Movement and a ministry which has led to a continuing widespread understanding between all the non-Roman Religious and other relationships throughout Europe. His work for Unity based on his love for Francis, and his care for countless visitors to Assisi was rewarded by the Archbishop of Canterbury who presented him with the highly prized Cross of St Augustine, given only to non-Anglicans, for his outstanding contribution to greater understanding between our Churches. And it all began with Patrick's habit!

My first visit to the Continent in 1951 was with a party of students – and I *didn't* take a habit. The centre of it was a week in Assisi with a week beforehand in Rome, and a week of relaxation in Florence afterwards. Three weeks for thirty pounds, fifteen for travel and fifteen for bed and board! Algy was in his element planning it all with me and for me. Lists of all the churches I *must* see in Rome, together with a present of two volumes of Alexander

Hare's definitive *Walks in Rome,* heavy, rewarding, and dated — "send your carriage to await you at the Forum". I took to reading extracts to the party while we lay on our beds for a siesta.

In Rome we were given a dormitory in the Monastery of San Gregorio which houses the Chair of St Gregory in which, we were told, he sat when he sent St Augustine to England. We all took turns having a sit in it! The monks were, on the whole, rather cool towards us until the evening that a messenger came from the Vatican with the invitation for a private audience with the Pope — Pius XII. Then what excitement — the mood changed. One problem was what to wear. We were travelling in very casual clothes indeed. So there was quite a flurry to make sure everyone was wearing long trousers, a shirt, a tie and something that corresponded to a jacket. This was well before Vatican II and protocol was a great deal stricter than it is now.

When we finally got there the following morning we were first put in a vast and most resplendent room full of clearly very distinguished people, the men either in clerical attire of various degrees of grandeur, morning dress with decorations, or dress uniforms, carrying plumed hats and so on. All our efforts, in contrast, seemed markedly inadequate. After a considerable time watching one another — some of the others were festooned with rows and rows of rosaries and holy objects they had brought for a Papal blessing — a rather grand member of the household in purple, wand in hand, came through the crowd and beckoning, took us away, past the Swiss Guards at the door. I assumed we had been placed in too high a station and were to be demoted, but no, it was a case of "friend come up higher". In fact we passed through two more rooms with decreasing numbers waiting for their audience until we were finally in a much smaller room with only one or two others. There we waited again for a very long time. Suddenly, almost silently and with only the slightest disturbance the Pope, all in white, walked in with two chaplains. The whole room full went down on one knee. Then he came round and spoke to us each in turn. He had very little English and seemed to have more to say about Oxford than Cambridge, but he handed us each a handsome medallion of himself and gave us his blessing.

We returned to San Gregorio worn out with heat and tiredness — but the monks were enthusiastic and had prepared a huge celebration meal. The wine was good — we slept well.

In Assisi we stayed in the guest house of the nuns at San Quirrico: little, dumpy Sisters who laughed a lot and bustled around. I have been there again more than once, and the same sisters, ageing with me, gave the same welcome. During the war, at great risk to themselves, they had given shelter to Jews fleeing from Nazi persecution, keeping them hidden, and at one point disguising them all as nuns!

I have been back to Assisi many times. Fr. Max Mizzi, who has lived for many years in Assisi, but has travelled widely in the interest of Church Unity, has worked wonders in establishing an ecumenical understanding between the Basilica, and indeed all the Roman Catholic Franciscans living there, and the Anglican Friars and other non-Roman Catholic religious orders. There is still some conservative reaction on the part of the older brothers, but I would always wear my habit now, and on various occasions have been treated with more respect than I deserve. For several years we had a brother living there, and others who stayed during the main tourist season. It was hoped they could help in a mission to non-Roman Catholic and English speaking visitors. It was only moderately successful. The Custos and the Assisi authorities have made over a church specifically for the use of non-Roman Catholics, and at first this seemed altogether generous and admirable. However the truth is that people visiting Assisi on pilgrimage, particularly if it is only briefly, want to pray in the great Basilica and at the tomb of Francis. I want to myself – so the generous gift is not used as much as it should be.

I represented the Society together with Br Angelo at the Mass to celebrate the 800th anniversary of the birth of Francis, and again when Pope John Paul II called for a day of Prayer for Peace, and representatives of all Religions assembled there. A bitter day with an icy wind blowing down from Monte Subasio. Having prayed in our separate Religious groups, Hindus, Moslems, Buddhists, Jews as well as all the various Christian groups, we all assembled in a vast crowd in front of the Basilica. For nearly three hours all prayed in turn for Peace. Olive branches were distributed to us by the young people of Assisi. Doves were released and the Pope and other Church leaders gave us a blessing. A memorable occasion. Bitterly cold I trudged back to the square. Having fasted with the others I felt justified in turning into a cafe for some coffee. Then, consternation – sitting in that prayerful gathering my pocket had been picked! Ticket, travellers cheques, money – all gone. I was suddenly the poorest friar in Assisi. How Francis would have loved it. He would probably have searched for the thief and fed us both. I was rescued by the Secretary of the Minister General of the O.F.M. – it cemented another friendship. In recent years the Ministers General of all the Orders have been outstandingly sympathetic and fraternally welcoming, and anxious to make us feel part of the Franciscan family.

Seeing Assisi for the first time was wonderful, and I brought back a little terra cotta statue of Our Lady which is in the Blessed Sacrament Chapel in Dorset.

After that, Florence was meant to be relaxation, and it was. I was to go to Florence many times in later years, when Bro Peter lived there with Abbot Aldenucci and the monks of San Miniato.

In the year following the 1951 trip Algy himself hatched a plan which was designed to enrich my ecumenical experience yet more. We would go to France. It would be a holiday and a spiritual pilgrimage. Anthony de Vere, an Oxford undergraduate whose father was a friend of Algy, would drive us all in a car, Michael Apps would come and keep us company and act as bursar, I would write the letters and make the arrangements, and Algy of course would supervise the whole thing, which meant many hours of changed plans, altered itineraries and all the familiar routine.

He insisted first that we must all meet in Paris "to get our bearings". I fancy that in the days of his youth he had done that more than once. In the end we managed to overrule him, and though he went to Paris it was agreed we would bring the car over and meet him at the "Hotel de la Poste" in Rouen. It was an almost disastrous decision. Three of us arrived in the afternoon, a good deal earlier than we expected. So I booked rooms for us all, we had some coffee and set out on a preliminary look around the town.

We returned to a storm. Algy had arrived during our absence, also booked some rooms and informed the hotel that he had three friends who would be arriving later! Then he sat down to wait — not an occupation in which he excelled. By the time we got back he was furious. "Where *have* you been?" "To look *round.*" "Look *round,* but dear man I told you to wait for *me*. I mean, I can't believe it" — and so on. Shamefacedly we slunk to our rooms only to appear for dinner.

Algy was to remind me of the incident the last time I saw him before he died. He was ill in bed and we sat for a very long time silent. He was holding my hand, his eyes were closed but I had an idea he wasn't quite asleep. As usual he was little more than a mound of clothes with a small lined face. It was getting dark, but I didn't want to disturb him. The room was a bit heavy with the smell of his medicine. He suddenly said, "I'm very sorry, you really must forgive me, I was *quite* wrong." I replied, "I've no idea what you mean." and he said, "That time in Rouen — I should never have lost my temper like that. Do forgive me." It was almost the last thing he ever said to me.

Bernard has given a very good account of the trip in Denis's book about Algy. For Algy himself it had enormous importance as it has ever since for me. He had during his time at Cerne Abbas been greatly influenced by French 17th Century spirituality, and I suppose I had come to share it with him. For me it was also the opening of a door to the wonderful world of French Romanesque and Gothic architecture. The high spot of the trip for him was the visit to Bec and Ars and our meeting with one of the great architects of the Ecumenical Movement, the Abbé Couturier.

The monks of Bec had only recently returned to the monastery, and were still in the early stages of its rehabilitation. Already they had established the groundwork of liturgy, the magnificent singing, and reformed Benedictine life which is so outstanding a feature of their monastery. Abbot Gramond welcomed us warmly, and Dom Philibert, who has since followed Gramond as Abbot and whose English is excellent, looked after us with singular courtesy. Algy was given a chapel where he could say Mass and for the first time I saw the advantage of a free-standing altar. It was for me the beginning of a friendship which has grown with the years, many visits and retreats, and a fulfilment, in which they happily share, in the establishment of a new Anglican venture in the Benedictine life for men and women at Burford.

Algy felt very much at home at Ars, as he did at Bec. When we arrived it was clear that something unusual was happening. There seemed a great many priests in soutanes walking around a bit solemnly and rather pointedly not talking to each other. A priests' retreat was in progress. We went to the church which had a number of them sitting in various places silently reading their Office. The place had the accustomed peace and calm of prayer.

Algy said "We must say Evensong." So I got the books and we went into a side chapel assuming we would follow the example of the other. Not a bit of it. Suddenly the high pitched voice of Algy boomed out "Psalms for the 23rd Evening", to my mind echoing to the farthest corner of the church. No one appeared to notice, but I felt acutely self-conscious and suggested I'd like to say the Office privately and preserve the silence. " Of course not dear man, I'm *sure* they don't mind, they know *exactly* what we are doing" and went relentlessly on.

He was equally happy at Paray le Monial. Devotion to the Sacred Heart of Jesus meant much to him − "first introduced to England by a chaplain of Cromwell" he would say. But Taizé was a different story. They too had only been there since the end of the war.

There was just a small group of monks, worshipping in the little parish church presided over by a youthful Roger Schutz and Max Thurian. There was a hostel for boys and Fr Roger's mother was much in evidence. The whole place radiated for me, the freshness and excitement of a movement of the Spirit that had swept up this group of young men of several nationalities who had the courage to harness all the simplicity of their singing and natural sense of beauty to the worship of God. I loved it and was thrilled to be a part of it. Not so Algy. He couldn't forget they were Protestants, Calvinists, not in the Catholic tradition. It was all so different in his eyes from the new life at Bec. Of course he was wonderfully polite and courteous − but he longed to get away, and a suggestion from me that we might stay another night was firmly rejected.

After that our meeting with the Abbé Couturier was a striking contrast. He was living in a small apartment in Lyons, where we were made warmly welcome. Algy had been in touch with him by post, and of course revered him as the Catholic promoter of the Week of Prayer for Christian Unity (though the origins in fact lie in the initiative of the Society of the Atonement, an American Franciscan foundation in the Roman Church which was originally Anglican.)

He showed us his little oratory with vestments and altar linens from Anglican Religious. The two men were alike in so many ways and they responded to the immediate spiritual and emotional appeal in each other, united by the same concern felt in the same way. We knelt for his blessing, and with mutual tears he knelt for Algy's. It was profoundly moving and we journeyed on for a while in silence.

On the way back Algy was *determined* we should visit Lisieux and the shrine of the Little Flower. I found it all a bit too much, and feeling, in any case, rather sick, remained most of the time in the car.

We returned to Paris. Algy left us to go home, while I stayed on for a day or two, determined to visit the parish of Abbé Michonaux to see, if I could, something of the Priest Workers. Some theological students in England had been swept off their feet by a wave of books describing in vivid and exciting terms the renewal of the church life and priesthood in the Roman Church in France. Maisie Ward's *France Pagan,* Abbé Michoneau's *Revolution in a City Parish, Mission to the Poorest* of Père Loewe and others had opened up ideas which gave a new and invigorating picture of the priesthood down among the industrial and agricultural workers that called for something similar in our own country. It seemed revolutionary — and indeed in the end that is how the authorities saw it in France and ultimately much of it was suppressed. In the years soon after the war it seemed at last that young priests could belong to the people, working alongside them and speaking for them. It went with revisions and experiments in liturgy long before Vatican II sanctioned it, and had youthful exuberance, revolutionary determination, and Gallic charm! I fell for it altogether.

S.C.M. friends had given me addresses in Paris, and I went off with two students to a typical working-class suburb for an evening meal with a family who were saying farewell to their parish priest, who was leaving the following day to work in the docks at Le Havre.

The tenement was bleak, the apartment on the third floor cramped, I was unexpected and, appearing in my habit, required additional explanation.

The family were shy and welcoming and the young priest, in an old blue sweater and black trousers, uncertain. It was a tight squeeze round a small table, and conversation was not at first very easy. I realised I had intruded on a personal affair — this family loved the priest, had wanted to say this sort of "goodbye" before he went off to his Mission, which was difficult in front of strangers. Little by little they relaxed and so did he. Soon he was hitting me on my back in a friendly way. I heard about his plans to be in the docks just as one of the workers. To begin with he would say nothing about being a priest.

He was a Socialist and an activist and the family (the father was about the same age) seemed a bit fearful for him. But we prayed together and his prayers were charged with a powerful and intimate sense of reality and closeness to God. I can understand how the ecclesiastical authorities later felt threatened by such men, and suppressed the movement, but for a while it represented to me a wonderful reflection of Christ the Worker and all that might come from such a conception. In England Gordon Hopkins at St Luke's, Pallion, Sunderland, and other priests in industrial parishes tried to establish a movement for young shipyard workers or steel or coal workers called 'The Christian Workers Union', based on the continental model of the 'Young Christian Workers'. Though in principle splendid, it was only successful in a rather limited way.

My visit to the Abbé Michoneau and his parish was exciting mainly because he himself was becoming a bit of a legend. He signed a copy of the prayer book he had written for his parish, and talked about his plans. In retrospect, I realise that the Parish

Commumion, started long before him at St John's Newcastle, and the 'Parish and People' Movement in our Anglican Church were a very worthy counterpart. Not *everything* new was French!

Throughout the fifties I continued visiting France with students from Cambridge. Never more than a car load, in cars that frequently showed signs of cracking under the strain. Crusty bread, cheese, fruit and wine for lunch – Eucharist celebrated in fields, Chartres revisited because its wonders never cease, Vezelay, and the numerous romanesque churches of the Auvergne. The cheap little hotels close to railway sidings with local people who looked at us sideways, oilcloth in the passages, uncertain water, and even more uncertain sanitation, the unbelievable clanking of trains and shunting in the night, and the dim street lamps that turned the whole thing into the setting for a French film.

In many ways, however, the most significant trip, and one which set my life in a bigger perspective and different direction, was to Switzerland in 1954. It was my also first flight.

Chapter Fifteen

Student Pastor and Preacher

In the 1950s the W.S.C.F. (World Student Christian Federation) was at the height of its power, coordinating Christian Student Movement activities in colleges and schools all over the world. It had attracted some outstanding leaders, and played a major role in the movement towards a united Christendom which had been given new drive and purpose in the post-war years. The rebuilding of Europe and the new international relationships which were being established at every sort of level, political, economic, social and artistic, as well as the revolutionary new approach to communication, gave new life and thought to the movement. There was also a revived attitude to the pastoral care of students.

An invitation came to take part in a conference in Switzerland for student pastors and chaplains from all over the world. I was a bit astonished to be thought of in these terms. It was my first encounter with the international student world – and the first time I'd been in an aeroplane.

The President of the Conference, Dr Visser 't Hooft, was a revered and shrewd father figure in the Student Movement. In the event I found myself a bit out of my depth. Asked to lead a section to discuss "Communication", we produced a long document which I presented, only to be gently but scathingly dismissed by the President. It was courteous, but it hurt, not least because I knew he was right. I had almost completely missed the point and produced a report which, quite brilliantly I felt sure, said almost nothing at all and failed to comment on the bewildering way in which new methods of communication were changing the whole progress of society with frightening speed.

What I did discover is that the 'Student Pastors' need loving care as much as anyone else and before the conference was over I seemed to have made some new friends on this basis, among them one who became the most intimate of all my contemporaries – an American, Sam Wylie. He started life as a Presbyterian, went into the Navy, became an Episcopalian and a priest, and at the

116

time I met him first had recently become Episcopalian Chaplain to Brown University, Providence, Rhode Island. I think we knew our friendship was going to be no ordinary one the first time we talked – though as usual I did much more of the talking than he did. As I impetuously plunged on, telling him my whole life story in brief, he smiled in his shy way, looking a bit hesitant and uncertain and mumbled a little in return. He did tell me about his wife Bea, whose parents had been missionaries in China and about his very young family, about his work, and the bewildering challenges of his new job.

He came over the following year for the Swanwick Conference, and we met there again before he went on to France. A typical American intellectual Francophile, he spoke the language with an impeccable accent. This time he did more of the talking, ending up by saying – "Will you come to Brown to share my job for a Semester?" It seemed an impossible idea – but to my surprise, Algy agreed. I would go in the beginning of 1957 – two years time. It looked a long way ahead. But Algy did not live to see me go.

Those two years were packed with experience. Algy as a reference point remained a significant feature in my life, but for advice and support from day to day, Lothian was a very present help in trouble, so was Ken Carey, and the beloved Bishop Edward Wynn. My diaries tell me how often I needed the assistance and love of these men and how much I drew on them and found strength from the knowledge that they were there. In retrospect I realise that the assurance I needed, I mean assurance also in the classical evangelical sense of the word – assurance of Faith – was given to me in the knowledge and trust that if it was true for them, not just one of them but all of them, and all of them in the end *in the same way,* then surely it could be true for me as well. I know I sometimes unconsciously copied them, as I did later many other men of a similar kind, R.O. Hall, Hugh Bishop, Michael Ramsey, to whom I gave an equal trust. Of course they were all very different, but the fundamental commitment to Christ in them was the same.

Well, I needed all their help. In Cambridge the ministry with undergraduates was growing. The Missions in parishes, visits to schools, camps, conferences, seemed to go at a rather breathless pace. Then in 1955 I was invited to share a Mission to the University of Newcastle with a prominent Methodist Minister. In this case it was, of course, familiar territory, and I accepted, knowing that the more theological input would come from him. But before that took place, and in some ways in preparation for it, the first invitation to present a reasoned argument for the faith came from the S.C.M. They had a crisis when the principal speaker for "Study Swanwick" said he couldn't come — would I give a series of four or five lectures on the theme of *"Reconciliation"*. I was pleased to be asked but daunted by the prospect.

The speaker who didn't turn up was Stephen Neill — and it was also his inability to go to Dublin for a Mission at Trinity College which gave me my first opportunity to prepare a series of Mission Addresses for a University as the Missioner. Malcolm Duncan, the student I met at St Andrews, who was by now a young Presbyterian Minister, came as my assistant.

It was an emergency, there was not a lot of time to prepare for it, and my father was dying. I'd been in Dublin before on a Parish Mission with Lothian at St Bartholomew's, so I knew it a little, and liked it a lot.

Trinity College Dublin — T.C.D. — has all the elegance and charm of the 18th Century. Spacious Georgian buildings, set in a city of fine streets, dignified, civilized houses with beautiful doors and fanlights. It also has the arrogance of a people who have allowed many of them to fall into decay and ruin, and have asserted their right to let them do so. The timeless charm of the Irish, the apparent indifference to beauty of an essentially beautiful people. The talk! The best conversations anywhere, "time stopping" talk, words sometimes for their own sake alone, gloriously exaggerated ideas that only make sense at three in the morning.

Apparently unimportant incidents crowd into my mind. On my way to find some lunch I could hear a girl singing. I passed through a dark passage with dirty milk bottles outside, and found a huddle of men crowding a door. They let me squeeze through to a barren lecture room packed with students who hid for the time being the chipped dark brown paint and general air of ill-contained deadness. In the middle was a piano and a girl with marvellous hair of dark copper, a striking face, the plainest of dresses and a voice of the greatest purity singing Schubert.

In hall at dinner we drank porter. Perhaps I drank too much, at any rate I found myself next to a venerable, elderly and rather eccentric don. More than a little nervous, I praised the *Lindisfarne Gospels* in, I fear, my usual exaggerated way, calling the book the greatest achievement of its kind. "What", he glared at me, "and have you never seen the *Book of Kells*?"- I admitted as much. "Then I shall put it in your hands, and then swear on your heart if it's not the greatest thing you've ever seen". He was the librarian, and he was as good as his words. I saw, and I swore!

Holiday in Salcombe, 1948, with my mother and brother-in-law, Edgar.

My father, 1939.

Brother Douglas and Brother Arthur (Brotherhood of St Francis of Assisi) with 'Wayfarers' in the courtyard of Flowers Farm, the Friary, Cerne Abbas. About 1930.

September 3rd 1939.

With fellow patients at Papworth in the doorway of my "hut", 1940–41.

Horton Military Hospital, Epsom French and English soldiers with Nurses, 1940.

Father Denis talking to Bishop Edward Wynne in the Garden of St Francis House, Cambridge.

Algy soon after becoming S.S.F. in 1940, in the courtyard at Cerne Abbas. As he was when I first met him.

With Father Denis and Brother Mark. Pilgrimage party en route, Durham 1950.

Keighley Campaign 1949. Left to right James, Michael, Charles and Algy —
who was rather ill at the time.

Father Algy — hasty departure, Brother Martin in attendance.

St Francis House, Lady Margaret Road, Cambridge. Michael, Cecil, Anselm, Denis, Lothian, Barnabas, Anthony.

St Francis House, Lady Margaret Road, Cambridge.

The Friary, Alnmouth.

Brothers at Alnmouth, 1963
Back Row: *John, Kevin, Aidan, Randall, Noel, Leslie.*
Front Row: *Wilfred, Michael, Edward.*

With Sam Wylie, Brown University, U.S.A. 1957.

With R.O. Hall, arriving in Hong Kong 1957.

With Bishop David Hand Eroro, Papua New Guinea, 1957.

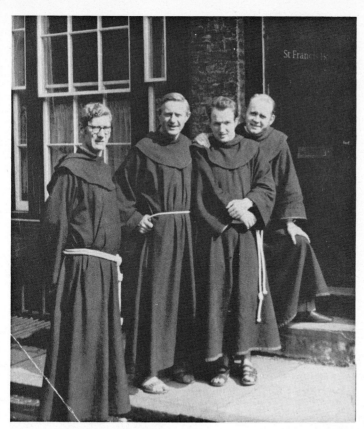

Outside St Francis House, Botolph Lane, Cambridge, 1971. Barnabas, Michael, John Wylan, Jonothan.

The Minster, Brother David S.S.F., Hilfield, 1960.

The great West Door of the Church, St Germans.

Installation at St Germans, 1978, with Brother Malcolm and Brother David.

Little Petherick, farmhouse kitchen, the home of Hinkston and Anne Wood.
With the choir from Keble College, Palm Sunday.

With Graham Leonard, Bishop of Truro, 1983.

With Archbishop Desmond Tutu, Bishop Donegan,
Archbishop Eames, and Canon Burgess Carr.
Ecumenical Service, Harlem, New York, March 1981.

Confirmation at H.M.S. 'Raleigh', Cornwall, 1983.

With the pupils of St Winnow Primary School.
Lostwithiel Cornwall, 'final' visit, April 1985. One of
many fine Church Schools in Cornwall.

Visiting Brothers in Papua New Guinea 1989. Welcoming party at Haruro —
Brother Silas on right, the one white Brother.

Non Roman Catholic Delegates to Conference of Major Religious Superiors,
Fr. Pedro Arrupe S.J. third from left, Villa Cavalletti.

Audience with Pope Paul VI after International Ecumenical Consultation for Major Religious Superiors, Rome 1977. Dom Rembert Weakland O.S.B. Abbot Primate of Benedictines, Brother Geoffrey S.S.F.M. Minister General Society of St Francis.

Audience after the Second International Ecumenical Consultation with Mother Honor. Margaret C.S.M.V. (the Wantage Sisters) and Father Roland Faley T.O. Reg. Minster General of The Franciscan Third Order Regular.

With Archbishop Michael Ramsay, returning from Westcott House Retreat, Walsingham 1976.

With Archbishop Paul Reeves and Brother Brian S.S.F., Minister General, Auckland, 1991.

The talks I gave were well attended, but how effective they were I really don't know. Even though, being protestant Ireland, I couldn't wear my habit, they were intrigued at the idea of a monk talking to them. I met and became very friendly with one of the great clan of rugger playing Pikes. Poor chap, his father and all his uncles, who all seemed to become Bishops or Deans, were distinguished rugger internationals and he was expected to follow in their footsteps. One of them, St John Pike later invited me to Belfast. That invitation was the beginning of a connection which was to have significant consequences for the Society later on.

The addresses in Newcastle and Dublin really formed the basis for a series of Mission addresses on the fundamentals of the Christian Faith which ultimately went with me all round the world. They were re-written again and again, given new illustrations, backgrounds, texts, anecdotes, until the final state was almost unrecognisable from the first.

I was in Belfast in November 1955 when Algy died. I had been invited to preach at St George's during Lent: three times a day for a week. I had also been booked to talk at Queen's University and various other meetings, It was a busy schedule and the brothers in England failed in their efforts to contact me.

So it was like a terrible accident. I just walked into St Francis House and the first brother who saw me – Leonard Hill – said "Father Algy is dead". Just that. It was sensible and required no rehearsal. He stood looking at me for a while, and tried to put his arm round me. I remember his anxious eyes trying to look right, an ugly kind face. I know the feeling, I've tried to do it myself. But I know too now the empty space that seemed suddenly all round me, the sudden knowledge that the expected has happened, nothing will ever be the same – and somehow it wasn't as I expected it at all. I had come home on a sunny afternoon to a bleak statement and a world that for a time seemed empty. The blow was sudden, unexpected. You know you are seriously wounded even though you feel nothing, only intense shock, and painless hurt, a spreading cold numbness. My first feelings when I regained them were "Oh why wasn't I there, why didn't they get me, tell me. Why them, and not me?" How strange that I could feel such jealousy at such a time.

So I went to my room, and after a while Lothian came with his dry words of comfort. Later I went round to Westcott and found Ken Carey, who saw at once something had happened and said "Is it Algy?" – and then he put "BUSY" on the door and he just stood by the fire and let me cry. A bit later he said "It's an awful bore but I've got to go and drink sherry with a lot of new men. You'd better come too. Have a wash." So I went and afterwards he said "Dear man, you did that very well". Later he wrote me a note in his slanting hand going across the pages, encouraging, sensitive, a little sentimental, sharing my sense of loss and adding -

"They told me Heraclitus, they told me you were dead,

They brought me bitter news to hear and bitter tears to shed;

I wept when I remembered how often you and I

Had tired the sun with talking and sent him down the sky" - very Cambridge, very Ken.

There was a Requiem for him at St Matthew's Westminster, the church in London he loved most of all, with its memorial chapel to Frank Weston, and an altar that commemorated St Francis. I found it almost unbearable, and difficult not to weep. Generally speaking I am not given to tears (In fact I once found in a Roman Missal a Mass for the gift of tears and persuaded a priest friend to say it on my behalf) but for a long time I couldn't speak easily of Algy without fear of weeping. Later there was another Requiem at Hilfield which Denis invited me to sing, an unexpected privilege, and we "buried" his ashes in the altar. Some years later they were put in the new graveyard where all the brothers are now buried.

Algy's death changed my life yet again. I suppose in one sense it liberated me to become myself, and not just a shadow of him. I have some of his books, the crucifix he always had in his room, cards and mementos of our anniversaries, holidays, journeys, and his numerous notes, letters and sermon outlines, but I was free to find myself. Yet his influence after his death has, in a way it is hard to describe, been even greater. Perhaps it is because I finally felt free to criticise him, to accept his love for all it was worth. Perhaps it is because in succeeding years I met so many others for whom Algy had been the beginning of life and I could share his life in them.

One practical result was that though Brother Douglas was still the Minister he was also an aging and frail man, so Denis became the Acting Assistant Minister as well as Father Guardian of Hilfield, still known at that time as Cerne Abbas. It was his decisions that dictated the next years of my life.

Chapter Sixteen

Round the World

The old Euston station was like a film set from the thirties. Steam belched from the boat train and the platform was crowded with passengers involved in tearful farewells and parting hugs and kisses. My mother, Bernard, (still in those days Michael Apps) and I must have seemed a somewhat "stiff upper-lip" group in comparison. There seemed a large party of mid-Europeans, women in black headscarves, men in dark buttoned up coats, lined faces, large eyes, huddled together in a strangely dignified fashion.

Michael and Jane looked determined — I was glad when it was over and I could settle back by myself. A lot had happened since the invitation to America and Algy's death, and an initial visit of three months had become a year's absence from England and a journey round the world. I was about to become, for the time being, the most travelled brother in the Community.

It began with an invitation from the S.C.M. in Australia to be the visiting preacher for Missions in all the Australian Universities; the S.C.M. grapevine had suggested my name. I didn't suppose for a moment that Denis would agree with this, but to my surprise he thought it a splendid idea. So I added three months in Australia to my time at Brown University, allowing also for visits to the Franciscans on Long Island, General Theological Seminary, the Medical Centre in Chicago, and San Francisco — a good jumping off point, via Honolulu, for Australia, which had already been visited by Bro Charles. He had made some Companions there, so there were Franciscan contacts to follow up as well.

Years before the Society had received a strong invitation from Bishop Phillip Strong to send brothers to New Guinea, but of course we just hadn't the resources in manpower. Now, of a sudden, Denis thought it might be a good idea if I were to go and have a look, talk it over with Phillip, and report back; perhaps the time had come to reconsider the invitation. So another two months were added to the journey.

121

The next unexpected addition came from the S.C.M. via Oxford. The President there at that time was a delightful undergraduate, Christopher Hall, who had sometimes discussed with me the possibility of being ordained. His father was the Bishop of Hong Kong – R.O. Hall, a famous name in missionary circles and even more widely recognised as the first Bishop to ordain a woman as a priest in the Anglican Communion. (It was a war time emergency – but also the product of a deeply held conviction.) R.O. was about to celebrate the thirtieth anniversary of his life as a missionary in China and the diocese wanted to know what to give him for a present. What he asked for was a Mission – a preaching mission in all the schools and churches in the Diocese! It was, I later discovered, absolutely typical of the man, and I came to love him as much as I loved his son.

He wrote to Christopher and said "Who do you suggest?" – so he came and asked me if I'd go, an irresistible temptation but it seemed to be asking too much of S.S.F. Apart from anything else – and it seems ridiculous to say it now – R.O. Hall was a missionary of the C.M.S. (Church Missionary Society) which was Evangelical, and even more, he had ordained that woman – so he was quite "unsound"! But Denis said "Yes", and yet more months were added to the trip, with an interlude in Manila to give a retreat for the theological students of the Philippine Independent Church.

Finally, the S.C.M. in India, hearing I was "on the move", and would not be too expensive, asked me to speak at their Conference in South India. What a chance to catch up with Algy, perhaps get to the Ashram in Poona, (which I did). So I left in January 1957 and got back for the Lent term in Cambridge a year later. The full story of that year would be another book. It put down markers for the rest of my life, gave me friendships which persist, so that I answer the door in Cambridge and there is someone saying "Do you remember me? Perth W.A. 1957". It gave me Chinese, Indian, American Godsons and daughters; gave me a world perspective economically and politically; a profound respect for other religions, an awareness of the complexity of our Church divisions, as well as easiness in being with other races, other cultures. Many of the students I came to know so well in all those places are now teachers, doctors, priests and bishops. We continue to meet because that travelling year seemed to establish me in the eyes of the Community as someone who would continue to do so, and I have, and the network of loving relationships has continued to spread all around the globe.

Most of all that year saw the certain beginning of the growth of the Society in America, Australia and New Guinea, though Denis had already visited the U.S.A. and Charles had been to Australia.

I nearly didn't get to America. It was the question of a visa, without which, of course, I couldn't get in. I filled in a form and went to the American Embassy in London where a minor consul said – "Thank you, Father, and will you now just sign this form?" – giving me a pen and indicating the place. I said "May I read it first", which surprised him a little. "Of course, you're welcome, but it's just a formality."

The form was lengthy, and required me to swear that I had never been a member, or in any way associated with a long list of organisations, mostly political. So I pointed to that section of the form and said "I'm sorry, but that prevents me from signing." He looked startled – and said, "You must see our Specialist". So I was passed to another Vice-Consul, a Mr Olenick, the tablet on his desk said so. I repeated my reservation. He looked severe and his answer sounded rehearsed "That automatically bars you from entry into the United States of America." However, it was July, and I wasn't going until January, there was plenty of time. How wrong! It was the time of McCarthy trials in California, Reds under the Beds, and the banishment of Charlie Chaplin. I was handed another form, a very long one. In the waiting room were others who looked as if they lived there, bags bulging with evidence to justify their application. So I took it away. They wanted to know every detail of my life and association, "Including being in the Boy Scouts and a tennis club?" "Of course" he replied unsmilingly. And every address at which I'd ever lived, and for how long, with dates.

I talked to the Socialist MP Tom Driberg, who I knew had been in the Communist Party, and somehow had been to America. He said "Always tell the truth, give away as little as you can. Don't appeal to the people you are going to – if you don't get in, *they* will be smeared. And it helps if you can be vouched for by someone fairly high up." So I said "Who did you get?" – "Oh", he replied, "I got the Prime Minister – but the Archbishop of Canterbury would do for you." So I filled in my forms and went back – three times, for different interviews with different people. I admitted to "association", never quite said I'd been a member. "Did you ever give money?" – well, I bought their publications, but anyone can do that." "So you read their literature – what have you read?" "*Das Kapital* – but you'll find that in every respectable American library" – and so on. I knew the Archbishop of York a good deal better than I knew Canterbury, so asked Michael Ramsey to write for me. "Poor old Michael," he replied, "so they think you're a Commie!" I think the letter helped, but by now it was December, and still no sign of a visa. Sam Wylie sensed something was wrong and wrote a cautious enquiring letter, to which I risked an equally cautious reply, saying there was a bit of a hitch over my visa for reasons he might understand.

More silence, and now it was early January. Suddenly I was recalled to the Embassy. They had had a message from Washington saying I could be given a visa – would I kindly just sign this form and they'd be glad to issue it. I was about to sign when I realised with a jolt, that it was exactly the same form as the one I refused to sign in the first place. With my heart in my mouth I explained and put the pen down. Consternation! – But we just *can't* issue a visa without *that* form being signed." "Then", I said" you'll have to do something to it to explain why I'm signing it". So they took it away, went into a huddle, a typist added some words, and they brought it back. I can't remember the precise wording, but it included the phrase, "The Reverend Michael Fisher is a Roman Catholic monk and we understand the respect in which he signs this form." So in the end it was still wrong – but I signed it just the same. They stamped a visa for me – and took my fingerprints.

I tried dining out on the story in America – but it wasn't funny. Too many people had been hurt by the almost paranoid fear of Communism which had been fanned into flames and destroyed some lives. Sam had found an influential friend in Washington, others were not so lucky.

So at last I got away from Liverpool, bound for St John, Newfoundland. I shared a cabin with a quiet, diffident man who seemed to have no family or friends, and was emigrating to Canada. It was winter, and the Atlantic soon had me confined to my cabin. Once I could get around I was besieged by Hungarian refugees. They had been invaded by Russia, and fled to England. Now they were on their way to a new life in Canada taking with them very few possessions. Anxious, fearful, and cut of by a language barrier, the sight of a priest in a habit seemed a Godsend, and I was overwhelmed. How to explain that I was a "Protestant" They all seemed to want me to say Mass for them, hear their confessions, be comforted for the family they had left behind, helped to grieve, be given hope. I eventually found an interpreter, but how could I help without hurting, or leaving them disillusioned? It took a long time, and as the sea was far from still I had, sometimes, to race away in a hurry. But I remember the proud men standing by their wives or mothers and the old ladies with black skirts, shawls and scarves who held my hands or smoothed their fingers over the back of them while we conveyed with warmth and nearness, smiles and sometimes tears, what could not be put into words.

By the last night of the voyage we had all got over the sickness, the Captain put on a huge party, we ate and drank through endless food and wine. There were streamers, caps, songs and dancing, hugs and kisses. I have never forgotten my Hungarian friends.

I went by train to Boston where Sam met me and we drove to Providence. He was nervous and anxious. The idea of bringing me over was expensive, and he feared a flop, so he was full of cautions. In fact it really *was* a risk. He took me to an old wooden house in Brown Street, close to the Campus, a typical New England building full of students, where he had taken a basement flat for me. Just ideal.

The next day it began — with an invitation to a party in the same house given by the "Brown Brunotes", a group of "Barbershop" close harmony singers! Once the ice had broken, I'd had my first Martini, and discovered I knew some of the words of some of the songs they were singing, I began to feel at home. Closely crew-cut, with button down shirts and the lanky charm and New England courtesy of the Ivy League, they were in the end not so different from their counterparts in England. They found my accent as amusing as the innovation of afternoon tea to which I invited them. More invitations came for other gatherings, clubs and to speak at various meetings. A habit *is* an attraction anywhere — on a University Campus in America thirty years ago politeness was overcome by curiosity. Sam began to relax. I had preachments and visits to churches and colleges, far and near, including a long visit to Dartmouth, which was more like Cambridge, England. I also went to Cambridge, Mass..

Geoffrey Beaumont, Chaplain of Trinity College, Cambridge, had just published his *Twentieth Century Folk Mass* and I had brought it with me, together with the manuscript copy of a number of the hymn tunes he had written. With the Brown Jazz Club and the "Brunotes", we "staged" a performance in the Cathedral for which I gave a running commentary, persuading a crowded congregation to join in. At that time it seemed a daring innovation, attracted a lot of attention and an article in *Time* magazine — the final accolade. After that I did it in all the universities as part of my mission programme. Geoffrey was a real pioneer. The music was not jazz, even though it was popularly called the "Jazz Mass", but the sort of foot-tapping, light romantic music of the musical stage, with hummable tunes and catchy syncopation. Some of his hymn tunes have survived and there have been many others written, creating a minor musical genre which now has a nostalgically dated sound. But in the remoter country places anywhere in the Anglican communion you can still find the "modern" or "jazz" tune for "O Jesus I have promised" or "Now thank we all our God" produced as something slightly daring.

Geoffrey was a splendid person and a loyal friend. He did lots of his evangelism playing the piano in pubs, and working on the "Footlights" revues. He once produced a chorus line for a musical in Cambridge who were all ordinands – which he regarded as a triumph! But behind the gin and tonics, the perpetual cigarettes, the endless rattling of the keyboard was a gentle, caring and very devout priest, who eventually became a monk at Mirfield. I did my best to pioneer his music in America and Australia – it just didn't work in Hong Kong!

There is no space to say just how important this time at Brown was for me, for all the lasting and loyal friendships. When I returned in 1992 to conduct a retreat for all the clergy in the Diocese many of those present were men and women I had first met as students thirty five years before.

I went from there to the Diocese of St. Louis where the Bishop, Hays Rockwell had also been at Brown on my first visits, and ended up helping to celebrate the 25th anniversary of the Rector of Yonkers who I met first at Dartmouth. I also had time with Bill and Henny Hale in their family home in Marlborough. In fact the whole Hale family made me, from 1957, one of the family. And there were many more.

Americans are very generous, and I left Brown with enough money to make the rest of my journey round the world a good deal easier than it might have been. I got used to being passed on like a parcel. There was always someone there to meet me at the station or airport and tickets or travel arrangements managed ahead of time. I'd made it clear that all I ever needed was bed and board and a ticket to my next destination – but everyone was kinder than that: and though I sometimes felt lonely and even homesick I never felt lost. In fact one problem was never being by myself. The programmes got fuller and fuller. I've never quite mastered the American custom of early breakfasts with a talk and even discussion, austere business lunches with bankers or business men and talks about God. This visit set up connections all across the country which led to regular return visits for parochial missions, retreats and conferences, and when I finally returned to England with a crew cut I was inevitably labelled "Americanised".

In New York I stayed at General Theological Seminary — which seemed a stuffy place until Norman Pittenger took me under his wing. New York! Unique and marvellous city. To go to America and *not* visit New York began to seem impossible. It's a good deal dirtier and more sinister now, but I have been back again and again. A ride through Central Park on a spring morning, to visit that infinite labyrinth of delight the Metropolitan Museum, with the Frick and the Guggenheim nearby. Within a block the fashionable life of Madison Avenue, and round the corner a Polish, German or Armenian neighbourhood with little stores, the crowd, chatter, bustle and undisturbed world of a past generation of emigrants. In the few days I was there I saw *"My Fair Lady"* which had just appeared on Broadway, and supported the "Brunotes" at a concert of student college groups in the Carnegie Hall where we all sweltered, and they appropriately sang "Too darn Hot!".

In Chicago one of the major hospitals had a chaplain who had invited me to give some talks on healing — but to pay my way had also fixed a variety of other opportunities — a sermon at Nashota House, a Catholic Theological College, a lecture at Seabury Weston Theological College, Evanston, and a preaching visit to a parish in Lake Forest, where all the rather wealthier people lived. I had dinner one evening with a group of people who had big names in the meat-packing industry, stayed another time in a house built by Frank Lloyd Wright, and found time to see the, to me, outstanding buildings of Mies Van der Roe.

I'd expressed a preference to travel by train to San Francisco on the California Zephyr. That was a treat. I had a "roomette", and when I tried to eat some mangoes I'd been given for the journey, and got smothered, rang for my "Zephyrette" — and a typical American blonde with flashing teeth who was highly amused to find a monk in a mess — and washed me down. It really was a great journey, trundling across a landscape that led to the Rockies and vast canyons. No one talked to me, so I slept, ate, read and gazed: and vowed that in future whenever I could I'd stick to trains. As a result I ended up crossing the Nullarbor Plain in Australia from Perth to Adelaide and in India did long, long journeys lying on my bunk and retreating into myself, with my thoughts and making time to be with God without interruption. I still do it when I can. I once had a carriage almost entirely to myself from Inverness to London — twelve hours. I'm sorry the trains are getting faster.

The jump from San Francisco to Honolulu was in one of the most beautiful planes I've known. Not, perhaps, as good as the Viscount, my " first" plane − but much larger and a lovely design, a Constellation. It seemed to me the perfect idea of an aeroplane. I expect by present standards it was noisy, though I don't remember that, it was certainly very comfortable, and for a while the Captain invited me to the flight deck. I went along with all the enthusiasm I had as a boy of ten when I was allowed in the cab of the Flying Scotsman going north. I'll never forget that either. And so to Australia, and missions in Brisbane, Perth, Adelaide, Melbourne, Sydney and Hobart.

Australian universities, rather like Oxford and Cambridge, seemed in the fifties to be going through an "age of faith." With the exception of Perth which was almost a disaster − the various halls were very full for the Mission addresses and there were endless extra meetings for questions and discussions. All the time offered for more private enquiry was taken up − and in many ways it remains a high spot in my experience of mission preaching.

I began in Brisbane, which was an informal affair and prepared me well for the rest of Australia. Next stop − Perth. My assistant missioner was Father John Lewis, a member of the S.S.M. (Society of the Sacred Mission). I rapidly came to the conclusion that he didn't really like "Pommies", and indeed in the end he said so. He also regarded it as an unnecessary extravagance to import a Missioner from England. It probably didn't help that I was a member of S.S.F., the rag, tag and bobtail of the Religious Orders. Perth itself seemed a long way from base in those days, and even the really lovely campus with its Scandinavian-style pool, could not quite compensate.

The first night was a disaster. I had prepared my address as carefully as I could, completely rewriting it, but it fell absolutely flat, and there was an embarrassing lack of response. So they were right, it *had* been unnecessary to import this flop. On the second night there were significantly fewer in the Hall. I went back to the college where I was staying. The Principal, Josh Reynolds, knew there was something wrong. Josh was a big man in every way. He had been a scholar at Oxford, had wide knowledge, and a calm unruffled gentleness that seemed, at the time, quite un-Australian. Talking to him I began to see I must approach my talks differently. What went down well in Dublin or Providence would not necessarily be equally acceptable in West Australia. After our talk I went to bed − but not to sleep, and by morning I knew I had got to start again with the third address. More anecdotal, more illustrations, more taken from personal experience, and much more directly challenging in terms of Christian conviction. I finished it not long before I gave it.

When it was over, and a spate of questions which followed, John Lewis said "Why couldn't you do it like that in the first place?" For the last two nights the audience grew a bit larger — but it was too late. So I went on to Adelaide — and the long journey, all alone in a remarkably comfortable German train, was just the break I needed.

I'll never forget Adelaide. Almost half the University came each lunch time for the talks, but the excitement had been heightened by a group of agnostic lecturers who had arranged an *anti*-mission. When I finished they began! They had transcripts of my talks (by now my heavily revised mission addresses) and, taking another hall had meetings to refute them. Everyone poured in. The S.S.M. priests (who had their monastery nearby, and included some distinguished scholars) came and sat with me in the front row. I was given the first opportunity to reply. Some of it was light-hearted fun — but a lot was serious dialogue, and all one could have possibly wished. I saw more students privately there than in any other university, and several remained friends. One is a non-stipendiary priest working for the B.B.C. in London — and it is a reminder when I hear his name given as producer, over thirty years later.

In Melbourne there was a new University Hall which had just been opened with a series of inaugural lectures by Toynbee. It was a bit intimidating to follow him. The "Jazz Mass" was also a big hit there. My talks were taken down from tapes by a student, Audrey Floate, who later joined the Sisters of the Church and finally became the Mother Superior. Long after the last time they had been given in Hong Kong they were published in Australia under the title (which I had used in all the Australian Universities) of *Christ Alive*. The Minister in England at that time refused to allow their publication here. Anyhow it wasn't much of a success as a book. I was told that, long after, there was a forgotten cupboard in Melbourne stacked with unsold copies. The last time I looked at it I felt grateful for the restrictions of the Minister.

In Sidney, I spoke in a large lecture room and the mission was given an unexpected boost by a student prank that in a sense quite literally back fired. Some of them had made a home-made bomb which was intended to frighten the audience soon after I had started my first address. I was just launching into my theme when there was a fierce explosion by one of the doors. It was too successful. The noise was tremendous, the door blown off its hinges, the lecture hall full of smoke and girls ran screaming. No one was hurt. I appealed for calm over the P.A. system and finally the culprits were apprehended, the audience returned — and I had a most rapt attention!

The publicity did the subsequent attendances no harm at all.

Charles was the only brother to have been in Australia before me. He had conducted some parish missions, and made some "Companions" (as associates of SSF are called). So before I left Australia I returned to Brisbane to meet some of them and conduct a retreat for students of the Theological College. The Bishop was welcoming, and discreetly sounded me out concerning the possibility of brothers coming to Australia. I was suitably cautious, but he was persistent, and took me to see a house on the outskirts of Brisbane almost in the bush. It had once had some brothers living in it — now it was empty. We could have it as a base. I said I thought there was little hope — but took some pictures of it. When a few years later we *did* go to Australia, I was able, a little to the surprise of others, to produce them, and it became the principal Friary of the Province.

That ended my time in Australia. I had some mixed feelings over the next part of my journey — to New Guinea — perhaps because Algy had a hand in this as well. In 1947 he was visiting the house in Cambridge and coincided with Philip Strong, at that time the Bishop of Papua New Guinea, who had come to a student meeting. They were old friends; had both been in parishes in the North East — and at the Wooller Camp.

At the end of his talk Philip turned to Algy and said "When are you going to send me some of your brothers", to which, it is said, Algy replied, "Dear Philip, how could I possibly say 'No' to you?" So here I was, in 1957, ten years later, the first one to explore the territory and report back on what was possible.

Chapter 17

A Friary in
Papua New Guinea?

Missionaries. I'd read about them in those old, dark brown missionary books – "illustrated". Pictures of men and women in white, with topees, outside mission churches and hospitals surrounded by "natives". Distinctions between black and white were very real then, not in the present antagonisms of racism, but in the old-fashioned paternalism of Victorian England when the missions were founded. When I got there it all seemed true – caught in a time warp, the pictures came alive. Port Moresby had an airport, the beginnings of a university and a flourishing port – but to me it seemed like Graham Greene country

After that I flew in a rather fragile-looking little plane over the mountains and inland to Popondetta. It was not much more than an airstrip and a trading post – where I bought a hat against the fierce sun.

Bishop David Hand, Philip Strong's Assistant, who met me, didn't look at all like the traditional "missionary". Big, burly, solid and florid, he might have been a rugger coach. Totally dedicated to Papua, and with a good intellect and powerful physique, he seemed tireless, determined and, when it came to it, stubborn. It was impossible not to admire the enthusiasm with which he approached life and his total commitment to the spread of the Gospel and the future of the Papuan people. But he could be exhausting! I set off to spend the next two months going back and forth over the whole territory with him. The country itself lived up to expectations – lush and exotic trees and shrubs, rough roads cut through great walls of jungle, the distant view of volcanic mountains, the heat, the sweat! It was sometimes very lovely, but always, for me at least, rather exhausting.

Most of our travelling was on the mission boat down the coast, but from time to time we took to the little plane the mission uses for travelling inland, at other times we went in a jeep or on foot. Many of the mission stations and villages are on the coast, and have qualities which seem to exist there in a special way. A deep blue sea, lovely sands, coral reefs and beautiful lagoons, a fringe of palms with thick jungle behind them, a collection of huts and houses, orderly and arranged. The people themselves were cour- teous and friendly with a real and ready smile of welcome. They seemed to have a grace and charm of manner, a very real sincerity, and a sort of dignity which made the barriers of language of little importance.

One reason for all this seemed to be that the Christian religion, as it has been brought to them, had become a part of their whole life, and was not just a superimposed veneer. It made a lot of the Christianity I know in England seem positively pre-Papuan. Of course there was another side to it. There is still sorcery, a lot of disease, illness, and under-nourishment, and the bigger towns that have grown up are bringing the people new, Western, problems. I saw some of this too.

The language question is considerable; dialects change from place to place, and I always preached through an interpreter. Each station usually had a school and a clinic or hospital as well as a big church. In the church everyone sat on the ground; there were decorations of tapa cloth, made from the bark of a tree and used for skirts by the women too. As we approached in the *St Lawrence,* the mission boat, the whole station lined up on the beach; we put ashore in a small boat, outrigger canoes sometimes setting out to meet us. For the final bit husky Papuans would lift the Bishop and me out of the boat and carry us to the shore. Great shouts of welcome greeted us as we arrived, and then we all knelt for the Bishop's blessing. Then *everyone* shook hands from greatest to smallest. After that came a talk with the missioner and others, after which it was announced when the service would be next morning – when I would say my "Words". In fact the service just happened when it was light. Many came a long way, or, having come the previous night, slept in a friend's house to be there in the morning. The congregation assembled early, and waited very patiently and quietly until it was time to begin, men and boys on one side, women on the other. All the mothers sat together at the back with their babies, who had their breakfast while they waited. After the Gospel I preached, and then the catechumens and hearers left. Nearly always we had a Eucharist – and the singing was splendid.

Sometimes there was some special problem for the Bishop to sort out. In one village it was a heathen man with two wives who had taken a third one – a Christian girl deserted by her husband. There was a very long talk indeed about this. The man looked extremely fierce, his hair in long strings covered with mud, many beads and other decorations on his otherwise rather naked body, and, when we finally left, brandishing quite a heavy-looking club – added by him for effect! In the end the girl went back to her village. Another time it was the case of a Christian teacher who thought he was going to die because of the effect of a sorcerer on him. David Hand preached a very fierce sermon about the wickedness of Satan and the power of God to overcome him. We took the man away with us, and eventually he recovered both faith and health.

After many stops, we reached Dogura, the centre of the mission, where Bishop Philip lived, It has a very fine Cathedral, a really tremendous church, built by the people themselves of concrete, lovely outside and large and cool inside. Bishop Strong had by that time been out there for twenty-three years – a real stretch.

I flew from Dogura back to Popondetta to visit several stations in that area and conducted a Quiet Day for the boys at the Martyrs' School. The school is dedicated to the New Guinea Martyrs: that is, the men and women who chose to stay with the mission when it was attacked by the Japanese, many of whom were put to death for their witness. One station I spent a night at was Gona, where the Japanese landed, and where Vivyan Redlinch, a priest from Cornwall, was beheaded on the beach. Round their waists the boys wore an "old school tie" of brilliant scarlet. They build their own houses, grow their own food in gardens which have been carved out of the jungle, and cook it. The standard of teaching in the school is very high, and so is the quality of the boys. During the Quiet Day itself they preserved a wonderful silence, disappearing into the jungle and being neither seen nor heard until it was time for another talk in the chapel! Many of the boys have since become prominent in the political and administrative life of the Government; others are Bishops, priests and teachers in the Church of New Guinea.

I flew on with a young Australian mission pilot up into the New Guinea highlands. The plane itself was a very small one indeed, and seemed capable of landing on a pocket-handkerchief – which it sometimes had to. Too small to fly over the mountains, we had to fly through them, the pilot enjoying my discomfort as he gaily pointed out where various planes had crashed! In fact we had to make several shots at it before we could get right through to Geroka, the small town that had been opened up in the highlands, and is the jumping-off ground for our own mission stations, further inland still. Until recently Geroka itself could only be reached by air.

In 1961 it was Geoffrey who led the group of brothers who cleared the "bush" and established the first Friary in New Guinea not far from Popondetta – where I met David Hand and bought my sun hat. There is also now a Friary in the highlands, and, together with those in the Solomon Islands, we now have over seventy brothers there who are all Melanesian, with the exception of three Europeans. In fact Geoffrey's pioneering work led to the creation of a Province which is now almost as large as the "home" Province in England.

After Papua New Guinea there came Manila. Humid, bustling, and seemingly overwhelmed with young people and students. It was in fact only one of several stops on my way to Hong Kong. I took a Retreat for the students and staff of the Episcopal Theological College in Manila, and was there for St Francis' Day which we celebrated in a special way. On the same day the first *Sputnik* was launched into space by Russia, an outstanding day in the history of western civilisation and man's first movement into space. The American staff of the college were reluctant to admit that Russia had stolen a lead on the U.S.A.

Before I left I asked a student to give me a hair cut. He seemed over impressed by this privilege, took a very long time, silently clipping away, and I finally emerged with my head virtually shaven like a Buddhist monk. Perhaps it was intended as a compliment.

It was certainly the first thing noticed by R.O. Hall, the Bishop of Hong Kong as I got off the plane!

R.O. – It's hard to explain how, once again, I was completely captivated. Perhaps I was already unconsciously looking for someone to "replace" Algy.

There is a handful of friends who have won my affection in a profound and human way that nothing could diminish or alter. But what I encountered in R.O., as in Algy, was really of another order, and I found it again only a few times – perhaps in Eric Abbott and Pedro Arrupe in particular. The outward ingredients were always the same. The attraction of academic ability, worn lightly but always available and used. The great humanity that can go with absolute dedication together with an almost ruthless energy and single-minded determination. A smiling beauty of personality, a freedom of spirit that disregarded pomp or position, - and a deep sense of the God-given world and His real presence in all His people. Great men of prayer.

R.O. had been in China most of his active life, and I was there at his invitation to celebrate it, with a preaching Mission in the whole Diocese for nearly three months. China and the Chinese people were everything to him. He understood the revolution, recognised that it could be for the ultimate good of the people and bitterly regretted that, at that time, he could not visit mainland China. The refugee position in Hong Kong was appalling, and he was tireless in his efforts to improve their conditions, and to build schools, hospitals and churches. He refused to live in the Bishop's house and only had an office in Hong Kong, preferring to have a small place at Shatin on the mainland, in what was then the country outside Kowloon. It wasn't always convenient for others, neither did the fun-loving Chinese always appreciate his spartan and disciplined approach, any more than the expatriate colony understood his indifference to their way of life, their hospitality, or at times their parties. He could be a thorn in the flesh to the authorities who saw him sometimes as dangerously "Red", even though no one would have disputed that he was clearly an English gentleman. He spoke hardly any Chinese and could just manage the Lord's Prayer and a blessing spontaneously. But he was absolutely loved by the Chinese people.

Of course it counted to have been there so long. The Chinese people understand age. Yet it was more than that. In the end they knew he loved them, they came first in his life, and he understood and felt as they felt. He didn't try to be Chinese but he had a deeply developed sense of their common humanity. They treated each other with trust and dignity, without pretence and without reserve.

The mission itself would have been impossible without the help of a remarkably capable interpreter who was both a priest and a journalist. Each week I had a series of services in Churches, schools, colleges − in "settlements", among the poorest and most impoverished people, and he came everywhere with me so that my sermons and addresses became a sort of "double act" in the pulpits and on the platforms. He enjoyed my jokes, often anticipated what I was going to say, and helped me to build up my sermons and speeches to best effect!

Each Friday I had the whole day off, and retired to the Bishop's house in the hills, with a small apartment in the garden painted blue. I woke in the morning to a Chinese landscape which sometimes, in the mist looked as if it had just been brushed in, and the rustle of bamboo growing outside my window − and nothing else but silence.

There were schools I returned to several times, all of them trying to meet the demands of the teeming mass of children. Some schools, which started very early in the morning, had three sessions, (as if there were three schools) until very late at night. Then the children in this desperately overcrowded city did their homework crowding round the street lights.

In the end I baptised a number of them, and several became my god-daughters and god-sons.

Some outstanding memories of my time there include a visit to Chung Chi College, close to the border with mainland China, to conduct a sort of Mission together with an I.V.F. (Inter Varsity Fellowship – very Evangelical) Missioner. Quite a large number of the students came to listen, again through an interpreter: but the most exciting event was a large lunch party, which lasted nearly three hours. It had been arranged in order that I should meet a very average cross section of the Non-Christian students in the College, and in this it was very successful. Some of them belonged to other religions, several of them were from Red China.

I suppose what stands out most of all in my mind is my visits to places down in the toughest part of the town, where the Church was working amongst the poorest and most distressed – the Holy Carpenter Church and the Saint James's Settlement, both small buildings and terribly overcrowded. At Holy Carpenter Church there was a hall used for everything: eating, working, worshipping, sleeping, and even as a place just to be in. It was turned into a Church for the Service I took – crowded out with men, many out of work, some of them ex-prisoners, all of them very attentive. We sang a hymn, I gave a talk, and then just stood in the middle and they asked questions; slowly at first and then quite rapidly. We could have gone on all night. Neither the Bishop (and this place was one of his special cares) or I wanted to leave. Such is the excellent courtesy of all Chinese people that before we left we were given a meal that I fear they could ill afford. It is impossible to describe just how wonderful a witness of Christian love was being shown on that tiny plot of land. St James's Settlement was a little different in that there were more old women and children but basically the purpose of the place was the same.

I had expected to leave for Canton, but the Chinese Government refused to let me have a visa, so I had a little extra time which was prolonged further by the failure of the B.O.A.C. to provide a plane for Singapore. It gave me the chance to do one or two things which I had not had time to do, like a visit to a Cantonese Opera. It goes on for many hours, and hardly ever stops; the orchestra are on the stage with everyone else. The show was magnificently dressed, very stylised in both singing and action; the fight between two Chinese Generals was superb and incredibly noisy. The audience chat together, have quite large meals and walk about throughout the performance. In fact, like everything else with the Chinese people, it is made a really family and social occasion. I absolutely loved it, but, after three hours, I'd had enough.

My journey to India was not without incident. I was finally transferred to First Class on another air line, sitting next to a dumpy, overdressed American lady of uncertain age. A widow, she was enjoying her widowhood travelling round the world. "I just go from place to place, round and round the world", she said, in between martinis. "Do you know what B.O.A.C. stands for − "Better on a Camel!" − she loved her joke and roared with laughter.

India had already become a legend in my mind. To get there at last meant following in Algy's footsteps. Then, after all the anticipation, I nearly didn't get in. We were held up in Singapore for a day or two, so I enjoyed the slightly faded splendour of the Raffles Hotel, and arrived several days later in Madras. The new India was rather suspicious of incoming Missionaries, and I had not the right papers. It was a little disconcerting to have my passport taken away for a while.

My main reason for being in India was to take part in the triennial conference of the Student Christian Movement of India, Pakistan and Ceylon. Several hundred students had assembled in the College at Guntur in South India. Some of them had travelled several days from Pakistan, under the leadership of an old friend, Ian Bennet, who was once in the S.C.M. in Cambridge, and now taught in Peshawar. Such is life in this sub-continent that part of the Pakistan contingent did not get beyond the border for political reasons and the Ceylon delegation could not leave at the end because of the terrible floods in that country. The Conference itself was magnificently well run by Harry Daniel, the General Secretary of the S.C.M., who was once a curate in Newcastle, and Renaka Mukerji, principal of the Women's Christian College in Madras. I gave a series of devotional addresses and one of the main lectures.

I managed a short visit to Hyderabad and Madras, and took a Retreat in Bangalore − which nearly came to a sudden end because of an attack of dysentery. That visit to India laid the foundation for a much longer visit three years later which included the next triennial conference in Lahore, thousands of miles north in Pakistan. It also gave me an abiding love for India, and the people of India, as a place which seemed naturally religious, and where the spiritual realities could be an assumed part of life much as, perhaps, England was in the Middle Ages.

Away for a year, much had happened in my absence that changed the course of our Society.

Chapter Eighteen

The Society –
After Algy and Douglas

Algy died before I left for America, and Douglas in 1957 while I was in New Guinea.

It had always been assumed that Denis would take over from Algy, and with the death of Douglas he had a clear field. As Guardian of the Friary at Cerne Abbas he was in a strong position. The Community was still small, and though he had encouraged me to explore possibilities in New Guinea it was difficult to see how brothers could be spared to go there. We had a house in the poorest area of the docks in Stepney, where Neville carried out perversely heroic work living close to poverty in a slum house that had more than the occasional rat, and a meeting room for unemployed dockers and others in the back yard, that not infrequently came to the attention of the police for the sickly sweet smell of the "cigarettes" the men were smoking.

Neville had been with the C.P.S.S. in India, and his natural bent was for the world of the literally deprived, sharing their life in that squalid street just as he had lived with the poorest in India. He was a Canadian with a lean and hungry look, a sense of New World charm, a wry smile and a stubborn streak that made him go right on doing what he thought he must do.

The house had once been a brothel, and the first brothers there stripping some obscene pictures from a wall found a picture of St Clare underneath! It was a heroic life lived with a degree of good natured understatement that inspired many to regard him as the most Franciscan of us all. They may have been right.

Further east in Plaistow we had taken over the old premises of the S.D.C. where the whole Franciscan movement in the Anglican Church had been started in 1893. Geoffrey was in charge there, and was busy rebuilding the church which had been bombed, whilst encouraging the parishioners. In addition there were the houses in Cambridge and Glasshampton.

There was also a sense of change in the air, which was to become much more evident a few years later.

138

There is no doubt but that Denis had many of the gifts that would make for a Minister in place of Douglas, even if he had a very different personality. He was still comparatively young, a dynamic man with the manner which is sometimes loosely called "charismatic". He could be a striking speaker and preacher who seemed never to have need of preparation, with a good voice, an engaging laugh, and a fine command of language. Above all, he really looked and acted the part. Perhaps that is what proved a disadvantage: the brothers expected a bit more than he could give.

At any rate with Algy and Douglas dead, the affairs of the Society were for several months, in his hands. Somehow it didn't quite work. I was still away when they elected a new Minister, and cast my vote by post. I voted for Denis, posted the letter, and instantly regretted it. To the dismay of Denis, the brothers elected David as Minister, while he remained Guardian of "The Mother House".

David Wynne-Owen had not seemed to me, at first, a 'typical' Franciscan. A very marked Welshman he'd been a curate and Vicar in the Midlands, Chaplain to Benedictine nuns, an Oblate of the Cowley Fathers — and appeared much more narrowly "high church" than most of us. A short, dark, puckish man with quick darting movements and a habit of swallowing his words. At some point he had ridden to hounds and was glad of his 'county' friends which in no way seemed to contradict his markedly socialist politics. He could make dogmatic statements about everything, and had at times fiercely partisan views. His devotion to his friends was absolute and life-long, protected and fought for if necessary. He was also capable of a sudden change of attitude which was totally bewildering. At one point, later on, he went to America an extreme Catholic, deploring the westward position, wedded to the old English Missal, the apotheosis of all that was catholic, clerical and correct. Once there, he saw the light of reform, and returned a chain-smoking liberal in a black roll-necked sweater, embracing every sort of change!

He had a deep love for God and the religious life, and saw it sometimes in somewhat stark terms. Prayer meant for him at least one hour, preferably two, in silence, in the morning and before anyone else was up. Enclosure (for the Sisters) demanded a rigidity which went well beyond many contemporary Roman models (at the profession for life of a nun he once turned to me and said "I've just shut her up inside — for good" — a somewhat ambiguous remark). Cleaning meant getting down on hands and knees and scrubbing, and at the age of ninety he was still doing it in the refectory at Glasshampton. That was the place he really loved, and where he wanted to finish his days. At heart he is very much a man of prayer.

He took over at a very difficult time. When I returned from India several brothers came to see me and talk about their sense of disillusionment and despair at the way things seemed to be going. David and Denis did not find life together at all easy. David had to find his feet as the Minister, and at the same time act as a buffer between contending personalities. Denis had inexplicably removed Geoffrey from Plaistow, where he was doing magnificent work, and was now filling in as a school chaplain. It seemed the only thing that I could do, as I had no authority and was not a member of the Chapter, was to appeal to the Bishop Protector, Robert Mortimer, the Bishop of Exeter.

The Bishop Protector in Franciscan terms corresponds roughly to the Visitor in other religious orders, but with us has always had greater significance. He is there roughly to protect the Order from the Church and the Church from the Order. He is a "go-between" in case of crisis and a final court of appeal and advice. The two I have worked most with in England have both been remarkably good and understanding in that role. The other was Mortimer's successor, John Eastaugh, Bishop of Hereford. Very contrasting characters. Mortimer was a Canon Lawyer, a distinguished scholar, a man of infinite patience and very little small talk, who found large gatherings boring and always left as soon as he decently could when he came for a profession or any other public occasion. On matters of the kind I went to see him about he was judicious, caring and exact and always betrayed a remarkably detailed knowledge of our rule and constitution. He was very generous with his hospitality in the Palace at Exeter. When he paid his final visit to the Friary just before his retirement I had arranged for Sister Angela, a very gifted sculptress and one of the enclosed Sisters at Freeland, to carve a present for him. It took the form of a small statue of St Francis and St Clare. It was very attractive, one of the best things she had done. We had a Solemn Mass, a small reception with refreshments, and then went into lunch. At the end of the meal I made a speech and gave him the statue. He rose to reply with drooping eyelids, and a tired look on his face, and said "Thank you very much", then glanced at the little model and added "my wife knows rather more about these things than I do", and absent mindedly put it down − into a large bowl of mayonnaise!

When we talked about the general malaise in the community he was helpful and understanding, recognising that the difficulties experienced by Denis and David were at the heart of it.

The nervous strain had clearly affected Denis, and it was arranged that he should resign as Guardian and go away for a prolonged rest. He finally settled with the Sisters at Walkerburn, the place so well known to Algy, and took up residence to recuperate and write a book — the biography of Fr Algy. It is anecdotal, has flashes of brilliance, though sometimes the voice of Denis seems more prominent that that of Algy. Together with the book on Br Douglas written by Francis they give a picture of the early years in Dorset and those two outstanding pioneers. The Franciscan revival in the Anglican Church has been remarkably well documented, and there has been one effort to bring together its many strands. (*see Appendix for brief Franciscan Bibliography.)*

During the time Denis remained Guardian at Cerne Abbas, David was already wondering who might take his place. Two brothers he greatly admired were Geoffrey and Oswald. In Churchmanship they were rather of the same Anglo-Catholic mould, having been brought up in churches with a catholic tradition. Oswald's home was in Walsingham, the site of the shrine of which he later became a Guardian. (His name is still above one of the stalls there.) Geoffrey, a Cambridge man, afterwards went to Chichester Theological College, and was a curate at St Stephen's Bournemouth. Above all in his eyes they were disciplined men of prayer with parochial experience, hard workers and organisers. Men you could rely on to build.

In the end Oswald became the Guardian of the Mother House, and Geoffrey was reserved for an even more exciting prospect.

Was it all David's doing? In the end yes. True there was a Chapter. In the earliest days this had consisted of all the life professed brothers, but as the community grew it became an elected body who legislated on behalf of the rest. There was at that time remarkably little communication with "the rest". We heard of elections and appointments and a few other things, but what "they" got up to was a mystery, and not one we were particularly interested in. You took what came from above. By now I had been professed for over ten years, but had never been offered any post of responsibility at all.

In effect the old Algy system continued working, and David decided who would do what. His decisions were often wise, far-sighted, unexpected — and accurate. The Chapter discussed it, and agreed. David was the right man at the right time, and saved the Society when it might well have been badly split.

Oswald brought a great wave of enthusiasm and confidence to the Friary in Dorset. The noviciate began growing rapidly, work was started for the care of men who were emotionally disturbed or in need of a temporary protective environment. The school for "maladjusted" boys at Hooke was encouraged and Owen, the Head-master, and brilliant innovator, had brothers with him to learn and acquire his skills. David, who seemed to require less sleep than most, spearheaded a healthy spiritual life by his own example. He was as understanding of human need as Algy had been and in some ways more open. He was clearly partial in his likes and dislikes, but unbounded in his sympathy and care even towards those for whom he could feel little affection or attraction: he was always ready to go the second, or third mile.

Francis, another favourite who had been with Algy at St Ives, was the novice master at Glasshampton. David had great regard for his spirituality and unaffected goodness, as well as for his intellect. At the Mother House he had Hugh. I'd known Hugh Fenwick since he came to Cerne Abbas as a soldier during the war. A brilliant engineer he was also a poet who had studied Kierkegaard. He could build walls, cook, sew, repair clocks − and a thousand other things, all with precision, speed, accuracy and very, very tidily. It was rather intimidating. The one thing he couldn't do that I could, was sing − he was tone deaf.

He later became the Novice Master, took charge of Glasshampton, and completely restored and rebuilt parts of it, including the very fine clock tower. He also redesigned the garden, kept pigs as well as poultry and tried to make the place self-supporting. At that time he had brothers with him who weren't much good at that sort of thing. His sometimes military manner didn't help. There was however one brother who proved helpful: and Hugh was heard to say "There are only three sorts of brothers in this place, fools, bloody fools, and Bro Cuthbert!" Cuthbert was a delightful brother who came from Co. Durham − alas, he eventually returned there.

With the benign and godly Lothian in Cambridge as Assistant Minister − and new leadership in the other houses, the Society was all set to "take off" and it did.

I plunged back into large campaigns in parishes, organising students and others to help me. The S.C.M. took up a lot of time, but now added to that were regular visits to America for Missions and preaching. I returned for a mission to Boston University and gave a course of talks at M.I.T. − Massachusetts Institute of Technology: my angel warned me not to talk about science in so august a place. I prepared by making a short retreat with the Cowley Fathers in Cambridge (Mass.) quite close by. At M.I.T. I restricted myself to talking about God. It turned out to be the least taxing of all my engagements. Those very kind and gentle men took me as seriously as I did them, and there was a very good dialogue.

The retreat was taxing at one point for another reason. I indicated to the Superior that I would like to make my confession. He said a Father could be available at any appropriate time, and indicated where. It was a small room at the end of a long corridor, and it seemed far from anything else. I soon discovered why. The priest in question was a saintly and elderly Fr Johnson who leant on a tall stick and was among other things a friend of Rose Macauley. Their correspondence was subsequently published. What I didn't know was that he was also stone deaf. After I'd been talking for a while he said "Speak up I can't hear you". A little later he said "I still can't hear you". I ended up roaring my sins at the top of my voice — a chastening experience.

David's determination to draw me into the administrative life of the community led to two appointments which he could make without consultation, and didn't require any election. The first was to be part of the "Mission Committee", which planned all the evangelistic work of the Society, Missions, Retreats, Conferences, etc. Then a little later he asked me to be his Assistant as Warden of the Community of St Clare, the enclosed sisters at Freeland. It meant regular visits to the Sisters, to hear their confessions. I had been instructed to give absolution, but never, under any circumstances, advice. The assumption, probably correct, was that I was too inexperienced in the Contemplative life to do this. Sisters who wished to do so could see me in the parlour for a personal talk.

At that time the physical enclosure was quite strict — the visitors' chapel, for instance, was so arranged that the sisters could not see or be seen by them. But there was no "grille'" and in many ways they were rather more emancipated that their Roman Catholic counterparts. I soon discovered that it was one thing to be involved with Algy in the foundation of the sisters, another thing altogether to be involved in the Community that had emerged. The first years with them were, for me, learning years, about the spirituality of the contemplative life, freedom, discipline, femininity, and a lot more, mostly about the labyrinth we call prayer. They became a point of reference, and I am still learning from them. There are one or to sisters who were there at the start, who have never left the convent for anything much more remarkable than having a tooth out. In that time I have travelled hundreds of thousands of miles round and round the world, endlessly talking. Yet when it comes to it I sometimes think that what I have learnt in that time could be summed up in a few sentences; while what they have learnt would be a library of knowledge. Until the time I ceased being Minister General I never ceased having a direct relationship with them in one capacity or another, and amidst all their fluctuating fortunes, departures, deaths, crises and triumphs — it was a life line keeping me in touch with reality.

·One thing they demonstrate is the wide vision Algy had right from the beginning — perhaps from his days in Poona — of establishing in the Anglican Church the threefold pattern of Franciscanism to be found in the three Orders. The First Order, with its fundamentally non-clerical character reflecting the original vision of St Francis; the Second Order — of St Clare — with its strict adherence to the enclosed contemplative life, and the Third Order for men and women in secular society living out, with integrity, the same Franciscan ideal.

With repeated returns to America, and a growing ministry in England, only the restraining love and care of Lothian, and the constant nagging of David, prevented me from going "over the top" at times, physically, mentally or emotionally. My spiritual life wandered a lot, depending on the amount of preparation to which I was committed for all the Bible Studies, sermons, retreats etc. I often cycled back very late and tired saying Compline out loud on the way. I came abruptly awake one morning at about 9.30 with Lothian standing over me and saying firmly, but not unkindly, "Are you bloody lazy, or bloody tired?" I should have said Mass that morning.

What lay ahead was the prospect of a return to India in 1960, and another visit to Hong Kong. Harry Daniel, who lived close to St Mark's Church in Bangalore, was the General Secretary of the Student Christian Movement of India, Pakistan and Ceylon. He had the idea that I might spend several months as a travelling missioner and visitor to branches of the S.C.M. all over the Sub-continent.

Chapter Nineteen

Return to India – "East of *What*?"

India through Western eyes and ears is something which Indians barely see. Even old India hands, the now very elderly former Indian Civil Servants, the old soldiers or missionaries, sometimes talk with a mixture of love, nostalgia and fierce possessiveness which bring only the response of a slightly private and courteous smile from those to whom it is one part of a native land. In such a vast continent there is no such thing as an "Indian". As well suppose a Bengali is a sufficient representative of India as to say a Cornishman or Northumbrian is "English".

The first thing I had to learn about India is its size and the infinite variety of its people. The scale of India never ceases to astonish, whether it is the teeming, seemingly chaotic masses of people, oxcarts, bicycles, rickshaws, cars, all seething with noise, bells, hooters, radios, shouts; with open drains, open air shops, outside traders; and so many children and young people; breaking through walls of heat, reflecting relentless light and the all-pervading smells that seem distinctive of India itself. And the dust. As the sun sinks it creates a mysterious world of screened light, a world of gauzy haze and refracted beauty. In those days, emaciated horses clip-clopped slowly by, the bells on their harness adding another evocative sound, the women flicked their saris, the burning cowpats send up an acrid smell, and it all goes on and on, in Delhi, Calcutta, Bombay, in all the cities. So many people crowd and jostle on the roads, waiting with infinite patience for buses, overloaded to bursting point, or on the platforms of the great cavernous stations with their fine Victorian facades.

But more of India is in the country – the even vaster plains, the endless roads, where the same haze of dust surrounds the erect figures walking slowly, deliberately, coming – going – it seems from nowhere to nowhere, as if the country of the villages will for ever win and predominate as the pace of India in spite of the rapidly growing world of Western style commerce in the cities.

In India for me there was always the indefinable but unmistakable sense of "religion" The shrines at the entrance to the villages, the stylised gods painted in bright primary colours with hands and arms in angular postures, eyes unblinkingly demanding my attention as I passed them – not, in the end, so very different from the primitive statues in the villages of Mexico or Spain, the cruder icons of Ethiopia or my own much beloved early Saxon and Romanesque carvings in France or England. This universal acknowledgement of that which is wholly other, the numinous, the need to express and acknowledge something in our lives which is also an intuition of eternal truths, seemed everywhere, alive. So much of such instinctive acknowledgement of spiritual need is ending up now in the auction room as the "Primal Vision", as John Taylor described it, recedes in favour of more sophisticated concepts of religious expression, or is swamped altogether by the secular world. In India it seemed not to be so. I wore my habit everywhere and appeared accepted without question as part of the landscape. I was nearly always staying with Indian families and students, and felt most at ease when they didn't try too hard to provide me, in their generosity, with European food and comforts.

For the first time on my travels I kept a diary throughout the whole trip until I left for Hong Kong. It is as well. Over the years my memory is of the pleasure I had in meeting so many people all over India, Pakistan and Ceylon – of warmth and love, of friendships which have persisted, and countless kindnesses. I also seem to have recorded how often I had "the runs", or a bad stomach, headaches and other painful ailments. It was tiring.

I arrived in Bombay and was handed a very detailed itinerary, a list of speaking engagements of alarming length and a large bundle of air and rail tickets! Harry's secretary clutched them in her hand all the way from Bangalore for fear of losing them.

Within a few hours, I was talking to meetings at Wilson College, the Bombay Christian Fellowship, a girls' school – and the Bishop, Bill Lash, at that time, 1960, the one remaining English member of the C.P.S.S. After that by train to Ahmednagar, leaving Bombay Central on the Dacca Express for Poona, and the excitement of my first long train journey in India, chugging steadily up through wonderful scenery into the hills. Then by crowded bus for over three hours to Ahmenagar like a great over-grown village with a college, a Christian foundation of over 1000 students, 160 of whom were Christians.

It was my second visit to Poona, and I was joined by Bill Lash for a visit to the Ashram. William Quinlan Lash was a man of great goodness, with a shy manner, who had absorbed the spirituality of India − if that can be said − by a surrender to the all-pervading sense of mystery, without in any way abandoning the grasp Christ had of him, or he of Christ. It seemed to liberate him to live and pray as part of India, while loving the particular Franciscan expression of it to which he had devoted his whole life. When he finally retired from India he became an Assistant Bishop in the diocese of Truro, and I visited him there several times, little realising I would eventually be going there myself.

As the time of his retirement from Cornwall drew near, I asked him (the suggestion came first from Denis, who never forgot that he had also once been in the Indian Brotherhood) − if he would consider coming to live with us. He did, and for many years brought the authentic understanding of one part of our origins into the life of the Society. Greatly loved for his eccentricities of speech, respected as a man of prayer, sought after as a spiritual director and retreat conductor, feared as a driver, winning friendship from the younger brothers and giving encouragement to the older ones. Never quite losing a certain detachment which made him hesitant to pass judgement or even advance an opinion at times. Not distant, yet standing back just a little. His immobile figure, sitting cross-legged on the floor of the chapel, his Indian shawl to keep out the draught, very still: it would never surprise me to see him there in Dorset at any time − it was the way I saw him in the Chapel in Poona.

The tour took me from Bombay to Bangalore and from there to destinations in Kerela and Ceylon, before returning to Bangalore, and then to Delhi, and on to Pakistan. In Lahore I comforted Ian Bennett, who ran the S.C.M. there, and whose wife eventually gave birth to twins; another Godson for me. Harry Daniel's wife also had a son, and I became his Godfather as well.

At Sialkot I took a mission in the school run by Malcolm Duncan, my Presbyterian friend from St Andrews and then went on to Rawalpindi, ending up at the Khyber Pass, and a distant view of Afghanistan.

It was there I met a small and very poor congregation of Anglicans, rather despised it seemed by the proud and magnificent Pathans who went everywhere with their rifles. Their parish priest was a gentleman who introduced me to his wife and children and his people. We had a meal, little chunks of fiercely cooked lamb and chappatis. Then he took me apart. "Did I know the Ashram in Poona?" I explained the connection, and I thought at first he would burst into tears. He had been there as a novice and had known all the brothers. Independence had come and with it the terrible events of partition. He had returned to his home, and eventually been ordained. He embraced and kissed me and I caught a look of loss on his face. I met ex-brothers of C.P.S.S. in other places — in Kerela, and in Assam, now widely scattered, and mention of the brothers and fathers all over the place.

There were odd incidents all along the line. In Karachi I gave a lecture in the university to a handful of students — and watched hundreds streaming past my lecture room on the way to sit at the feet of Stephen Spender. Back in Delhi I found myself billed on the same night as him once again.

Travelling from Bangalore to Tiripatur the train stopped at a small town where students were waiting for me with garlands. I explained apologetically that I had no plan to stay there. It quickly became clear that they knew this but it did not stop them piling into the train, complete with hampers of food, travelling with me for an hour or two while we feasted and I led a Bible study. We sang songs, laughed, clapped our hands, the crowd from the carriages and corridor always changing so that I could meet them all. Then they got off the train, I prayed with them on the platform — and they walked back home, I suppose for hours!

After Delhi — which took in an extended tour, including the mandatory visit to the breathtaking Taj Mahal, I moved on to Calcutta, staying with the Oxford Mission to Calcutta, an Anglican Order for men and women recruited in the first place from a background of the University. At Barisal their house in Bangladesh, I took their seven day retreat, involving fifteen addresses, something I'd never done before. The journey there by train to Dacca, and then by paddle steamer on the great wide Bramaputra seemed like a journey into time-past, the bustling boat with its vast wheels, the crowds, the flyblown "first class" dining room — and all the traffic of the river. So many boats of so many sizes and shapes, for cattle or crops, for fishing or ferrying. The vast moving "drain of India", a source of life, a terrifying threat when it floods.

Barisal was an island of peace, the accustomed calm of the brothers and sisters re-assuring and, after so much aloneness, vastly refreshing. Before I left there the school children gave me a beautiful carved boat and an address.

I returned to Calcutta and then, by plane to Dacca on the way to Shillong right up in the foothills of the Himalayas. I set off at first light by bus, part of a long convoy of cars, trucks, lorries, buses. This was the first "gate". The road wound up through mountains and offered no possibility of passing, so those coming down from Shillong had to wait for our arrival in the early afternoon. The whole convoy stopped half way for tea, and I found the clammy air was already much cooler. Tea indeed — there were endless plantations, and the tea shop of my youth in Clapham came alive. "Assam" — and "Darjeeling" which lay further on. The road sometimes seemed a bit perilous and I wondered what happened in the case of a breakdown.

My great hope in Shillong was that I would meet Verrier Elwin, one of the original C.P.S.S. Oxford group. An anthropologist, he left them to continue his interest in the Gonds of Central India, finally married one, gave up his priest's orders and his Christianity, wrote a definitive book on that particular tribe, and was now the Minister for Tribal Affairs in Nehru's government. He was living there. It was all arranged but in a rather "Indian" fashion somehow it didn't happen. Perhaps hearing who I was, he preferred otherwise; perhaps the Bishop (who had never seemed enthusiastic) "re-arranged" things. Whatever the reason I missed him and was very sorry. He wrote one of the best biographies of St Francis in our language and had much to do with the wording of *"The Principles"*. I knew that Algy had loved him and often spoke of him.

So I went to Baripani in the hills a few miles from Shillong and a Christian College that had been established there for the tribal people, Nagas, Kasis, and so on. Its inspiration was a wiry Yorkshireman who had been Principal of Scotch College in Calcutta.

Assam has a high percentage of Christians, converted by Presbyterians, Baptists and Roman Catholics — but not many Anglicans. The college was supported by them all, and greatly respected the Anglican Bishop.

The students seemed to turn up each term, walking from their villages, all in distinctive hand-woven shawls. Fiercely independent, and rightly proud, accustomed to a hard climate and with great dignity as well as a most disarming sense of humour, they really seemed very different from any of the other people I had met.

They had no artificial light, so the timetable ran from daybreak to dusk, and I just lived with them. The principal — John Taylor — was so deeply respected in Indian educational circles that he had managed to recruit a remarkable group of teachers from all over India, and the standards were high. The college had only been going for a few years, and they were still living in huts while the building of something more substantial was going on. We talked politics, and European culture as well as religion, and finally, the Nagas put a shawl on me and made me "one of them!" They were in conflict with the government, demanding independence and urged me to support them in any way I could, even by approaching the Prime Minister.

·I met some of them later when I returned to Lahore for the Triennial Conference of the S.C.M. where they renewed their pleading for my support, as well as our new-found friendship. The astonishing thing is that before I left India I *was* actually able to take their case to the Prime Minister! The presence at the conference of those who got through, was something of a miracle. They had gone to great lengths to find enough money for the journey − right across India, and then at the border had been treated with such suspicion. I heard of their plight and came down from Lahore to see what I could do. My passport just said I was a "monk" − and my habit proved it − so I seemed able to pass backwards and forwards across the frontier with impunity. Not all of them got through and a number of students from various parts of India just slept in a school for a few days, and went sorrowfully home.

There were a few more visits, with old memories. Two or three days with Murray Rogers − in his little pocket of monastic life, sleeping in a separate hut in the bush and waking up frightened by the sound of appalling screams, as if a baby were being beaten. Fortunately this was not the case − it was just the screeching of peacocks in the bush! And at Ranchi, going late one evening to visit a school for the handicapped and in the dark bewildered by a strange brushing sound on the verandah. When my eyes grew accustomed to the dark I was astonished to find a group of boys making cane baskets. But how could they do it in the dark so rapidly and skilfully − of course, they were all blind.

And so to stay with the Cambridge Mission to Delhi, roughly speaking the corresponding religious order to the Oxford Mission in Calcutta. Some of them were old friends and it was good to be "at home". Harry Daniel had prepared my way yet again, to meet Mrs Alva, a Christian Minister in Nehru's government, and then to meet the great man himself. "He will be very interested to hear what you have been doing − and there is the Cambridge connection". I somehow doubted it.

Harry's zeal was almost my disaster. Mrs Alva, Deputy Minister for Home Affairs, the only Christian in the Cabinet, invited me to dinner the night before to meet various people of influence. She was charming, and the meal very Indian, was superb and endless. So I arrived back late and most uncomfortable. As the night wore on the situation became much worse and I felt very, very sick. By morning I was a wreck. I was to see him at 11.0 a.m. and had been told "if he doesn't like you, you will be out in three minutes, very politely. If he wants to talk you could be there a long time". I was shown into a small reception room which was thankfully cool, and looked round to find a lavatory in case of emergency. Too early, I sat still and concentrated on calming my stomach. What do I do if I am sick on the carpet?

Suddenly the door opened, a secretary took me into a room, and there he was, standing by a desk, dressed as I had always seen him in pictures, down to the tiny rosebud in his coat. He was however taller than I had expected and strangely still.

He beckoned me into the chair opposite his desk, and sat down himself. The room was large and uncluttered, with a window, wide open and a merciful breeze gently blowing on my face. On a shelf behind him was a thermos flask – the inevitable tea I suppose. He put his hands together under his chin and just looked at me. It seemed as if he should speak first so I just waited, and looked at him. A large, heavy face, with hooded eyes. A face that was not in any way vague – the face, I thought, of an actor. It seemed a very long time before he spoke while I became more conscious of the curtain blowing gently and some distant sounds. His eyes weren't 'penetrating', just looking.

"Well, Father Michael, and what have you been doing?"

I tried to describe my journey and the many corners of India I had visited, talked about colleges in general and the Christian mission in particular. He let me chatter on, never changing the position of his hands under his chin – and looking at me. In my own impetuous way I tried to say something about the particular people and places that had specially caught my imagination – the hospital in Vellore, the Syrian Orthodox Seminary in Kerela where I took a retreat for the students, the problems at the border – and of course the cause of the Nagas. He said how much India was indebted to the Christian Missions and mentioned the Cambridge Mission to Delhi. And he talked of England and all it had meant to him. He asked me if I could speak Hindi, and gently rebuked me for trying to communicate in a country without first learning its language.

At one point I said to him – "Of course, sir, in the East ..."

He did not let me go further, but leant a little forward and interrupted:

"Excuse me, Father, but East of *what*?"

That rebuke I did deserve.

He asked me about myself (the three minutes had long since passed) and I tried to describe the origin of my vocation, in which he seemed to take a real interest, indeed by this time he had relaxed, and was sitting back, seemingly looking at the corner of the room beyond me. I thought it might be a signal to go — but suddenly he returned to the Nagas, and then to the whole India problem at that time, of its borders, China and threats to peace. He stood and walked a little, and went on talking as if he were clearing his head of ideas. Then after some minutes he came back, I stood and we shook hands. He had a warmth that communicated itself as he said "I am going over to the parliament building, would you care to come with me?" But I just dare not risk disaster and sorrowfully declined.

The following day I saw in the newspaper that he had made a major statement on defence and the borders. So perhaps he had been rehearsing his speech after all.

Chapter Twenty

Alnmouth – in the land of Cetlic Saints

With some Naga students I climbed a hill and looked out towards the Himalayas. It would have been impossible to be unmoved by the truly majestic beauty, a sense of space and something like wonder. Most of all I felt strongly that this was a place where I knew I was engaged in work that God meant me to do. It was probably a response to the warmth and natural friendship of the students as well. I was very glad to be there. So an invitation from the Principal to consider staying or returning as the Chaplain for a year sounded almost like an answer to prayer. I said it seemed unlikely, but I would write home to David. After all I had no absolute commitments, and sensed my time was running out in Cambridge.

By the time a reply came I was in Masulipatam – many miles away. David said he was glad I was enjoying myself, but had consulted Oswald and they agreed that it was time the Community opened a Friary in the North East – I was expected on my return to find a house in Northumberland and begin working there. So that was the end of Assam for me.

I left India for Hong Kong to follow up the Mission of 1957. Soon after my arrival there R.O. Hall said "Is there any chance that your Society would let you stay here as a Missioner, for the schools, for about a year or so?" In reply I told him about Assam, and the reply from David. R.O. who had been a Vicar on Tyneside laughed "Your Father David knows you too well. The one thing that will get you back to England is the Geordies!" This was true enough.

I was back in Cambridge for the Lent term in 1961, and started exploring in Northumberland as soon as it was over. My base for the search was Howick Hall. Lord Grey and his family had been supporters of the Society ever since they had given us the camp site on their land on the coast near Howick.

With a small committee we began to attract support for a Friary in the North East, and to attend to practical details. We looked at over thirty houses – old vicarages, stately homes, a wing of

153

Auckland Castle, an ancient priory. (David said, "I only give you a year before the first suicide if you go there") Then suddenly I was sent the prospectus for a house on top of the cliffs at Alnmouth – Lint Close. Built at the turn of the century by a man in shipping, it had been added to after the First War. We went to see it on a dreary Sunday afternoon. On the death of its original owners it had been turned into a sort of club, but this had failed and it stood empty and rather forlorn with a tangled garden: but from the moment we entered it seemed right.

Now in the place of two old people and a few servants it can hold thirty. We eventually planned for it to have about fifteen friars and fifteen guests. The spacious drawing room with great wide windows looking out over the sea is the most beautiful and prayerful Chapel, while the big library above needed no alteration. A summer house connected by a short cloister is a chapel for the Blessed Sacrament, and the life of the Friary reproduced in many ways the varieties of apostolates found at Hilfield in Dorset. However its influence is even wider. After crossing the Tyne it is the only substantial Anglican house of men Religious in the North of England or Scotland, and has become a resource for parishes and priests, all sorts of lay groups and individuals, for conferences, retreats, holidays or general spiritual refreshment and renewal. It also entertains a large number of "men of the roads".

Now there are three offshoots – in Edinburgh and Glasgow and much nearer at hand, the hermitage at Shepherd's Law on a lonely hill in sight of Cheviot, founded and built by Bro Harold.

I had little idea of all this when I went there with a small group of brothers, arriving on August 15th, the Assumption ("A good day to go north", someone said). Edward, my second in command, had been a Colonial – and enjoyed getting things done. Aidan, from Tyneside, had been in a parachute corps and is a man of many practical gifts. Randall had been in the army in North Africa – so the empty house in which we camped out assumed at first the manner and style of a barracks – a point emphasised when the occupant of the other big house in Alnmouth, Brigadier Sir George Walter, rode up on a horse the following morning to blink through a monocle and say, in a somewhat military manner "I say, anything I can do for you?" In fact he did a great many things for us. The other member of the advance party was Wilfred. Partially blind he had a passion for cleaning and polishing, for chiming clocks, and as a result of coming to Alnmouth, gardening. Laid out in terraces, the garden had once been in an ornate Italian style, with many charming statues, pots, pools. Much of the garden had totally disappeared under weeds, or been vandalised. With a party of helpers whom he tyrannised into back-breaking activity, Wilfred cleared, replanted, redesigned it, and became a local celebrity for his roses. His reputation went far beyond our garden and there is at least one rose named after him.

The five years at Alnmouth were amongst the happiest in my life. We were formally made a Friary soon after the house was opened and bit by bit it became beautiful and workable. The whole area is resonant with the lives of the saints who lived and worked there in the early years of Christendom in the North East and are still a vital source of inspiration. The people have an openness and generosity of heart which is exceptional and unique. Forged in the crucible of poverty and hardship, the world of mining, shipping, fishing and a hard land, pretensions are stripped away. Unemployment may now have compensations that were unknown in the past, but people who work with their hands are lost and ashamed when they cannot use them. Natural pride and reticence prevent then from wearing their hearts on their sleeve, but the men and women of the North are naturally and deeply heartfelt in their emotions, give their friendship freely, but are fiercely independent if it is betrayed. For someone who has always needed to know he is loved, and is fearful of rejection, the North East is a good place to be.

As Guardian of Alnmouth I was also for the first time automatically a member of the Chapter and able to share in the decision making of the Community. To begin with we were regarded as a rather experimental lot and distinctly the poor relations. Alnmouth seemed a useful place to send anyone who was proving difficult or awkward elsewhere. When I had asked for Aidan and Randall there had been no problem, as they were difficult to fit in anywhere else, and later they were joined by Leslie who was also proving a nuisance. All these three had only just finished their noviciate, and after three years we all went to Dorset for their profession in life vows. It was a great occasion.

But on that occasion, and some subsequent ones it became clear that a sort of rivalry was growing up between the two Friaries. Alnmouth was growing in numbers all the time. We were getting our first enquiries from those who might come and join the community. As a result of our innovations we were regarded with some suspicion, not least because we had a "central" altar in the Chapel. It seems incredible now that such things could have mattered so much. For me it was nothing new, I had first seen it at Bec Abbey ten years before — and determined I would do the same when I got the chance. But this was well before Vatican II, and David, supported by some young brothers in Dorset, was prone to follow R.C. practice in England when he could. For a time we couldn't see eye to eye and only met each other under slightly strained circumstances at Chapter Meetings or at Freeland. No doubt I was as much, or more to blame than he was,in racing ahead with these changes.

One Chapter meeting was an absolute disaster for me. I had preached a couple of times at Gordonstoun while Prince Charles was there, and came to know him a little. We corresponded a bit and perhaps as a consequence there was a telephone call one morning at Alnmouth which I asked a brother to take. He said in a rather strangled voice "It's Buckingham Palace" I said "Stop joking" – but it was an equerry asking if I could be free to accept an invitation for lunch. I looked up the date and to my horror saw that it coincided with a Chapter Meeting. So I replied "I'm very sorry. I suppose I couldn't come on another day" The reply came "I'm afraid the Queen would be rather busy on any other day" – so I said "Yes".

David had a rule that nothing, absolutely nothing but extreme sickness, could prevent attendance at a Chapter meeting. I knew I was in trouble. I rang Oswald and told him what I had done – but he just laughed and said "Brazen it out!" The response from David was all I expected and our relationship, already a little strained, was made a bit worse. In the end I didn't tell a soul what I was doing, left the Chapter apologetically half way through and dashed off to London. I arrived in time to go to Lyons for a cup of tea, rang my mother who only said "Have you got a clean handkerchief?" and hailing a taxi said "Buckingham Palace". The driver looked a little doubtful, but took me just the same.

The pace of life at Alnmouth increased. Missions, retreats, visits to America, more and more people, and growing interest in the community all began to take its toll. I first realised something might be wrong at a public meeting in Newcastle. It was our Annual Franciscan Festival, with a packed service and a large gathering for talks afterwards. I stood on the platform with plenty to say, but somehow the words would not come out right. I knew I was confused, my head was not so much aching as feeling clouded and heavy. I feared I would dry up altogether, in fact a worse thing was happening and I couldn't be sure I was making sense. I sat down intolerably tired and wondering if I could ever stand up again.

A day or two later a friend rang to suggest a ride and drove over that afternoon. We sat a bit later looking out over the sea. She had been at the meeting and I suppose Edward had discussed what had been as evident to them as it was now to me, that an accumulation of emotion and physical strain was taking its toll. She said "I'm not quite sure what a nervous breakdown is, but I rather think you could be near it". Edward later suggested I should have a word with Frank Johnson, a young doctor I had known first as a student. So I went off to rest and recuperate at Cley in Norfolk – driven there by another faithful friend, Eric Zachau. Jane came to cook and make sure I took my pills and had my sleep. It was the autumn, quiet, and a bit out of season. I learned a lot about myself, and something about the way we live which, perhaps, I could not have learnt in any other way, and returned wiser, and with a better perspective on life.

Edward with his loyalty and quite unselfish but unswerving friendship nursed me through this and several other crises of identity or insecurity. That brief Guardianship which was such a creative opportunity building up a new Friary – not just the building but very much more importantly, an increasing family of brothers, guests, men and women who were in need of counselling or help, learning how to direct and guide without unnaturally controlling and dominating all – became another period of formation in leadership.

The 'rivalry' with Dorset had other origins as well. As Alnmouth flourished and grew in confidence a malaise set in at Hilfield. Oswald was developing his work for men who were in emotional or mental need; but there were too many of them and the balance of life in the Friary was upset. The novices were not getting as much attention as they needed, and a general sense of disorder set in. Brothers left the Society. There was talk of retrenchment, closing houses to support the Mother House. The first to go was at Cambridge. Several Chapter brothers had never been really happy with a house in the University. It appeared to them "unfranciscan", elitist and a ministry to the already privileged, and we nearly left Cambridge altogether; but I talked with some of the old Cambridge hands, and a rearguard action was set in motion.

The brothers at St Bene't's church also got going. So in the end we left the house, but moved into another much smaller one – and have been there ever since.

Rumour had it that a section of the Chapter were determined to close Alnmouth as being too great a drain on our resources. I was sent by the Brothers at Alnmouth to the next Chapter Meeting with a batch of carefully marshalled statistics. How many sermons preached, how many visitors, numbers of retreats and so on, ready to defend to the last ditch. It wasn't needed. In fact, Alnmouth was approved of, while the problems of Hilfield were discussed to a painful degree. I returned relieved but worried. Oswald had indicated to me that he was not sure how long he could go on as Guardian. David was saying nothing, and our relationship was merely polite. I returned North heavy-hearted even though our future there seemed secure for the present.

Several weeks later I had a sudden call from David. Would I see him in London? He was to attend a major Benedictine celebration in the Abbey. So I met him at Waterloo, and we walked along the Embankment. He indicated in a generous way that he needed some help. He thought Oswald was moving towards a decision to ask for Leave of Absence from the Society — indeed he might leave us altogether. Would I be prepared to take over at the Mother House?

That was in March 1966. By the summer I was in Hilfield and for a while acting as both Guardian and Novice Master. Once I was firmly in place David decided to pay an extended visit to Papua New Guinea, and appointed me Deputy Minister to act on his behalf.

So I returned to Dorset — and Edward took over at Alnmouth.

Chapter Twenty-One

In Algy's room –
with a thousand echoes

I walked into Algy's room, shut the door, and just looked around. No one had questioned that as the Guardian I would occupy that room. To me however it seemed at first uncanny, unreal, almost an intrusion. Of course it was different, bare and a little bleak, but I could almost catch the once familiar, sharp smell of his medicine, and when I opened a window the noise of the old lattice brought back a thousand echoes. I was in his place.

Things were still somewhat confused. I was to be the acting Guardian until Oswald had finally made up his mind, even though in truth we both knew he would leave the Community. His departure sent a shock wave through the Society. A few months later he formally broke his connection with us, and this news together with my permanent appointment in his place was told to the assembled brethren in the Chapel. As we came out, a tearful and angry young brother who loved and admired Oswald came up and said "I hate you – and I always will". There was a lot of pain and understandably some of it was taken out on me.

The Friary was not a happy place. One house was full with men in need of help, often acute, and in some cases we were trying to tackle psychological problems beyond our skill. The disturbance and destructive power was not very well-contained. A general sense of permissiveness had spilled over in the noviciate which was a large and ill-assorted collection of not always happy or disciplined men, some of them now with a sense of grievance and discontent. We tried to establish a sense of confidence, of community trust. I was treated with suspicion by some and as a saviour by others. We needed to get organised and believe in ourselves again.

Novices left, some because they didn't like the new regime, others because we just could not discern a vocation and encouraged them to go. But there was a loyal group of 'old timers' who recognised the need for change and, before long, supported alterations in the time table and all the other obvious things that it seemed had to be done.

Less obvious but requiring even more trust was the acceptance of a style which tried to get things done on a basis of mutual love and shared responsibility.

It was the summer of 1966. The sixties were a time of experiment – and the "Swinging Sixties" of secular society could invade the world of the religious communities. We are often asked how it is that the Franciscans almost alone among the Anglican religious Orders avoided the rapid depletion of novitiates, departure of middle-aged friars and all the other insecurities that followed on from the influence of Vatican II – a decline that meant the death of many sisterhoods and a radical change in the fortunes of such distinguished and admired communities as the Cowley Fathers. The answer lies to a considerable extent in the decisions we made in the latter part of the sixties concerning our life style and the adaptation of fundamental Franciscan spirituality to the world in which we were living. That too was a painful process.

The pattern of life at the Friary in Dorset went on – with a few changes and increasing confidence. Though some novices left a number of young men came to take their place. By 1969 I was able to hold a novices' conference with twenty-six in the group photograph at the end of it. It was the first one, and I have had the picture on my desk ever since. Fourteen of them are still in the Community, although sadly two of them have since died. One of them I helped to nurse when I could during his last week. I had known him since he came as a postulant and for a while he drove me everywhere. Since his death I have always been conscious of the intimate pain of any father who watches a dying son.

Perhaps one "innovation" was the awakening sense of family life. Many of those coming to us were in their late teens and early twenties, while I was nearly fifty – old enough to be accepted as "Father" – conscious as I always have been since I first met Algy of Aelred's final words in a letter to one of his young monks: "My son in age, my friend in love". Among them were one or two who had been ill-treated by their own fathers, neglected or ignored, or had never known a father at all. There developed an openness in speech and exchange of ideas that would never have been possible in "the old days".

A series of Chapter meetings led to even more radical decisions. The first was a General Chapter of all the professed brothers held in blazing summer light and designed to bring the brothers together from the various houses to rediscover their solidarity as a Community, and renew their Franciscan vision.

Simon came from Australia where he was the Guardian of a new Friary in Brisbane. I had first met him just after I became a novice and we became intimate friends, spending wonderful holidays at his home in Marlowe. He gave one of the last talks at the Chapter — a memorable personal statement about himself, his vision of God and his vision for all of us. It gave us all, though we possibly did not quite realise it at the time, a new freedom of expression among ourselves. He returned to Australia, and a year later, slipped on a climbing trip and was killed. That was also a terrible shock

It was at this Chapter that Peter, a rogue elephant among us, proposed that in future we should drop the distinction of calling priests "Father", and do as St Francis did, calling everyone "Brother". It may not sound much — but not all the power of the many thousands of Roman Catholic friars has ever been able to persuade the Vatican to let *them* do the same, and with us it was a hotly debated issue, but was finally accepted. The consequences were quite remarkable, even if those outside the Community found it confusing. It didn't just demote the priests or give status to the brothers; it actually made us look at each other in a new and more realistic way. It is also more honestly what we are: a Brotherhood.

However, this was only blazing the trail for another Chapter meeting at which we were to approve a new Constitution to meet the changing situation. The Community was growing. There were now houses in London, Cambridge, Alnmouth, Glasshampton and the school, as well as overseas development in New Guinea and Australia, and invitations were coming for other places at home and abroad. There were those headed by Hugh, the Novice Master and a powerful advocate, who believed it was important to build up large strong centres of friars, preferably in the cities. I was very doubtful about this and much preferred the concept of small houses of four or five brothers each with a distinctive task or evangelistic opportunity. This was the model we finally settled on, but Hugh felt badly defeated.

His sense of defeat was severely compounded a little later. Not only had we dropped the title "Father" for priests — a decision with which he greatly disagreed — but it was now proposed that all the roles in the Community reserved for priests should be opened up to the non-ordained: Minister (the head of a Province or the whole Order), Guardian (the head of a Friary) or Novice Master. This is also something forbidden by Canon Law in the Roman Catholic Church. Hugh affirmed that, for instance, it would be quite out of the question in his view for a priest novice to be under obedience to a Novice Master who was a lay Brother. There was a long and some-times angry debate, but we finally agreed to alter the Constitution accordingly. In effect we were affirming that S.S.F. is, unlike the R.C. Friars and the majority of Anglican religious orders, a *non-*clerical community. This had far-reaching consequences.

Hugh found it hard to take. He had already supervised the rebuilding and extension of the Friary chapel in Dorset − now he threw himself into extensive restoration of the Monastery at Glasshampton, doing much of the work himself. The result was impressive − but he became increasingly isolated from us. The crunch came when he was asked to supervise the reprinting of the new Rule and Constitution, which specified all the changes that had been made. It was a lovely production, well printed on fine paper, with several copies bound in leather. He brought a copy and left it with me. A little later I browsed through it − and couldn't believe my eyes, in fact I thought he must have brought me one of the old copies by mistake. Not a word had been changed.

When I asked for an explanation of this costly mistake, he said "I thought it was the only way I could bring you to your senses and show you how you are misleading the Community." Clearly it was quite deliberate. We were due to begin another session of the Chapter Meeting, the Brothers were all waiting. So we walked to it in silence. I prayed, and saw I had a hard thing to do, and explained to the Chapter Hugh's disobedience, and his expla-nation. He apologised to us and asked permission to leave the room. After that it was only a matter of time before he left the Society altogether.

So we lost Oswald and Hugh, and one or two more who left with them. They were both strong personalities, and for a while I found myself Novice Master as well as Guardian. I enjoyed it more than I thought I would, but it was hard-going.

As we moved into the seventies the concept of the small houses ("a house is not a building, it is a group of four or five brothers") really took off. Bernard House in Dorset which had housed the men with emotional and psychiatric problems became a home for a dozen delinquent, deprived or difficult lads sent us by the local probation offices and others. This later developed into a house at Ashton under Lyme for ex-Borstal Boys which pioneered an idea of group therapy in which four brothers and four or six young men from prison lived together. It could be hell, and some brothers had break-downs before we learnt how to do it − but there were some wonderful redemptions, and several successful marriages from the house. Later we opened several more small houses; on a severely deprived housing estate on the outskirts of Edinburgh; in Birmingham for unemployed homeless youths; in Canterbury in a sixteenth-century gatehouse to involve ourselves in ecumenical contacts; in North Wales where Silyn, a Welsh-speaking Welshman who had been the Guardian at Hilfield, opened a house to minister to his own people in Welsh in London we had house in Soho for several years and in the Paddington area some brothers started in a "squat" but ended up in something a little more substantial; and in Belfast.

I had continued visiting Belfast for preaching, to visit some of our associates and talk to a clergy conference. On one visit there was a message waiting. "Mother Teresa is visiting her sisters in the Ballymurphy. She wants to meet you. 8.0. tomorrow morning." I explained to my hostess and she replied "I'll never allow you to go there, you'll be shot." I said that if they wouldn't take me, I'd walk by myself: but I was going. I was wearing an army duffle coat which they made me discard, and we drove off into what seemed the strangely deserted streets of this Catholic stronghold. We found the little house close to the presbytery where the sisters lived. Mother Teresa was sitting on a low stool, with two other Indian Sisters wearing their distinctive white saris with a blue edge. She looked small and shrivelled like a walnut, with bright eyes. There were no preliminaries. We drank tea and she talked as if we had always known each other. Her fears for Northern Ireland, the expectations she had for her sisters there, and then, quite suddenly, "And of course brother you will bring your brothers here too, and we will both work for peace on either side." It was said without any question or doubt in her mind, not so much a suggestion as a command, with a slight smile. I explained that it was a concern I shared with her, but we were only few in number. We talked of other things, and I left to return through the to me somewhat threatening streets.

A little later at a meeting in London a priest with a parish in the Lower Falls said to me "Come over and help us" — and we did, and have been in the thick of it ever since.

Ironically not very long after our encounter, Mother Teresa fell foul of the parish priest. I fancy it was a question of authority where the control of the sisters was concerned. At any rate, one day she descended on them with a bunch of air tickets in her hand, they packed their meagre possessions, and she just took them off. So we never "worked together". I didn't see her again until we were close to each other in the packed cathedral in Assisi on the day the Pope called us all together to pray for Peace. On that occasion, when she tried to creep in unobserved, she got even more applause than the Pope himself.

By the end of the sixties the Society was expanding in several directions. In Africa, pioneer exploring by Peter and Francis led us to take over an old Mission at Fiwila, over a hundred miles into the bush from Kabwe in central Zambia: We also had brothers in the Solomon Islands, where Geoffrey was responding to a challenge from the Bishop; in New Zealand; and most notably in America, where it seemed a merger might take place with the American Episcopalian Order of St Francis, until now quite separate from us. I found myself once again, travelling to new places.

Chapter Twenty-Two

Franciscans in America and Exploring Africa

The Order of St Francis in America was started in 1919 by the Reverend Claude Crookston, later known as Fr Joseph. I first met him in 1957, after my time at Brown University, Rhode Island. I had supposed that it would be polite and right to stay in their Friary on Long Island and went there for rest and recuperation. It was quite an experience. Fr Joseph belonged to the old school and was a man of great integrity and quite uncompromising Anglican Catholicity – not least in all the outward observances of the religious life as he understood it. His relentless praying reminded me forcibly of Fr Algy; they were much of the same stock, though he hadn't quite the same sense of humour. I thought it was right for me to go to him for Confession. It was a formidable business. The Chapel had traditional confessional boxes and to me Fr Joseph's style seemed somewhat inquisitorial. Perhaps I deserved or needed it. I certainly felt I'd been put through the wringer, and vowed I'd never expose myself to the experience again.

Joseph and the brothers were courteous and generous on that occasion. They also made it clear that there could be no possible hope of S.S.F. and O.S.F. getting together. I returned several times in later years but nothing developed until Fr Joseph gave way as Minister and was succeeded by Fr Paul, who was much more agreeable to the possibility of a merger. One of my problems was Bro David, the Minister in England, who was at that time distinctly "anti-American". However, early in 1966 I persuaded him to return from a visit to Australia via America and visit Little Portion Friary on Long Island with me. He and Paul got on like a house on fire. David was converted to America and the American way of life, and returned to England as enthusiastic as I was to promote a new relationship between the two Communities.

In 1967 I attended their Chapter meeting at which they formally decided to approach the S.S.F. At our subsequent meeting in England the merger was agreed. The Order of St Francis became the American Province of the Society of St Francis, and brothers from England went to live with them while some of them came to stay with us.

There were other far-reaching consequences. We began to recognise that with our steady spread to other countries, particularly in the South Pacific, it would be of practical advantage for the Society to be organised on a regional basis. So we became eventually four Provinces: European, American, Australian/New Zealand, and Pacific Islands (Papua New Guinea, and the Solomon Islands). Each had a Provincial Minister and David became Minister General. I became the Provincial in England, David took off to live in America, and I was left with by far the largest Province and a very free hand.

I continued to live at Hilfield and, as our various houses increased, travelled around visiting them from there. Eventually it seemed sensible to live in a more central place, and I moved to London, first, for two rather extraordinary years, to St Paul's Knightsbridge, and then to Plaistow, which I made my home until, in 1979, I moved to Cornwall.

In most respects those twelve years as first Deputy Minister, and then Provincial, proved the fulfilment for me of all the expectations fostered by Algy. As a preacher I had opportunities to share my thoughts on big occasions in prominent London Churches, St Paul's and the Abbey, as well as the little but no less important places elsewhere. My style changed. I wrote and rewrote my sermons, and valued the opportunity for evangelism.

As the Minister of the English Province there were opportunities to become more widely involved in the ecumenical movement, not least with Roman Catholic religious, representing the Society in conferences and discussions of all kinds. Many of the undergraduates I had known in the fifties were now, twenty years later, moving into all sorts of positions of responsibility and the old S.C.M. network drew us together.

With the growth of the Society it became increasingly difficult to arrange my time so that no one got neglected or left out. I had a succession of loyal brothers who acted as my secretary/driver — friend and companion as well. We spent a great deal of time 'on the road'. Apart from the houses for the brothers scattered all over Britain, I had become Warden of both our enclosed Sisters of St Clare at Freeland and our active sisters, the Community of St Francis, in Somerset.

As has been said before, the history of the Franciscan Movement in the Anglican Church is of a large number of independent religious orders, none of them ever very large, who all gradually faded away or merged with the Society of

St Francis. The fruits of all this began to show clearly during these years.

The African element had its origins in a tentative move made by the old Society of Divine Compassion. The last of its members to go to Africa died at Fiwila in Zambia in 1965 just before we took over. As a romantic outpost of 'foreign' mission it was all you could have imagined. At the end of many miles of rough track its buildings of mud bricks, made from giant ant hills, had a warm baked dull red glow. There was a school, a leprosarium, a hospital, a long low church.

I visited them soon after I took over and on several subsequent occasions. It needed mechanics, and Stephen and Aidan did wonders with the trucks. Nurses and Sisters went out to run the hospital. It was a remote and costly life, and it was also living in the past. One task we faced was its necessary "Africanisation."

I became absorbed with Africa. With Aidan, who ran a parish on the copper belt, I recognised all the problems of industrialised society competing with a largely agricultural and rural country and drawing the young men from the land to the town. I visited Johannesburg and talked over questions of the religious life in Africa with the Mirfield fathers there – who took me to visit Soweto. I had conversations of another kind with Adrian Hastings, and stayed for some time with Bishop John Maund in Lesotho, where he hoped we would open a Friary. So did I. The Basuto seemed to me the most likeable people I had met in Africa – but when it was discussed by the Chapter they looked kindly at me – and opted instead for Tanzania.

There were good reasons for this. During my time at Alnmouth we came to know a group of medical students who were determined to go to Africa as a team of missionaries, among them Frank Johnson who had for a while looked after me. They stuck to their guns until they were qualified, and then looked round for somewhere that seemed to be calling them, But the call didn't come. As their spiritual guide I also looked around. I had met Trevor Huddleston once or twice – so finally wrote to him in Masasi, Southern Tanzania, where he was then the Bishop. His response was immediate "I don't know where we'll get the money from – but please do come". So they went and worked together in the hospital there. One of them had thought about the religious life and began gathering a group of young men from the villages round the hospital. I went to spend Holy Week with them. It was unforgettable. There were six of them from various villages, all places of great poverty. They spoke very little English, so I spoke almost all the time through an interpreter, but somehow the message got through, and it was agreed that once we had plans for a friary they would join us.

The plans in question were being supervised by Desmond, a brother from the West Indies, who became a novice in England, and went to work in Fiwila. With the closure of Fiwila he was to be the founder of the new Friary in Tanzania.

After much debate we accepted a large piece of land near Dar es Salaam which had been given to the Bishop long ago as a place for the resettlement of slaves from Zanzibar.

Desmond was a vigorous worker. The first houses were all of bush material, and the furnishings of the simplest. But how simple can you be? An old retired bishop said to me "You think you have made them poor friars – but you've made them princes!" In the admission service for our Society we say to each brother "In future calling nothing your own", but when the first aspirants came from Masasi they had little more than the clothes they stood up in and a pocket comb.

To condense the story of Dar es Salaam, where the Friary was built, is to distort it. I blame myself for the mistakes we made, principally my failure to grasp the nettle when I felt instinctively that we were going wrong. I have always found it difficult to contradict others or to say or do the unpopular thing. Some mistakes were the product of ignorance, but most of them were the result of trying to do too much, too soon and without the massive resources such a venture demands. We did start with native-style buildings – but the chapel we added was rather grand. The expatriate brothers all learned Swahili – but it didn't help much to overcome their western sophistication. There were two black brothers, Desmond and an American, but bridging the gap between them and the lads from Masasi, Zambia and Zimbabwe was not easy. When Desmond returned to England to finish his academic training as a priest, his successor seemed totally logical. He was a white brother who was born and educated in Rhodesia, had known and lived close to black Africans all his life. In fact it didn't work out at all. Behind his back his black brothers called him "Smith" and in the end he became very ill and had to return to England. (He eventually recovered, left the community, is happily married and does a distinguished job in animal conservation.)

So we appointed an African brother. I had my doubts but hoped it would restore morale among the others. In fact it was again asking much too much too soon, and it led to a series of disasters. The friary contained brothers from different countries –

Tanzania, Zimbabwe, Zambia, Zaire and even different tribes. With a European in charge they were united. But with an African Guardian there was rivalry and distrust – which could become virulent. The brothers in England grew restless at the very considerable drain on our financial resources. When my successor took over in 1979 one of the first things he did was to visit Tanzania and did all he could to encourage the venture returning several times. But in the end he was obliged to initiate the winding up of the whole project.

Several expatriate brothers stuck it out to the last, and two of them went back to Masasi to begin again. Only this time it was the Africans who dictated the pace, the style, the intention. It was very humble, very rural, and grew out of the soil of one of the poorest places in a poor nation. Once again Anselm did all he could to support them.

Long before going there I had grown to admire the writings and personal example of Julius Nyerere, the founder of modern Tanzania. When the opportunity came to meet him, I went almost in the spirit of a pilgrim, It was Aidan who arranged it. On leaving Fiwila he became "Missions to Seamen" Chaplain in the port of Dar es Salaam, with a finger in every possible pie in Dar.

We drove out to the President's house near the coast. Inevitably the grounds were surrounded by a high wire fence, but I was a little surprised that the gate had few guards, and we were waved through after a glance at our papers. I suppose a message had been phoned through because a young man in a smart dark suit came out to meet us as we drove up in Aidan's battered Landrover.

The house was a modest bungalow and we went up some steps on to a long verandah. There seemed no guards, though I later thought I detected one or two behind pillars on one side. Nyerere was sitting in a rocking chair in the far corner with his secretary, an English woman who lived in the Salvation Army Hostel and the one who had arranged it all. There was hardly any other furniture, just a big space and a shiny polished floor.

He sprang energetically to his feet and came across the room, hand outstretched and smiling broadly. I remember thinking incongruously "How vulnerable he is. If I had a gun now no-one could stop me using it", but perhaps the guards were smarter than I thought. He returned to his rocking chair and we sat down and talked. He wanted to know all about the Society in Africa. At that time I was still very optimistic about the future and said so, though I continued "Of course there are only twelve men there", at which he roared with laughter, swung back in his chair and said "I seem to remember something rather remarkable happening once with only twelve men!" Then he went on to talk about his own deep religious convictions.

I said how much I admired the principles on which he had based his future for his country, but, when I tried to be more explicit about political ideas and recent conflict he had experienced with the West, his face became blank. The secretary steered us back towards the common place. I expect she had done it before.

We finally left Tanzania, but our connections with Africa are far from over. The Third Order flourishes, inspired by Archbishop Desmond Tutu who never fails to acknowledge his membership, and his loyalty to the Franciscan ideal.

And Geoffrey. When I succeeded him as Minister General he had already started recruiting for an independent African brotherhood, the first of whom have been professed. The Friary is now at Penhalonga, Zimbabwe, where the Mirfield Fathers once lived. His Bishop is another member of the Third Order — and the Brotherhood has adapted the old title of the first Anglican Franciscans, who lived in the house where Geoffrey was once the Guardian — at Plaistow, and call themselves the Brotherhood of the Divine Compassion.

Chapter Twenty-Three

Monks and Nuns – Unity through the eyes of a great Jesuit

Plaistow is in the old "East End" of London – sometimes called "London over the Border". It was once the heart of the dock-lands – until they deserted it for the mouth of the Thames, and left the whole area with a paralysing uncertainty of purpose from which it has not yet fully recovered.

42 Balaam Street, Plaistow was the old home of the Society of Divine Compassion. Beginning as a pleasant Georgian town house, it is the one 'listed' building in the area, built probably for a gentleman in shipping, it has a large garden and a pleasing if severe front. Unfortunately it also gets an awful battering from the heavy traffic that rumbles past it now – and quite a battering from the brothers as well, with repeated interior changes and alterations. Always full, with constant comings and goings of people in need, or people staying a night on their way through London, it somehow captures a sense of cockney charm and charity. It is remarkably free from the middle-class tarnish of most Anglicanism, and during the years I lived there I grew to be unsurprised by anything at all – we had some great times. I moved there from Knightsbridge in 1974.

I had been there only a short while when something entirely unexpected happened, delivered by Graham Leonard, at that time Bishop of Willesden. We had met from time to time and I was attracted by his mixture of Catholic zeal and Evangelical enthusiasm. He was Chairman of the Council of the U.S.P.G. (United Society for the Propagation of the Gospel – one of the major Missionary Societies of the Anglican Church), of which I was automatically a member as a Religious Superior. I have never been good at silent membership of committees, and Graham and I had agreed publicly on one or two issues, including a plan which was afoot to consider some sort of a merger of U.S.P.G. with the other great missionary body, the Church Missionary Society – (C.M.S. is as 'evangelical' as the U.S.P.G. is 'catholic'). There was a residential

171

conference of the two Councils, and I was invited to do a series
of Bible Studies on *The Holy Spirit*. John Taylor, at that time
the General Secretary of the C.M.S. – he later became Bishop of
Winchester – was also showing enthusiasm over the idea of some
kind of merger. A lovable, sensitive theologian with a poet's ear
whose *Primal Vision* is one of the best and most discerning books
on Africa and whose *Go Between God* is a profound examination
of our understanding of the Holy Spirit, he became a warm and
much valued friend.

Well, it may have been because of all that, while I was staying in
Somerset for a few days rest, there came a totally unexpected phone
call from Graham,. "I've had an idea, I'm sure it is the guidance of
the Holy Spirit. I think you should be the next General Secretary
of the U.S.P.G.". The position had just fallen vacant due to the
elevation of Ian Shevell to the See of Newcastle, N.S.W. In a slight
state of shock I said there wasn't a hope, but he insisted I think
about it. So I did and talked it over with friends and brothers.

It seemed out of the question. It meant giving up being Provincial
Minister, living in London apart from the brethren and taking on a
wholly new way of life. I *did* know by now many of the countries
served by the U.S.P.G., and for that matter some of its personnel:
but it wasn't for me. So I wrote and said no.

The next thing was a letter from Michael Ramsey, writing as
President, and suggesting that I should think again and possibly
recognise U.S.P.G. as the greater claim, a ministry for the whole
Church, and so on. I took the letter to the Sisters at Freeland, talked
it over once again with Eric Abbott, who since Algy's death had been
my Spiritual Director. He advised caution, but an increasing number
of those I spoke to seemed to think that if the Archbishop asked
you to do something you probably should. So we had a Chapter
Meeting and I put it to them.

Some were angrily against it, a few very much in favour. Too
much for my comfort, I thought! In the end I rang Graham, –
but he had gone to Japan. So I wrote and said "Yes". By this time
months had passed. It was after Easter, but I felt no resurrection,
only a heartbreaking weakness, and a feeling of failure. It was all
to be formally announced to the Annual U.S.P.G. Conference on
Whit Monday, and to the Brothers' Chapter, meeting on the same
day in Dorset.

I went to Compton Durville to be with the sisters the week before.
By Friday I knew it was all a mistake. I talked it over with them –
and they prayed with me. The only thing to do, they said, was to
own up – I was wrong.

I rang U.S.P.G. to be told Graham was too busy to see me – but I persisted and went to London on the Saturday. On Sunday – Pentecost – I went to Mass at St Bride's, Fleet Street. As we drove back in the early morning through Trafalgar Square I spotted a large circle of men and women, amongst them two brown habits. The pigeons were circling, the sun brilliantly bright. They had all just come from a joyful charismatic service – and were dancing!

In the afternoon I saw Graham. I was feeling very "strung up". I had rehearsed my speech – "You don't really know anything about me. I could be a Communist! I've not been properly interviewed. I've no idea of the job. I know nothing of the staff – in fact, it has largely all been done on telephone conversations and letters from the Archbishop, and anyhow I know in my heart it is not right. I still have things to do in S.S.F. and I cannot leave them." – and so on it was all unfair and incoherent of me. In the middle of the flood a secretary came in with a copy of the Press release for the following day. Graham just said quietly "We'll not be needing that now". He was courteous, kind, manifestly a bit shocked – gave me tea, and before I left, said "Oh, and by the way, *are* you a Communist?" I think his enquiry was genuine. I felt guilty and conscious of letting down, Graham, the U.S.P.G. and the brothers by my indecision.

I attended the Chapter meeting, which was to have been my last – and told them what I had done. The majority seemed genuinely pleased, one or two others who had hoped for another Minister with perhaps more liberal views were disappointed. I went to see Michael Ramsey who made it clear that he was very glad I'd stayed on as Minister. "You mustn't get trapped behind a desk." And later he wrote a loving letter. Interesting, that when he wrote saying I should consider doing it I got a formal typed letter via a secretary, but when I *didn't* do it he wrote at length in his own hand!

Michael Ramsey had a deep and instinctive understanding of the Religious Life. His connections with S.S.F. sprang in part from Cambridge, not only through his personal family connection and University association but not least because he was at one time Vicar of St Bene't's, the church which the friars have run for the past fifty years. Since our meeting in Durham he had encouraged me to assume that I could turn to him in time of need. He was invariably available, gave shrewd and discerning advice, remembered with accuracy the needs of the brothers and radiated love and friendship with unembarrassing generosity.

When in 1971 we celebrated the fiftieth year of our foundation with a Solemn Eucharist in Wesminster Abbey, over a thousand people turned up, and he came to preach a sermon of character-istic clarity and charm. At the reception afterwards he stood eating sandwiches in an apparently absent-minded way while crowds eddied and flowed round his rather rock-like figure.

A bit later there was another massive occasion in Canterbury to celebrate the 750th anniversary of the coming of Friars to England. It concluded with an open air Eucharist for the Anglicans, with the "Community of Celebration" leading the singing. In the sunlight with the guitars and the crowds of young people he towered among them and waved his arms a little too (those were the charismatic days!). In the afternoon the Cathedral was packed to the doors with people of all denominations who had come from all over England. The choirs, the organ, the colour, the crowd – and Michael Ramsey, every inch the 100th Archbishop and successor to Anselm, stood at the top of the Nave crossing resplendent in gold and welcoming the Min-isters General of all the Roman Catholic and Anglican Franciscan Orders, and all the Provincials.

At an altogether different level he invited me to take the last retreat for ordinands in Canterbury before his retirement. We all lived in the Palace with him – and I had assumed he would leave me to get on with it, but no, at the first address I looked up, and there he was. There was an additional cause for alarm. I had planned to quote from one of his own books, in a somewhat playful way. Should I now? I went ahead. He heard it all right, and for a moment his head came up slightly, and I saw his eyebrows fluttering furiously. I think he was laughing. He came to all the addresses, all the meals, wearing a scapular and keeping complete silence with us all throughout, conveying somehow the sense that he was just one of us. It is no fancy to say you could be conscious of his prayers.

The year after he retired I returned again to Canterbury Cathedral to give the Holy Week addresses. On the first evening as I announced my text from the pulpit, I noticed two large Bibles being opened, as if two doves had suddenly spread their wings just beneath me. I couldn't help glancing down and to my slight astonishment saw his successor, the recently installed Archbishop, Donald Coggan and his wife. They came each night and invited me to tea. He suggested he did not know much about Anglican Religious or the Franciscans, but seemed eager to discover more, and it was the beginning of another, unexpected friendship. He valued the evangelical background of the Society, its emphasis on preaching and its commitment to Mission.

In 1978 I was surprised one morning to find in the post a letter from Lambeth in which the Archbishop proposed conferring on me

a Lambeth Degree of Master of Arts. I had to look it up to find
out what he was talking about.

Miss Benedicta Whistler was receiving a degree also, and we
assembled at Lambeth with the twelve guests each we had been
encouraged to invite. Twelve – a bit difficult. Close family, some
brothers, one or two friends. It was all rather formal and dignified
as we were led into the Chapel. I was glad I had had a chance to
see the service beforehand. All in Latin, but at least I knew just
enough not to stumble too much – and have a general idea of the
meaning.

A gown, a hood, bands and a square – all borrowed plumes. I
knelt, was tapped on the shoulder, received the hood (a Cambridge
M.A., following the University of the Archbishop) and was given
a truly splendid vellum document written all over by hand assuring
me of the degree that had been conferred, signed and sealed. Donald
Coggan said "Don't forget it's a real degree". His avuncular manner
is quite genuine and his warm friendship real. He seemed as glad
as I was – even though there has never been much opportunity or
reason for wearing the hood.

Both Archbishops seemed to appreciate and support the ecumenical interest I was developing with the Roman Catholic Church.
Being Provincial Minister gave me a new springboard for this work.
If the S.S.F. takes rather lightly the idea of hierarchy (and I've no
quarrel with that) the R.C. Church takes it very seriously indeed,
and even an Anglican Provincial can gain a formal respect unknown
to him in his own Community.

It began with the death of Bro Peter in 1969. Because of ill-
health, he had been living in Florence at the Benedictine Monastery of San Miniato, in the care of Abbot Aldinucci. He had
a fatal heart attack on Florence station, and I went to Florence
for his Requiem. The Abbot was very generous and the Mass in
the Basilica was attended by a crowd of Religious, notably the
Friars from Fiesole. I later stayed at San Miniato several times,
and the Abbot, who has a passion for Church Unity, invited me
for the Week of Prayer. We spoke to groups of Religious and in
various churches both there and in Rome, Arrezo, Perugia, and on
one occasion in the depths of winter, La Verna, where I gave some
talks to the novices. And I met the Atonement Fathers in Rome.

The Society of the Atonement was originally an Anglican
Franciscan Order in America. Founders of the Week of Prayer
for Christian Unity, they seceded to Rome in 1909, and were permitted by the Authorities to remain a Franciscan Order dedicated
to the promotion of Church Unity. It was probably this which

accounted for a letter I had from them later suggesting I might come to Italy in 1971, at their expense, to take part in the annual conference of Major Religious Superiors held every summer at the Villa Cavalletti, the large estate of the Jesuits twenty miles outside Rome near Frascati. The Abbot of Nashdom had also been invited, and the superior of the Jesus Bruderschaft, a Lutheran Brotherhood in Germany. We would be there as non-Roman Catholic Observers.

They arranged for me to stay with the Third Order Regulars, a Franciscan Order, at the Monastery of SS Cosmos and Damian — and their Minister General acted as my guide and sponsor at the Conference.

What an opportunity! Patrick made me a new habit and I set off for Rome. Fr Louis Secondo, the General of the Third Order Regular, turned out to be a charming and gentle American, as was his Assistant, Roland Faley. The monastery became my home address in Rome, and I was regularly accepted there wholly as a brother, sharing their life.

We travelled by car in our habits — so it was a shock when I walked into the conference to discover we were almost the only habited Religious. It was a long low room and we sat in a huge oval, over a hundred men, representing all the major religious orders in the Roman Catholic Church, thirty thousand Jesuits, forty thousand Franciscans, Missionary Orders, teaching Orders and so on. There are probably about three hundred thousand male Religious in the Roman Catholic Church — a very powerful group: so the conference is carefully observed by Vatican officials, letters of greeting are sent to the Pope and the Congregation of Religious plays a prominent part in any decision making that takes place. It was the first time non-Roman Catholics had been present. They were almost all of them in black suits, looking like the Board of Coca Cola or I.C.I. I felt ludicrously conspicuous in my shining new habit. But it is what I wear — so I wore it — and oddly enough the only comments were ones of approval.

And what about Communion? On the first day I attended the Mass, but didn't receive. One of the Superiors came to me afterwards: "Is anything wrong — You didn't share communion with us". I explained my reluctance, and he put his arm round me and said "Oh but you must if you feel you can." — so I did after that, and it became clear that there were others who were glad.

At the heart of the conference was the President, the Superior General of the Jesuits, Fr Pedro Arrupe. How to speak of him? A Basque with a striking Spanish nose, he spoke eight languages fluently, including Japanese, he was also a Doctor of Theology and a Doctor of Medicine. He was the Novice Master in Japan when the bomb fell on Hiroshima, and was one of the first into the ruins leading a team for medical care and rescue. Fearless in the cause of Justice and Peace, a man of prayer and discipline, progressive and innovative in his thoughts, prophetic in his speech, and compassionate in his understanding and care of the Society of Jesus. His modesty and discipline were reflected in a true simplicity and humility. Whilst all the other Superiors moved away from the tables after a meal he quite unassumingly helped the Basque sisters who looked after us to clear up. A Jesuit to his fingertips, he was gentle, strong, and fearless. The Pope found him difficult – and his obedience to the Pope was sometimes strained, even though his loyalty was absolute.

He knew rather little about Anglican Religious but was glad to know more. For my part I felt I had met a man I would follow anywhere and trust absolutely. He took up the cause of Unity among Religious with great enthusiasm, and I found I was invited to the Annual Conference year after year – in the end I attended for ten years. During that time I was, on one occasion, invited to be one of the principal speakers.

Fr Arrupe's main contribution was the idea of a permanent group of Religious Superiors, Roman Catholic and Non-Roman Catholic, who would meet each year to discuss in depth the ways in which Monks and Nuns might be a sign to the Church and the world of the Unity for which all Christians should long. He talked this over with me and asked if I would act as the Co-Convener, to enlist the support of non-Roman Catholic Superiors. It involved many more trips to Rome – and led to the International Ecumenical Conference of Major Religious Superiors. We met for the first time at the invitation of Dom Rembert Weakland, at that time Abbot Primate of the Benedictines at the monastery of S. Anselmo in Rome. The Consultation was welcomed at the Sacred Congregation for Religious and the Secretariat for Unity, and was received in special audience by Pope Paul. There was an exciting sense that the Solemn Vows of Religion could form a foundation for new dialogue, as the Churches reach towards visible unity. As Pope John Paul said to them, on another occasion "Who more than Religious should experience in prayer the urgency not only of manifesting unity, but also of living in it the fullness of truth and charity" It has met regularly ever since; not only in Rome, but in England, Jerusalem, and America. It is, for me, the greatest honour that my name is associated with his as co-Founder.

We often met in Rome, and I took to talking over other things with him. He always seemed to have time, to give individual attention, and I came to have a deep love and admiration for him. Meeting Jesuits in many parts of the world I find that the mention of his name is enough – it is like a passport, admitting me to a territory of faith and love which is naturally shared through him. He seemed remarkably true to the spirit of Ignatius Loyola himself, at least as far as I have understood him. It was on his recommendation that I was invited to contribute a paper at Loyola itself – my first visit to that Jesuit stronghold in Spain – at another Ecumenical Conference for Religious, organised by the wiry, indefatigable Fr Martin de Zaballa, Ecumenical Officer to the Bishop of Bilbao. That was a confusing occasion – but I shall never forget the stately and elegant dancing of the Basque boys in the Basilica in honour of the Host just after the consecration in the middle of High Mass. Such an astonishingly eloquent and dignified tribute of worship to our Lord.

Fr Arrupe had a serious stroke, and his place as Superior General was taken by someone of equal strength, but cast perhaps in a slightly more conventional mould. The last time I saw him his speech had returned – but his only language was Spanish, and little of that. He smiled and seemed to understand me – and gave me a blessing. He lived on, cared for in a corner of the vast fortress of Jesuits in Rome – not far from St Peter's – where he died in February 1991. He lives on in the love and loyalty of the Jesuit priests, who like the martyrs in Latin America, give their lives for the faith which he so fearlessly shared with them.

Chapter Twenty-Four

Brothers and Sisters growing together – Expansion and Experiment

The seventies were a time of expansion. In 1972 Geoffrey replaced David as Minister General and went into orbit, buying a "round the world" ticket each year for himself and his secretary, and the two of them just went from country to country, friary to friary, taking in visits to Franciscan Tertiaries in Hong Kong, Malaysia, India, Africa and elsewhere en route. It was a punishing schedule – but he survived, though his secretaries found it a bit wearing. Having started all the work in the Pacific, he inevitably spend a lot of time there, encouraging growth in Papua New Guinea and the Solomon Islands in particular. The Friary at Brisbane was also growing and the brothers in New Zealand were struggling to get established.

In America, as elsewhere, the recurring problem was one of leadership: discovering it, encouraging it and then preventing it from crumbling. This was to prove particularly difficult in America and Australia. Attending Chapter Meetings I saw something of all these places from time to time, but my chief concern was the growth and establishment of the Community in Britain, where we now had houses in all four countries. There was also a concern for the Community of St Francis, the First Order Sisters and the Second Order at Freeland, both of them discovering new ways of expressing their Franciscan vocation. It was a great idea, having Sisters, almost a mixed community. What we did not realise well enough as brothers, was the way our Sisters, like all thoughtful women, were part of a new and deeper understanding of womanhood, femininity, and the achievement of equal emotional, spiritual and psychological status. The whole awakening of women to their real role in the world as equal partners with men meant for them a constant exploring of possibilities, potentials and powers which has kept them in a state of heightened awareness and experiment. So much was liberated that in the past had been repressed and frustrated, and all the old relationships with men were challenged. Inevitably and understandably this new found freedom to act and speak in their own right as women sometimes sounded exaggerated and even aggressive, and some men, having nothing of a similar kind in their own experience, could feel threatened and retreat into an equally exaggerated chauvinism. If that is true of life in general how much more so might it be when heightened by the sharper definitions of the vows of poverty, obedience and chastity.

So the Sisters took over all the authority and organisation of their own Order (which had in any case always retained the title "The Community of St Francis" under the general umbrella of all the orders of the Society of St Francis) establishing complete autonomy while using the same Rule and Constitution − and the brothers stood back, wearing the same mediaeval habit as they have always worn while they watched the Sisters express all their freedom by constant experiment with what they wore, losing their veils and wimples, skirts getting shorter and shorter, until like the majority of their Roman Catholic counterparts the habit sometimes disappeared altogether. Of course the real changes were much deeper, signalled by the first Sister in America to be ordained priest, followed by others in England who were ordained deacon, led by the Provincial, Elizabeth.

We have had brothers and sisters living in the same house as a "family" together, helping one another to a better knowledge of themselves, quarrelling and disagreeing, in much the same way any family might, feeling their way towards personal freedom and finding fulfilment in prayer and service as Franciscans. As a consequence of all this heart-searching and enquiry at the personal level and in conferences and Chapters − of a kind wholly unknown at the time I became a friar − I sometimes find it hard to accept the large number of greatly loved brothers and sisters who have left, but I am sometimes astonished at the larger number, growing in maturity, who *remain*. There is also a flourishing 'old boy' network of teachers, social workers, priests, nurses, all sorts, who continue to regard S.S.F. as in some way the place where they came to life, and turn up with wives or husbands or friends to claim a continuing solidarity with us.

Little by little the brothers began to discover and come to terms with their masculinity − though they might not feel the need to admit as much, or put it in that way − and ceased to be threatened by what they discovered about themselves, each other, or the Sisters. A very few appear to remain entrenched misogynists, but many more have discovered that they had little to fear and have begun to accept their vulnerability, no longer imposing hasty judgements on themselves or others. Such honesty is not easy, and self-conscious introspection could be a menace, but it is redeemed by a steady move towards a deepening spiritual awareness and conscious devotion to God.

Year after year I travelled round visiting all the houses, coping as far as I could with crises, wearing out a succession of faithful secretary-drivers. These emotional factors were by no means the only ones to be faced. More frequently there were the inevitable questions of how brothers and sisters might learn how to live, pray and work together as they faced the particular demands of our very varied apostolates. The claims and demands of the world and the Church regularly clashed with the insight, understanding, and abilities of the brothers. Some things were just not possible, no matter how hard we tried, and our failure to live up to the possibly unreasonable expectation of others could be frustrating and disillusioning. It could also be exhausting.

Then rather unexpectedly a note came – very confidential – from the Archbishop's Appointments Secretary. We had a very guarded talk about his job, and the appointment of Bishops about which he advised the Archbishop. A little while later there was a note from Donald Coggan, suggesting a talk at Lambeth. I told Tristam, the First Order Secretary, and Jeremy my personal secretary (he is now a prison chaplain and doing a splendid job) but no-one else. He dropped me there and I climbed the great flight of stairs in the main hall, a Victorian addition which never quite achieved the grandeur it was meant to convey. At its head is a wide corridor, flanked with portraits of past Archbishops, great canvasses in gilt frames against a background of gloomy paper and much polish. The drawing rooms on either side are vast, high-ceilinged, formal, and somehow with their stuffed sofas and settees demanding bishops in gaiters and ladies in Edwardian frills and bustles!

The Archbishop was in fact in a small study upstairs and he gave me tea and talked about the Society, wanting to know how it was getting on. He talked also about himself a little, and sounded dismayed at the superficial way in which he had been described in the Press. His eyes twinkled behind his thin gold-rimmed glasses. "And you", he said "how are you getting on after ten years in this job?" My present term of office was coming to an end – it seemed likely I would be re-elected. I told him frankly that it becomes harder to remain fresh and innovative, and avoid getting stuck in a repetitive groove, just keeping things going. I could not quite feel for him what I felt for Michael Ramsey, but I did value his absolute sincerity, his warm human concern and a sort of saintly integrity which seemed all one with what I knew of his evangelical background. We squatted forward in our chairs and he prayed for us both – then I knelt and asked him for a blessing.

Some time later John Eastaugh, the Bishop of Hereford and Protector of S.S.F., "took me aside". As a matter of fact he gave me dinner at the Athenaeum. "I've heard your name mentioned", he said, "in relation to a new Suffragan Bishopric, but I don't think it's for you at your age." Well, taking on an industrial area with a million people did seem, formidable, and in any case I knew he was only 'sounding me out' − and I trusted John's judgement. So nothing more happened and I tried to forget about it. I hadn't sought it, and felt quite ambivalent. One or two vacancies occurred and were filled. I got on with the job, which included a Chapter Meeting and letters from various quarters asking us for help, to open houses and generally extend ourselves.

Among them was a letter from Graham Leonard, the first time we had been in touch since the debacle over the U.S.P.G. I had felt uncomfortable, and longed for some sign of reconciliation, and suddenly here it was, a request − would we consider opening a house for wayfarers in Cornwall? There were some stables at the Convent, of which he was Warden, which would be ideal in Truro. (I later discovered that this idea, which had much merit, had not quite been cleared by the Rev. Mother, who didn't like the idea at all!) Well, there had been a Franciscan house for wayfarers in Cornwall in the thirties, founded by Bro Douglas himself. My enthusiasm was as instant as Graham's, but the Chapter first counselled caution, and finally said No. We just hadn't the resources, so I had to say "No" to Graham again − even though it was of course primarily a Chapter decision.

I decided the only thing was to go and see him and explain, face to face. I think I had a need to be reconciled, and get right with him. So I travelled to Truro. He met me at the station himself, and insisted on driving me round the city so that I could see the Cathedral. Then we went to the Convent of the Epiphany and Mother Constance gave us tea. We had met once before, but this time I detected anxiety. It was all a bit uncomfortable as I was shown the stables, with another sister trailing behind and muttering "It's quite wrong, it will never do". So it must have been a vast relief to them both when I finally got round to saying we couldn't do it.

Graham took it very well, almost jovially, and said come out into the garden. So we went and walked up and down, and he lit his pipe and I wished so much I had mine. And that was when he asked if I would consider being Bishop of St Germans. He said, out of the blue, "I once asked you to do something for me, and your answer was "No" - and you were right. I asked the wrong question. Now I want to ask you something again, and I think it's the right question. Will you consider becoming my Suffragan Bishop" Once again his intuitions were at work — and though I gave a *very* cautious reply almost at once his enthusiasm and impetuosity spurred him to action!

What I didn't know, until he told me very much later, was that quite by chance the Archbishop's Appointments Secretary had been there only the day before to discuss the appointment and had shown him a list of suggested names which had mine among them. To Graham that was a signal from the Holy Spirit — all unknowingly, I had arrived for an interview!

When I was finally able to consult the Chapter brothers they were generally generous and supportive, though some had mixed feelings, and, when the whole community heard, one or two were hostile. I asked if I might have two brothers to live with me in Cornwall, and there was some relief when I suggested the names of David Columba and Malcolm, two lay brothers I have known since they first joined the Society, and for whom I had a high regard.

The whole question of brothers becoming Bishops came to a head a year or two later. There had been requests in other parts of the world, and an anxiety was expressed finally in a Chapter decision (which became front page news in the *Church Times*) to the effect that brothers would generally not be available.

Soon after my meeting with Graham Leonard I talked at length with Eric Abbott. He had no doubt it was right, but understood my fears that it might mean some sort of separation from the Society.

Eric was in his day undoubtedly one of the great spiritual directors of our Church. Firmly based in the Anglican Catholic tradition he belonged to that world of Tractarian truth and balance, discipline and generous love which cannot be imitated and springs from a life of prayer and trust in God. He was a gentle and patient listener who never seemed hurried. His comments were shrewd, and could in a few words sometimes pierce a deception or unmask a half truth. Algy saw him not long before his death, and told me I could always turn to him. Soon after I went to see him at Keble College, Oxford, where he was the Warden, and he was a comfort and help in the painful process of adjustment. The best way to learn how to be a spiritual director is to have a good one yourself — and when he died Eric seemed as irreplaceable as Algy had been.

Three of my closest friends gave me a beautiful and simple Victorian ring, and Eric blessed it. The service in St Paul's on 25th April, 1979 brought together more of my brethren, family, and friends than I have ever had in one place, and the party in Plaistow afterwards was a grand 'send off' to Cornwall.

David and Malcolm hired a van and went round collecting furniture from friends and we all finally met in a spacious Edwardian villa in Truro.

Chapter Twenty-Five

Living beyond the Tamar –
a taste of "Cornish High"

It's a long way off if you start from London, or almost anywhere. Driving down it seems as if you are nearly there when you reach Exeter – but that is only half way in miles, and much less in imagination. Cross the Tamar and you are in another country: a fact of which the Cornish are proud, and never cease to remind the English. I thought the Celtic fringe would be like Northumberland, and in some ways it is, but the Cornish are more wary about taking you to their hearts, though once there you belong for ever. Coggan had said "You will just love them, and they will love you" and it seemed true almost from the start.

We arrived in early summer. David got going in the garden, and helped by Malcolm organised and redecorated the house. I was instantly involved in the unfamiliar world of Diocesan committees, Synods, my first Induction (in the Scilly Islands), Confirmations, and the wholly unfamiliar episcopal world with its time-honoured protocol and customs. A friend gave me *Barchester Towers* as a handbook for my new job – and I found it true, indeed quite unbelievably true. The Cathedral Dean and Canons, the Archdeacons and Rural deans all became friends of the most courteous and generous kind. Graham Leonard's chaplain took me in hand to instruct me in the niceties of liturgy and ritual with an enthusiasm and quite relentless determination that betrayed his training as a teacher as well as a priest of the catholic school. I still feel I dare not step out of line in case he is watching.

The prevailing Churchmanship throughout Cornwall has been called "Cornish High". In fact it is a type of Tractarian catholicism of the kind I first knew as a boy, doctrinally strict, restrained in ritual, with a strong sense of dignity and hierarchy coupled with friendly even familiar respect. Graham's system of parish visits meant that between us we spent a day in almost every parish each year – a full day, and David who helped to organise services, drove me all over the county and shared in the pastoral side of the visits. I got to know the farming community well, listened

185

to all the farming programmes on the radio, and tried to be intelligent about farming affairs. There were some families I came to know very well, and shared their life by marrying their sons and daughters and baptising their children.

We plunged into the life of the diocese and county — St John's Ambulance, Multiple Sclerosis Society (as President I reclaimed all my early concern for M.S., making new friends among patients and their families) and there was the newly built Hospice and many other things. Graham went to Australia on a visit of some length, and later had a sabbatical, so I had a few months running the diocese. I was welcomed again by Mother Constance at the Convent of the Epiphany, and later, as their Warden, assisted them in their move to a new house — leaving behind the very large Victorian building on which both Sedding and Comper had worked.

Later, I had a fall and fractured an ankle. It coincided with an interregnum, which presented interesting problems when confined to crutches and a wheelchair.

I learnt a lot from Graham. Our paths had crossed a little — we both grew up in Clapham. He was at Westcott, and married in St Benet's, Cambridge. Working beside him was a revelation. He was working very hard, taking on more and more. As a Bishop he was absolutely professional and never really off the job. He has never lost the ingrained attitude of his evangelical upbringing, and that legalistic and rather black and white approach to the faith characteristic of doctrinaire evangelicals, coloured his approach to catholicism. It gave him, a clarity of vision and an absolute approach to everything he examined.

I attended a small conference for newly appointed suffragans at which we were asked the question "Does your Diocesan treat you as a Curate or a colleague" I was the only one there who could genuinely say that Graham treated me always as a colleague. Indeed he assumed too readily that I would just get on with it, and was not always good at letting me know his latest decisions and intentions. It led to a crisis between us. We came out the other side of it closer friends and my admiration for him had grown.

Fairly early on I was elected to the House of Bishops and became part of General Synod. I was then invited to be Chairman of the Social Policy Committee of the Board for Social Responsibility — of which Graham was Chairman. It seemed a bit like another Graham inspiration though he assured me it was not!

As chairman I was occasionally the speaker in synod for a variety of social issues, *Housing and Homelessness, The Death Grant, Capital Punishment, Abortion,* — all things about which I feel strongly. But most important of all, I felt I at last had what I had always hoped for, a public platform where I could share in some of these human issues and possibly play a small part in the shaping of national affairs. At the time I joined the Board for Social Responsibility the Report on Homosexuality was being debated; and shortly after that there was the lengthy discussion which led to the Report *The Church and the Bomb*. Graham was a first-class Chairman. When he moved to the Board of Education, his place was taken by Hugh Montefiore. The Westcott House network seemed still in operation (He was succeeded by Ronnie Bowlby). In fact, one great pleasure of the General Synod was the large number of men and women there who had been at Oxford and Cambridge in the fifties, many of them playing a prominent part in the S.C.M. in those days. Sometimes it was almost too much like a Swanwick Conference! I would have to say I relished it, and with Barnabas and Bernard also there, it seemed as if S.S.F. had a valid role to play.

To do so much commuting from Cornwall had its costs however. Truro *is* a long way off, and I was often more tired than I cared to admit. Even more seriously, it became difficult to meet the proper claims of Cornwall as well as those in London.

Graham was replaced by Peter Mumford. We had known each other since he was an undergraduate and the transition was an easy one. It was less easy for me when David went off to Queen's, Birmingham, to train for the priesthood. (He was later followed by Malcolm. Luke Underwood who became my driver later trained for the non-stipendiary ministry – so the Truro house made an unexpected contribution to the Church of three priests.)

Peter was as tireless as Graham though his style was a little different. As time passed my connections in the diocese grew and repeated visits to parishes and people led to a sense of happy belonging and a sort of tradition. On Palm Sunday I usually went to "Little Petherick" one of the most beautiful small churches in Cornwall, restored and made gloriously and strikingly beautiful in the mediaeval manner by Comper, richly endowed with ancient copes and chasubles and on the occasion packed to the doors, with the choir of Keble College, the Patrons brought by their Chaplain Geoffrey Rowall, to sing the Passion. Later there was a riotous luncheon party for the Choir and others in the large farmhouse kitchen of Anne and Hinkston Wood. All their sons took part in the services. At Michaelmas it was St Michael's Mount, on Easter Sunday, St German's of course. On Mondays, any Monday, it might be a visit from a modest Methodist Grandmother who came with her daughter and a basket full of freshly baked Cornish pasties.

By the kind of holy accident which surely can be seen as purpose, I was led to the village of Sancreed, beyond Penzance and not far from Land's End. Once the home of St Credan, this tiny cluster of houses and ancient church was in later days one of the homes of the Newlyn school of painters – some of whom are buried there. Now the old vicarage is the studio of a latter day English Impressionist, John Miller. His instinctive Franciscanism shown in his love of nature, expressed in his brilliant painting, is coupled with a love of people which is expressed in the generosity with which he shares his home with all comers, not least those in need of comfort, rescue, or care. His love of God finds expression in the oratory in his house and in the church next door. For a long time he and Michael Truscott a potter, painter and gifted picture restorer, have lived out a life of Franciscan generosity in this remote corner of Cornwall, welcoming others to share their instinct and insight – among them one who has become a Franciscan Brother – and welcoming me. A place for silence, security and renewed strength. John encouraged me to paint – very therapeutic. Discovering Sancreed was one of the many enrichments of my time in Cornwall, and one which relieved a little the sense of loss and separation from S.S.F.

After six years I began to wonder how much longer I should go on. On my sixty-fifth birthday we had a party with sixty-five guests, and a few more. My next door neighbours, Maurice and Eve, whose marriage I had blessed in our chapel, made a splendid cake with sixty-five candles. I couldn't quite see myself going on until 70, and signalled as much to Peter. The Archbishop, Robert Runcie was understanding – he also sprang the surprise of inviting me to be the Bishop to Prisons, which I could not resist, it was so much the sort of thing I believed in, I said 'Yes'.

Then late in 1984 Anselm, the Provincial Minister, paid an unexpected visit. He had been at the Chapter Meeting of the First Order Brothers and Sisters in San Francisco, where Geoffrey, after twelve years as Minister General, had suggested he might not go on. There was to be an election. Anselm had been commissioned to ask me whether I was prepared to be nominated, and whether my health could stand it. I had recently had a check-up, felt marvellously fit and energetic and said as much. I privately thought there was little likelihood of my being nominated. I had been out of things for over six years – I also remembered vividly the disapproval that had been expressed by some over my becoming a Bishop.

The final election took place the following March and the votes had to be counted by the Protector General, Bishop Paul Moore of New York. I was going to preach at St James-Madison Avenue, and was asked if I would take the voting papers with me. That sealed packet contained my possible future – and the American brothers were astonished I had been entrusted with it! Immediately on arrival we contacted the Bishop's Office – to discover that the Bishop was having a holiday and rest in the Bahamas, and under no circumstances could he be disturbed. We explained the unusual nature of our demand and suggested urgency. To no avail. He would be returning for Holy Week – the day after I left New York. The secretaries were adamant, the brothers furious but we had to wait. Eventually there was a flurry of telephone calls and telex messages, and Bro Tristam, the General Secretary, rang me early one morning in Truro to say I was the new Minister General. Then there were more letters and telephone calls. Among them a loving note from Denis remarking that at last I was taking the place of Algy.

Soon after that my retirement from Cornwall was announced, though it was not to take effect until September. Ahead lay a long hot summer of farewells. It didn't happen.

The House of Bishops had some painful and serious decisions to make, and the Archbishop called a special meeting in a "secret" place, in fact Manchester. It was a warm day in June, and I travelled by train. About half way there I began to feel hot and cold, as if I had a fever. By the time I arrived my temperature was over 100, and the following day it was 103. I had to leave, but Truro seemed too far to go, so I rang the brothers at Paddington and asked to go there.

The next few days are a haze. A doctor came and gave me antibiotics and brothers brought me food. Pamela Hill, a close doctor friend, came and sat with me for hours. A lot of the time I seemed to be in a hallucinatory dream or nightmare, it kept recurring, receding always a little out of reach; sometimes horrifyingly real and then drifting away. Sometimes I was frightened and for the first time in my life I felt certain I might die. Night and day had no meaning and I was afraid to lose consciousness. For the past few weeks I had been busier than ever before. For some of the time I had been alone in the house, and then Brother Simeon had come to stay for a while. He is an S.R.N. – and warned me I was doing too much. So my resistance was lower. I had been preoccupied at times with thoughts of death. During the past recent years I had taken three funerals – for my mother, for Pam's husband Norman, and for Bob, the father of one of my most intimate friends. They had all affected me deeply. Now I wondered if I might die as well. I longed to get back to Truro, and once there went to bed and Simeon nursed me. He became very unhappy with my condition.

The Medical Officer of our Hospice is an old friend and when he was called, diagnosed pneumonia and took me off to his own home. That is really how my time in Cornwall ended. I recovered enough for a farewell luncheon with the Bishop and the Cathedral staff, a little party in our house and a wonderful service in the cathedral: but packing up, finishing up, in fact all the departing, was overshadowed for me by chronic tiredness and weakness.

In the middle of it all I was driven up to London for the service at which I became the Minister General. My temperature shot up again that evening, but I was so flushed everyone said how well I looked.

Friends in Truro heroically came to help with the clearing up. Pamela did wonders in cleaning, David, Malcolm and Julian were always at hand and finally the house was spotless, and empty, as we drove away. The Cornish episode was over.

In the years since I left, I find I miss Cornwall more and more and visit it when I can. Yet I know I can never be 'Cornish'; I went there much too late in life. In retrospect I realise that if my time in Cornwall means so much to me, it is because I did so much learning and growing there.

Going to Cornwall was a big upheaval, emotionally, physically, spiritually. There was so much to learn, about the structure of the Church of England, about a Diocese or about parishes. We knew virtually no one, so it was all beginning from scratch, finding out about being a Bishop as I went along. Some of it was familiar enough, after all, as I have said, Cornwall had something in common with the Celtic fringe elsewhere. But it is not Northumberland or Scotland. It is, very particularly, itself, and I was, to begin with, often lonely, and unsure of myself. Putting on a good face, but wondering, and leaning heavily on David and Malcolm. No one tells you how to be a Bishop, it is assumed you will some how know all about it. Those who have come up through the ranks, parish priest, canon, archdeacon, etc. have something to go on. I had nothing of that kind. At first we would ring up home and family, brothers and friends up country as if we were exiles in a foreign land: but that diminished in time as we more and more came to "belong".

What persisted as if for the first time was a nagging question, or two questions, in the back of my mind, basic questions of faith. It was of course wonderful to have a new world to work in, preaching all over the county, often several times a week, confirming, talking to conferences of school sixth formers or the like, discussing, explaining, sharing the faith, allowing my enthusiasm to overflow in cascades of words, making endless work for my secretary "Mrs J." or Malcolm to type out. Yet the question was *there* — in what way did I *really* believe in God, and how, if at all, did it relate to the things I said about Him?

I am no philosopher, and though theologically intelligent, no theologian. I manage, generally speaking, because I can use the right words in the right way, and usually know what they mean. I also read a lot and I think I know enough to know when I *don't* know. From time to time I tried to discuss my feeling with my friends, who seemed to think that my faith was quite unquestionable. All my life I had, apparently, taken the existence of God for granted, virtually without question. And now? Now I felt a bit like Stevie Smith's drowning man

> "Much further out than you thought
> And not waving but drowning"

- Drowning in Matthew Arnold's *Sea of Faith*. People are people — everywhere, and those I saw from the pulpit, met in the parishes, or who came to see me in my house were mostly involved in the pains and triumphs of the human situation in such a way that a *definition* of faith was rarely required, but rather reconciliation and reassurance. What I wanted to communicate was not just an answer to problems, but the power of love to resolve and reconcile, give new hope and strength to continue. To me it seemed that there *is* a power of love so great that no adequate words can describe it, so we call it the Love of God, partly no doubt because there are also no adequate words to describe *Him;* and so great that you might continue to talk of Him in that way even if you doubted whether He existed at all. Indeed a good deal of the difficulty for me had come to centre on the very idea of God "existing". In the meantime, human need can respond to unselfish human love and human sacrifice, and the evidence for that is all round us if only we can look with undemanding eyes. There had never been a shortage of human love in my life and it could have totally destroyed me — indeed it nearly has on one or two occasions — if I had not been led to see that human love can also be divine, the other side of the same coin. To be wholly vulnerable to human love, yet one with the divine imperative — that was a tricky business. It cannot be calculated or contrived, there is no standard technique. It requires, in most people, experience, the experience of failure as well as success. It knows nothing of "self" in any way, and in the end there is only one model. Christians only have Christ; for *all* men and women there is only Jesus. It is because of Him "Everything became a You and nothing was an It"

Countless writers, finding themselves in the School of Christ, have left me in no doubt as to the validity of love demonstrated in this way. It *is* possible to "put on Christ", or rather let the life of Christ be reflected in our own lives. Not to become clones of Christ. It is remarkable how much men and women who in this sense are becoming truly Christian, Christlike, are also becoming more and more the unique person they were always meant to be. As unique in their way as Jesus was in His.

I am sure it is the reason why I have grown in my love of St Francis, St Vincent de Paul and many others. In the end it was the example of Jesus that propelled me along the path of love, made me on occasion over bold, using my human love for what I believed to be divine ends. Sometimes, though I hope never intentionally, in ways that could seem dishonest, confusing the means and ends in the interest of looking for a response to me, rather than a wholly unselfish response to God. There have been mistakes, pains, penitence, reconciliations, resolutions. There have been wounds as well

It costs so much to love with the unselfishness that never confuses others. To be deceived by a longing for reassurance − or use our own needs to make demands which others will meet only out of a confused sense of affection or loyalty. One of my spiritual directors once said "love passionately those who are given to you by God − and never let them go." I am not sure. Sometimes love can grow selfish, and letting go be the only way left of loving.

Yet somehow one expression of that love never quite got lost. I was led to it near the beginning of my Christian life, by Algy Robertson at the time when I joined the Society of St Francis, and others had confirmed me in it. By experiment I know it to be possible, and by experience, sometimes painful experience, I know it to be true. Jesus had said "I have not called you servants. I have called you friends. You are my friends."

Friendship for me became one major key among others to my understanding of love. Algy and I talked about it a lot, we read about it, and wrote about it. In retrospect, I recognise how much he valued our own developing and deepening friendship, while I was looking for an answer to the waves of liberating love I began to feel for so many of my new Christian friends which I no longer wanted just to take for granted. During the war I came by chance on a new translation, printed on grey wartime paper, of the treatise by Aelred of Rievaulx on *Christian Friendship,* and introduced it to Algy. It said so clearly and deeply all I instinctively felt. So it went on, and friendship with God became an ultimate goal and experience of Faith.

Then in Cornwall another doubt began to assert itself. At a

time when I was beginning again to nail down the idea of God as Creator, helped in particular by Teilhard de Chardin, and God as Father helped, as much as anything, by putting the idea to the test in my prayers, why should the persistent nagging thought appear and refuse to go away — "Jesus is man" I can understand, but his miracle, the Incarnation, — "Jesus is God" — what do you really and truly make of *that* if you are honest"? Put like this it must seem naive in the extreme. Over the past forty years I'd preached it enough, and sung endless hymns with meaning, of which it was the core and central idea.

I eventually took the question to Br Barnabas, by then Rylands Professor of Biblical Exegesis at Manchester, and a beloved friend in the Society, one of the oldest. It actually took a bit of courage to come out with what seemed such a feeble "problem", though very real to me, and his answer, in his rather precise academic voice, was at first distinctly deflating. "Yes, I quite see what you're saying. Of course the Christological problem is *the* difficulty we are all faced with." All very well. I know that a good many heresies have centred round it in the past, those who have said Jesus is God, but not quite man, or Man and not quite God, with many other variations on the theme involving the Holy Spirit. I wasn't interested in being identified with a heresy, and Barnabas, recognising that too, was infinitely sympathetic and caring, and really tried to feel what I was feeling.

At that time a whole range of theologians were questioning the biblical basis of the Incarnation, evidence for the Resurrection and many of the fundamental doctrines that many had held dear. They were little help to me, either way. Some things did help. If, for instance, it was good enough for Augustine, Francis, Keble, or Michael Ramsey, surely it should be good enough for me, so — "take it on faith"! But it didn't quite work.

Then, by some sort of "holy accident" as Charles Williams would have called it, I began looking again at the books of John Robinson. It was no doubt because a friend, Robert Atwell, was just about to become a Chaplain at Trinity College, Cambridge, where John was Dean. I'd known John Robinson in the fifties, so I began picking up the threads of an old friendship. John had written a whole series of controversial books, beginning with *In the End God* and including the notorious *Honest to God*. I'd never found that other than helpful and it had encouraged me to think again, and reread, Tillich and Bonhoeffer in particular — good S.C.M. stuff. But it was *The Human Face of God* which really captured my imagination and "spoke" to me. At last here was someone who seemed to understand my dilemma in my way.

St Paul in the Second Epistle to the Corinthians says "We are the imposters who speak the truth" (*N.E.B.*) and that is just how I had felt, in some ways a complete fraud, now it was a comfort to know there was someone who could see through the mask to the face behind, and not flinch. It didn't answer the question completely for me, but I no longer felt dishonest to entertain it and still continue my ministry. (At the time I saw Barnabas I had seriously wondered whether it was honest for a Minister in the Society of St Francis to continue holding office, and entertain such doubts.) At least now I could see there was no alternative: but some new questions had appeared.

All my life I had, I suppose, taken my belief in God for granted, even during my "agnostic" years in the Young Communist League. How had it grown, where had it come from? And my vocation as a Friar, might I have done just as much in another walk of life?

I see now that while I was in Cornwall the whole question of death sometimes loomed large, though I little realised its significance. "Leaving" the Society of St Francis, of which I had been Provincial Minister for many years, (though of course I was still a member, and had two brothers living with me) was in some ways a very real bereavement. I had been deeply involved with every single brother and sister. Now that was the responsibility of someone else, and it was for me to be seen to be taking a back seat. From the time I went to Cornwall I became acutely aware that my mother had not much longer to live, and I was preoccupied at that time with preparing myself for her death. There was more to it. Perhaps my faith, in the widest sense of that word involving not only faith in God but faith in man, had to die as well. Possibly that dying and living was the story of my whole life until now. And then, just before I left there seemed the possibility of dying myself.

The ultimate motivation of my life had apparently been my faith in God but now I felt compelled to ask myself where it had come from. Until the last few years I had taken God for granted, and never seriously questioned Him. Now I found myself asking what my life has been in relation to Him. Was it all a rationalisation of my own emotional insecurity, a justification of my own need to be sure that I could love and be loved, a need which a God of Love met, either directly through prayer and sacraments, or through other people? A God who, if He didn't exist, would have to be invented for the sake of people like me? My appreciation of God, and all the expressions of faith depended largely, it seemed, on my ability to demonstrate my feelings.

It may sound naive – but I think Cornwall gave me back my faith, a 'wilderness' where I found new love and trust and that "Death shall have no dominion".

Chapter Twenty-Six

Cambridge once more

In the summer Cambridge, like all famous and beautiful European cities, is a mass of tourists, visitors, parties of school children, day trippers from London. Bus loads tumble out to be led in parties into the city. Frequently their first point of interest is a narrow winding lane with a beautiful church and garden on one side and a row of medieval cottages on the other. As the garden gives way to the high wall of the garden for the Master of Corpus Christi – the college owns the lane and its houses – so the little houses are replaced by tall narrow Georgian town houses. They are in fact *very* narrow – just a basement, and then four rooms piled on top of one another with a winding staircase, like a light-house.

In my room on the first floor of number 14, I hear the parties approach, the high-pitched voice explains pedantically and with sharp Teutonic severity, "And here we stop. (under my window) In this house is the Franciscan Monks. You can know them by their long brown robes. See, there is a notice which reads that they give tea and food to the poor men who come to the door. The monks take services in the ancient church – which we shall see soon." Well it is all more or less true – though the poor old men are more frequently these days teenagers who have run away from home and are sleeping rough. So they pass on to be taken down Free School Lane and told about Rutherford, and the discovery of DNA and the Double Helix in the Cavendish Laboratories that used to be there; and then on and into the small church of St Bene't's, with its fine Saxon tower, for which the brothers are responsible and in which they worship. The church gate is only a few yards from the spot where I picked up the colony bus for Papworth the first time I came here, as a soldier on my way to the Sanatorium, over fifty years ago.

In 1985 I returned to Cambridge on a hot day in late September, to settle in with a group of brothers who had also just arrived, and were discovering new tasks as well as the inevitably sensitive prospect of learning how to live with one another. I had lived with two of them before. Reginald, just returned from being Provincial Minister in the Pacific, had been with me in the old house in the fifties, and Tristam, who was Provincial Secretary with me in London. We have a friendship which was cemented when he did a fine job helping us to withdraw from Zambia. Now he was General Secretary of the Society and my right-hand man, there to save me when possible from making a fool of myself.

There were still many friends from the fifties in the town, university and parish. Worshipping in St Bene't's was a renewal and when the Diocesan Bishop, Peter Walker, invited me to be the Assistant Bishop I was happy to rediscover connections in the Diocese, the beauty – and the coldness – of its glorious cathedral at Ely, and continue a part time ministry through Confirmations.

Peter shared my affection for Ken Carey and had at one time followed him as Principal of Westcott House. He and his wife Jean were close friends of Fr. Lothian. We also shared an enthusiasm for poetry – and in particular for WH Arden on whom he is something of an authority. To be offered a part in his work was a particular mark of love and trust.

I was Minister General. Not a lot of administration goes with the job: it is more a case of being a Father in God and friend to the Society throughout the world: representing the provinces to each other, and giving, if it is possible, some vision for the future while ministering pastorally in the present. My previous experience had given me countless 'contacts' in all the Provinces, men and women always ready to help, which proved invaluable.

My predecessor had done the job by being always on the move – living out of suitcases. I knew I couldn't do that, though visiting the other provinces was essential. In some way I was committed to redefining the role.

I planned early on to pay an extensive visit to the Brothers in the Solomon Islands, Papua New Guinea, and Australia and New Zealand – returning via America. I hoped I could do this at least every two years, with additional visits to Africa and America. Well it didn't quite work out, though I got to them all in my first two years, had amazing journeys, gave time to the rapidly growing Pacific Islands Province – now the second largest in the Society – and shared a good deal with the Americans for whom I felt a particular concern, having played so big a part in their union with us.

I was particularly glad to make what turned out to be my last visit to Africa. Much had happened during my time in Cornwall, and the Friary at Mtoni Shamba near Dar es Salaam in Tanzania had come to and end. However, two of the remaining European brothers were convinced a new start should be made, on more African lines, and were now in Masasi in Southern Tanzania. A brave venture.

Br Geoffrey on his retirement as Minister General had opted to go to Central Africa to begin the foundation of a Franciscan community for black Africans. After much searching he had been given a former theological college not far from Harare in Zimbabwe.

I set off to visit them both, accompanied by Bro Chad of the American Province who had been offered as my secretary, driver and travelling companion. All went well on our trip to Zimbabwe, and we were impressed by the small group of African brothers that had already been gathered by Geoffrey. We visited some townships, and preached to a large congregation in the open air on a hot day in a setting which reminded me of old missionary films. That beginning, in spite of occasional problems, has gone on flourishing and they have already had their first professions. Once there were sufficient of them to be formally constituted a Community they took the name "Brotherhood of the Divine Compassion" — an echo of the first Franciscan Order in the Anglican Church.

We moved on to Tanzania. The plane was late, and we arrived in the dark. The splendid modern airport in Dar es Salaam is difficult for the authorities to live up to — and there was a power cut, so it was lit only by occasional oil lamps. Peering at our passports the Tanzanian officials found Chad an object of suspicion, not helped by their English being somewhat rudimentary and his accent having a marked New Jersey twang. His papers were not right either. What was he doing? Why was he going to Masasi (which borders Mozambique and is a protected area)? Any how, what *was* he? Chad tried to explain — calling himself a Friar, only it came out as 'Freer', and even I had difficulty in explaining. In the end we were there over two hours, and only got away when someone was sent from the theological college to explain it all in Swahili.

It was twenty years since I was last in Masasi — but little had changed. There is a tarmac road almost to the coast and quite free from pot-holes, after all, there are so few cars it is hardly used. The Bishop, whom I had originally known as a curate in Wallsend on Tyne in the fifties, gave us a warm welcome. James Anthony had gathered a group of young men living an austere and simple life, and building their own little monastery. Every morning they were up to sing Mattins in the dark, so that at first light they could go to their gardens where they grew vegetables, maize etc. Breakfast came later. They sang everything in Swahili and accompanied themselves on native percussion instruments. They had come from all over Tanzania – and were obliged when they joined only to bring a mattock, and indeed often turned up with that and nothing else, not even shoes or a change of clothes.

Papua New Guinea and the Solomon Islands are another matter. It had all changed so much since my first visit in 1957. Both countries were now independent. Boys I met at the Martyrs' School in Papua New Guinea were now prominent citizens: Bishops and priests, teachers, government officials. A trip to the highlands was a revelation. In thirty years Goroka had become a thriving township, though the blend of highland villagers wearing native clothes and carrying spears, with Papuans in sophisticated western clothes remains. Along the paths were I once struggled through the rain with Bishop Hand there was now a tarmac road, and the brothers had opened a small house in this growth centre of the territory. There were however problems. In Lae, local conflict, together with the looting of shops and burning of houses, had imposed a curfew. Tribal conflicts contrasted with the very westernised hotel in which I had afternoon tea with the Bishop.

Yet the lifestyle of the main Friaries both there and in the Solomons reflects the work of Hilfield, Dorset – in the fifties. It is not surprising. Geoffrey built well and strong, creating a tradition based on what he had grown up with in England – and our Melanesian brothers are loyal.

In fact to see all that had happened in the other Provinces since my first visit to those countries in 1957 filled me with amazement and thankfulness to God. The Solomon Island in particular has grown astonishingly under the imaginative leadership of Br Giles.

One difficulty was my health. When I returned to Cambridge I was taken in hand by a G.P. whom I had first known as a student at King's. As long-time friends we were able to face together that the pneumonia had left some permanent damage; a consultant at Addenbrooke's diagnosed Bronchiactisis. Well, lots of people live with that.

In retrospect I see those years as frustrated by my battle with my body: repeated visits to the hospital, the tolerance of brothers who lived with my preoccupation with my temperature, antibiotics and need for rest. I seemed at my best away in other countries, where the warm dry heat suited me, but often my return meant a return also to the medical routine.

That was not the only battle. I fancy I inherited my parents sense of 'service'. I was 'in service' to God and S.S.F., and couldn't be allowed to let them down in any way. Cancelled engagements,

altered plans – including one (to me) crucial visit to the Solomons
and P.N.G. caused real grief and guilt. It was more than a sense
of failure, it seemed more like a betrayal. I felt I was living under
false pretences – after all, I had been asked before they elected
me if I would be fit enough.

The lowest spot was in Trinidad. I went to visit Desmond –
later Bishop of Belize – hoping to help him. In fact it was not
much good. I began feeling ill again. In the heat of the afternoon
the phone went. Desmond said "It's for you, from England". And
there loud and clear (it always is!) was Tristam in Cambridge. "Sorry
to give you bad news, the hospital has just been on to say your tests
have proved positive, the T.B. has reactivated."

So my life had turned full circle. I was back in Cambridge, and
with the T.B. I had turned up with in 1940. Of course the treatment
now is very different and with drugs I was cured in eight months.
However the original T.B. had left its mark and it became clear that
I would have to return to Papworth for an operation to remove from
my lung all the accumulated consequences of my visit there forty-five
years before. Reassurance was given me in an unexpected way.

Some months before, I had received a personal latter from Archbishop Runcie concerning the Lambeth Conference. He told me the
Primates of the Anglican Communion would be coming, twenty
eight of them, and he wanted to invite them all to Lambeth to
share in a Retreat, a spiritual preparation together before it began.
Would I conduct the retreat? He put it lovingly and personally,
and it was impossible to say 'No' to such a privilege even though
the prospect was daunting.

I hadn't reckoned that as the day drew nearer my health would
deteriorate so rapidly. The cough got worse and worse, and its consequences were difficult to cope with. The virus grew less and less
amenable to antibiotics, and after a scan it became clear that only
major surgery could offer any hope. The surgeon was honest about
the possible risks, and the extent of the operation, and wanted to get
on with it. "Could I come in right away?" I explained without going
into any detail that there was a little job I had promised to do for
the Archbishop – could I do that first? "Well", he said "when do
you finish?" "July 17th" I replied – it was a Saturday. "Right",
he said, "I'll do you on the Monday."

I made a retreat myself with the Cowley Fathers, wrote the
addresses and went for a short rest to Sancreed. Living in
Lambeth had a certain unreality, but my mind seemed suddenly quite calm and clear. I knew what God had given me to
say, and the silence was a creative assurance of His presence.

The Archbishop seemed always to be gently encouraging all the other Bishops with his still, purple figure, often first to arrive and last to leave in the chapel. The nights for me were a torment, a wretched business but the peace and prayer was very powerful.

Of course nobody knew what lay ahead for me. The addresses were as much for my own reassurance, and the prayers so much for my own strength that I ended with a sense of gratitude and at peace.

When it was over I stood with the Archbishop at the top of the stairs while he waited for the car to take him to Canterbury and the greatest undertaking of his episcopate. He said "Well Michael, and what are you going on to?" I said "I'm going to see my sister in Worthing, and then straight into hospital for a little operation." It was a silly conceit to make so light of it. Later Peter Walker told him all about it, and there was quite a flurry at the hospital when flowers came from the Archbishop of Canterbury. It was a good moment too when the surgeon said to me afterwards, "Well *that* went well." and I replied "It should have done, you had five hundred Bishops praying for you!"

I went back to Sancreed for a long convalescence − a *long,* long time of sitting and learning to be. That too, in retrospect, seemed a time of retreat − not running away from, but running towards. Well, there wasn't much running! In truth those weeks at Sancreed I now recognise as a major turning point in my life, a spiritual landmark. At first I felt too weak to do anything, read, write or paint. I just sat, and while John and Michael did their work in their studios I did the only thing I could do, made the discovery again of waiting on God; letting God discover me, praying in me. Gradually as I grew stronger, I found him still waiting for me every morning, travelling with me through the day. Most days I spent nearly all the time alone, but never alone, and certainly not lonely. I even found myself resenting the intrusion of old friends who came to visit me. I began to understand some things about prayer to which I had often given lip service in the past but were now becoming an inseparable part of me. In time I also began to know that I need not be physically alone to be alone with God in this way. Nevertheless the "discovery" was so real I promised myself that whenever possible I would always take one day a week as a "Sancreed" day; and to my astonishment − and with the help of my good friends David and Elizabeth Walser − most of the time I have: in a room at the top of their house, free from phones and doorbells, overlooking the garden. It is remarkably generous of them.

Towards the end of my six years as Minister General, I attended a Chapter Meeting in England. I looked round, and realised suddenly that the only brothers from earlier times present now were the Provincial, Anselm, and myself, and we were about to go out of office. None there apart from us had ever known Br Douglas or Fr Algy, never known the Founders. In fact they were mostly brothers who joined in the late sixties and early seventies – the rebel years. Of course it shows, their attitudes and freedom, for thought and action, are the life which invades the whole Province. It was a moment of truth for me, and an exciting hope for the future.

At another level I recognise another change which is no less important. My style of leadership was I suppose inevitably formed by the benevolent autocracy of Algy, his fatherly care and highly personal pastoral concern. It is a role which includes a 'Mr Fixit' element that rushes all over the place to deal with crises, and can create a too dependent attitude in the brothers. Br Anselm, my successor as Provincial had been for many years headmaster of St. Francis School a few miles away from the Friary of Dorset. This was a residential school for what in those days were called maladjusted boys. A man of real compassion he seemed to allow people to learn by their mistakes, though it must have sometimes been very painful for him. In terms of S.S.F. it has undoubtedly been profitable in producing a Society of monks who really do act in a mature way, relate their life towards God to their particular vocation as friars, and have a sense of responsibility. Such generalisations are dangerous, and there are disadvantages and losses, but the growth of the Society seems related to the possibility of men joining us without a fear of losing their identity, dignity or maturity, while at the same time discovering how this can be related in practical ways to Franciscan Spirituality. Much of this developed during his twelve years as Provincial Minister.

The hopes for the immediate future seems to include reaching out towards the underprivileged. This would have pleased the heart of Bro Douglas. In reality for instance to a little band of Papuan brothers living in a mosquito-infested bit of swamp land on the outskirts of Lae on the coast of Papua New Guinea; to a large house in Brooklyn in a neighbourhood which is as tough as you can find; to 'Family Link', the hostel which ministers to the parents and dependants of AIDS sufferers in San Francisco; to a little group living on a housing scheme in Glasgow where murder is not unknown and drugs an overwhelming ever-present problem. Side by side with this work the Society accepts a stream of men and women who are hoping to turn away from the pressures of a society encouraged only to think in terms of cost effectiveness and financial security in order to embrace the greater reality of investment in humanity and the vision of God's love for us, a decision which expresses itself in consciousness of the solid power of goodness and justice, sacrifice and truth which in so many different ways is reflected in the life of St Francis.

It is also a new discovery for some – and a reassuring one – that Francis began his spiritual awakening as a hermit. It was prayer and waiting on God that provided the springboard for his apparently so active life. The conflict he felt at times between those two sides of his calling is often reflected in the new generation of men and women whose imagination is attracted by him today.

Six years is not very long, and yet I can already see them as years of consolidation, and exploration of new ways in which the Franciscan vocation can be expressed. Perhaps because we remain consciously a non-clerical Order, (even if a third of the brothers are priests), we are welcoming men and women to test their vocation who bring with them a strong sense of the secular world from which they are distancing themselves. They know the undermining power of money for its own sake, of misplaced love, or ruthless ambition. They are neither fools nor failures. For some the choice for God has often a painful reality because they have only recently come to know Him, and frequently are free from any sort of ecclesiastical or "churchy" conditioning. "Street wise" in their secularity they challenge our settled presuppositions, prejudices and sometimes unthinking acceptance of all that we suppose to be right or possible – or because that is the way it has always been.

By no means all of those who come with such high hopes and sharp visions stay. A significant number do, and as a consequence the gaps in our ranks are filled, and there are brothers and sisters available to share in the pastoral, preaching and prayerful ministries as the elderly die and "retire".

The last to die of the men who began with Bro Douglas was Kenneth. Almost to the end he remained alert, and celebrating sixty years in profession, living still at Hilfield which he had known all his life – and where he started, wayfaring with the early brothers, and became an indefatigable missioner in hopfields, prisons, Borstals, schools and parishes all over the country. A natural and engaging preacher, remarkably consistent and a reminder of our foundations. I saw him for the last time just after he had moved into a new nursing home for the elderly who need nursing care. The move had its irony. In the early days, on joining the Society we each agreed that in old age we would finish our days in the workhouse to avoid being a liability to the brethren. The nearest was at Cerne Abbas, a very stark "Dickensian" building, more like a prison. It later became a bleak and most uncomfortable Youth Hostel. This is now the very comfortable, light and well-equipped nursing home in which Kenneth was given loving and skilful care before he died. So he is the only one, so far, actually to keep to the undertaking he made sixty years before. It could be said that he got the last laugh!

Of those who started with Algy only Francis remains – a hermit living a life of prayer at Stroud in Australia. Still hammering out Bach on an old piano, still reflecting the enterprise, surrender and charm of B.K., the Sangha, and Cerne Abbas in the first days of the merger with Douglas, and later the consistent prayerfulness and ascetic reality of Glasshampton where he was Novice Master, and to which David said that, under Francis, he owed everything.

Of the Brotherhood of the Holy Cross there is only Arnold, who continued for years a ministry to young men, deprived or in difficulties, at our school or in Birmingham.

Of the Society of the Divine Compassion only the house remains in Plaistow, the jumble of East End life flowing in and out of it, the cockney twang, the rumbling lorries, the human life lived always close to crisis, the humour and the hurt. It seems the place where St Francis would feel most readily at home.

For the time being, there is for me always the little house in Botolph Lane to come home to, sharing with one brother almost my age, one in his early fifties and another in his early thirties – the age I was when I came to live in Cambridge as a brother. Only the religious life could have thrown us together!

From there I go for drives through the mists and fog of the fens along straight flat roads with only a dyke or a ditch on either side to remote villages and the excitement of a Confirmation or the blessing of new bells, a 'harvest' or a festival. These fen folk of few words, stubborn pride and warm acceptance, dressed with such care for the occasion, renew my faith when it flags and are as much a blessing as the young women and men I meet in the University. I find I had not just returned – but travelled on,

> "I shall remember this with a sigh
> somewhere ages and ages hence
> Two roads diverged in a wood and I
> I took the one less travelled by,
> And that has made all the difference."

Conclusions

I was walking down Prince's Street in Edinburgh on a brilliant day in August, Among the crowd of shoppers and sightseers, I felt more than a little conspicuous in my habit. Suddenly, standing in front of me, there was a young woman, dressed generally in green with a head of hair like blazing bronze in the sunlight. She said – *"Why did you do it?"* – her voice was a little too loud, too nervous, and a passer-by noticed. I supposed she meant, why did I become a Friar, but it was no place to talk. We were outside McVitie's (alas, no more) and I suggested a cup of tea. I never saw her again and though I tried to tell her then, I am not sure whether I am much nearer an answer now, though that encounter was over forty years ago.

To explain why any of the brothers lead this life is, I suppose, to try to define the faith, the belief, we each of us have in God, though many of the reasons why I became a Franciscan appear to be entirely unrelated to God, at least in any direct way. Ambition, the need for a safe life, the need to be wanted, accepted, trusted and loved, the need to escape. They probably all played some part for me. Yet to become a monk for those reasons alone is surely to run the danger of being condemned to torment, isolation, frustration and diminishment. And that can happen sometimes even now, unless or until, you encounter God. "You have made us for yourself, and our hearts are restless until they find their rest in you". That certainly is true – even if informed and understood restlessness remains. I find myself closer to Pascal, "You would not seek me if you had not already found me." It has taken me all these years, greatly enriched by the opportunity for stillness given me (by God?), through illnesses and operations with all the recovery they demanded, to recognise the few truly significant moments of truth in my relation with God, and His with me.

There is the business of prayer and God knowing me there. It takes a long time – a lifetime. I am still finding out about just being still, really still, until I am no longer aware of being still but only knowing in my deepest self that God is there, and was

205

always there before I ever tried deliberately to know Him. Then there is the question of silence. It is possible to discover a silence so absolute that it becomes a creative reality in itself, and not just the cessation of noise. And this is only the beginning. We also have to wait and, as R.S. Thomas has said, "the meaning is in the waiting". Indeed, only if we are prepared to wait may we discover that prayer is not just the saying of prayers, but a recognition of the God who prays in us. He who is the Divine Glory, the Majesty, continues to be incarnate, become man, be born and broken in us. It is there, it was always there for my instruction, in the psalms, in the scriptures, in the example of countless men and women in all the ages of the Church. Present in the lives of John and Paul, Benedict, Francis, Aelred, Ignatius, Wesley, Newman, Douglas and Algy. So why did it take so long to be at least regarded as possible by me and in me?

So far as the routine of the Religious life is concerned I am fortunate never really to have found the saying of the Offices very difficult — though I much prefer to say them with others. The order, the rhythm of psalms and hymns, readings and prayers, four times a day (it was seven when I started). I joined in, no doubt partly from loyalty, discipline, even fear. It was one way of knowing I was doing my job. And anyhow, I *liked* it. Then there are the other set times for prayer. In a life of so much travelling this could get lost; or only seem real at the point where it was related to other people, and their needs.

As to preaching, I have often found myself preaching for myself, answering some of my own needs, seeking assurances, that I am not forgotten by God. Of course there is a professional side to all this. Sermons are still written and re-written because I want them to be as good as I can make them. I still search for approval, but greater even than that is a longing not to be a fraud, not to preach just for the gallery but for God. Honesty has never been easy because of my old need to please. So God finds me in my preaching as well as in my prayer.

What has grown is the inescapable reality of God, and the possibility of meeting him. For all these years I have been meeting him, though all too frequently my own heart got in the way, or made a prior claim. He was always there, speaking to me, but I could not always hear — perhaps I like the sound of my own voice too much. There are vivid flashes to remind me of times when I saw Him only too clearly; a back street in Karachi, a terrible sewer that choked me with its smell, and the old people sitting and lying beside it, as it ran past the little church I had come to visit. Or driving on a hilly track in Lesotho with John Maund, the Bishop, who stopped to take on a crowd of men and women, all in their brightly coloured blankets, until the truck was a mass of colour and laughter – all shaking together; or with a sister dying of cancer at Freeland, and seeming to take us some part of the way with her. This, and so much anxiety, fear, love, pain and joy seen in faces of many colours in so many countries. He was there, in them all.

Charles Williams, whose books still mean much to me, talks of the importance of "recognition" and "exchange". This sight of God, this truly accepting that we are accepted, is an act of trust that took so long to put wholly to the trial of test and surrender. Yet "we shall see him as he is" *can* be a reality here and now. It is sometimes harder to accept that he sees *us* as we are, and loves us just the same. This meeting Him in others, seeing them as far as we can as He sees them: unconsciously finding him in each other can be an important preliminary to prayer, even prayer itself.

Above all things – to acknowledge the absolute priority of God our Creator, our Father and Jesus as our Saviour and Friend in the power of the Spirit is to become aware that all prayer is a response to His initiative in each one of us. It can lead us from the restrictions of our all too human lives into a sharing of his transcendent Being, in Love and Glory.

As to prayer itself, this being with God. All the retreats, the Schools of Prayer, all the books on spirituality, all the techniques and Directors can only indicate some general ideas. Time, and space, and silence; patience and loving concern; the knowledge that He has chosen us long before we respond, and that all praying is a response to that love. An awareness that all we have is His and "You can't take it with you"; and that in reality, the true end of life lies beyond death. Yet this world in all the expressions of His Creation is for the enjoying because it is His world, the place of His presence, and we are His dwelling too. In prayer we can discover an exchange of love with Him. "My true love hath my heart and I have his, By just exchange one to the other given" may be a secular sonnet – it is also a holy truth. And in that exchange we begin to see His world and the people of His world through His eyes, love them with His love, pray with His prayer.

So why did I do it? Perhaps because all unconsciously I was led by God to look for him, in His love for the poor and dispossessed, yet meet Him also in the rich as well; in the clever as well as the simple; and in the infinite diversity of men and women he permitted me to love as He loves them and me. Above all, to find Him in a family of Franciscans who in their vulnerability shared mine, recognising

God in one another, but also in the romantic violence of a love that at its best tries to share the human suffering of the world, and permit us to share it with Him – to share Him.

There is a rashness, and a folly in this, but for some people perhaps there seems no other way to live in this world, No other way to be saved; and so far as salvation is concerned, it still seems to me at times a rather close thing!

I once gave a retreat to the Sisters at Compton Durville on some words of St Paul, and I know that, whatever it did for them, it made a change in my life. Perhaps it explains a little why it was possible even for me to become a Friar – and in spite of the failures I know too well, face the future with confidence and fear, with love and hope.

He said:
"We are the imposters who speak the truth
the unknown men whom all men know
Dying we still live on
Disciplined by suffering we are not done to death
In our sorrows we have always cause for joy
Poor ourselves we bring wealth many
Penniless we own the world."

Index